French History

A Captivating Guide to the History of France, Charlemagne, and Notre-Dame de Paris

Free Bonus from Captivating History (Available for a Limited time)

Hi History Lovers!

Now you have a chance to join our exclusive history list so you can get your first history ebook for free as well as discounts and a potential to get more history books for free! Simply visit the link below to join.

Captivatinghistory.com/ebook

Also, make sure to follow us on Facebook, Twitter and Youtube by searching for Captivating History.

Table of Content

Part 1: History of France

A Captivating Guide to French History

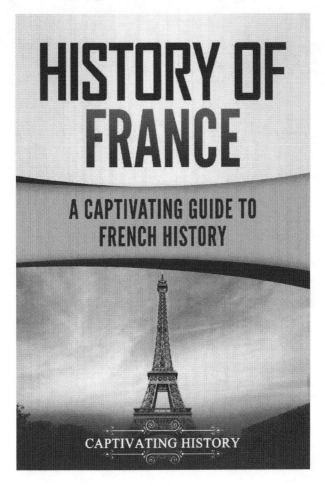

Introduction – Let's Go to Lascaux!

In September of 1940, two months after France fell to Hitler, a group of teenagers was out walking in the woods near the village of Montignac in the Dordogne region of southwestern France. The story goes that the boys were out looking for reported buried treasure at the end of an underground tunnel somewhere in the area. The legend had been going around for years, but this group of boys was sure they were onto something when they (or their dog, in one version) found a large hole in the ground.

The boys gathered around the hole, dropping rocks into it to get an idea of how deep it might be. Thinking it wasn't all that deep, they made their way one by one down a narrow shaft that went down about fifty feet. When they got to the bottom, they found themselves in a dimly lit cave covered with an amazing assortment of paintings. The boys weren't sure exactly what they were looking at, but they were pretty sure it was unique. After going promising each other to keep their findings a secret, they went back the next day and then decided they could make money off of what they had found. They decided to charge admission to some of their local friends and acquaintances.

Word spread, and hundreds of locals came to see the paintings, each with a theory about what they were and how they got there. Word finally got to a member of a local prehistory society whose members collected fossils and examined caves in the area. When he went down the hole, he felt sure he was looking at prehistoric paintings and instructed the boys to not let anyone else in until he could notify a local expert. This is the story behind the discovery of the amazing cave paintings of Lascaux.

One small sample of the Lascaux cave paintings.

The Lascaux paintings are estimated to be between 15,000 to 17,000 years old. Today, only recognized experts can go into the original cave to study the paintings. The climate is very carefully controlled because in the years after their discovery, thousands of people went to see the paintings, some even touching them. Others faded due to the amount of condensation and carbon dioxide caused by the visitors' breathing. The caves were closed to the public in 1963. In 2016, an amazing reconstruction of the paintings was created in a site nearby.

Were the inhabitants of the Lascaux caves "French"? Of course not. But the paintings at Lascaux and elsewhere in France prove that the land we call France has had a long history of human habitation going back thousands of years. It also appears those residents have had the same taste for art and culture that the people of France have always been noted for. Captivating History's *History of France* will introduce you to one of the most fascinating and influential nations in the world. French history is so involved and so intricate that it would (and has) taken forests to provide the paper to write it all on. For this book, we're going to introduce you to some of the greatest Frenchmen and women in history, and while you're getting to know them, we hope you get a feeling for the time and events that they lived in or perhaps even created themselves.

Chapter 1 – Just the Facts

Modern France and the American state of Texas are about the same size (France is 248,573 mi², while Texas is 268,597 mi²). That gives you an idea of the size of the United States as a whole compared to the largest country in Europe, discounting, as some do, Russia and Ukraine.

France has been both blessed and cursed by its location and topography. As you can see from the topographical map above, France is surrounded by water on three sides: the North Sea/English Channel on the northern coast, the Atlantic Ocean to the west, and the Mediterranean Sea to the south. These bodies of water provide great riches in terms of fish and other resources, and they have allowed France to establish seaborne trade throughout its history. These waterways have also allowed the country to project power not only in Europe but also around the world. This has been a great blessing, as they have allowed France to become one of the richest and most powerful countries in the world.

Unfortunately for the French, those waterways also expose the nation to invaders from overseas, though, in one case in 1944, the invasion from overseas was welcomed. Most notably, France's long English Channel coast exposes it to the country that had been its mortal enemy for centuries: England/Great Britain. However, times change, and France and England are close allies today.

In the Middle Ages, France's long coastlines exposed it to the ravages of the Vikings. This was made worse by the incredible number of navigable rivers that flow through France. The most famous French river, the Seine, flows from the English Channel directly to and through Paris—a fact discovered early on by the Norse invaders. The Seine, other large rivers (such as the Loire), and their many branches allowed the Vikings easy and rapid access to the interior of the country.

The rivers of France are also a blessing. They bring water deep into the heart of the country, and before the advent of trucks, cars, and planes, they were the primary economic highways of the country, bringing goods from one area to another. As you can see by the large amounts of green on the map, France is an incredibly fertile country, growing not only abundant crops but, as any chef will tell you, also some of the best natural ingredients in the world.

Another mixed blessing is France's location vis-à-vis the other nations of western Europe. We've already mentioned England, with whom France has gone to war countless times over the centuries. Today, France borders eight countries, though, at other times in history, French territory was either larger or smaller, as was the number of bordering nations. Three of those countries are quite small: Luxembourg, Andorra, and Monaco. The other five are Belgium, Italy, Spain, Switzerland, and Germany. Germany, which has only been a united nation state since 1871, has been a thorn in the side of France (to put it *very* mildly) since its inception, though at times, various German states (mostly on the French border) aligned themselves with France.

Since the French Revolution and the rise of Napoleon Bonaparte, the French and the Germans (before the Germans unified into the large and powerful state of Prussia) have fought four or five major wars, depending on how you divide historical eras. Between 1789 and 1815, the French and many of the German principalities fought a series of conflicts that saw France overrun virtually all of modern-day Germany. From 1870 to 1871, the Germans, under Prussian leadership, invaded France as part of their plan to unite all the German-speaking peoples into one nation. The Franco-Prussian War was a disaster for France. Some forty years later, World War I began, and the Germans invaded France yet again, conquering and occupying its richest regions for four years but never subduing the French nation. In 1940, the Germans under Hitler conquered France and subjected her to brutal occupation for four years. Today, France and Germany, thankfully, are among the closest allies on the planet.

France was the most populous nation in Europe up to the time of Napoleon and a bit beyond, which, combined with other factors, gave it great strength. Today, the population of France is just under sixty-eight million people, a number that has held steady for about a century.

The majority of the population is ethnically French, although there are sizable ethnically German populations in its east. Since the end of the French colonial period (circa 1945–1961), the nation has seen an influx of immigrants from former French colonies in Southeast Asia, Africa, and the Middle East. Some 7 to 9 percent of the population is Muslim, which, in recent years, has become a national issue. Some argue for limits on immigration even though generations of French Muslims are native-born, and others argue that the French are prejudiced against foreigners and, in particular, Muslims.

France has been and still is overwhelmingly Roman Catholic, though the number of people calling themselves "non-believers" has grown since the late 19th century. A small but culturally significant population of French Jews and Buddhists lives throughout the country, mostly in the larger cities, and most of the country's population as a whole is urban (around 81 percent).

France has one of the largest gross domestic product (GDP) in the world at nearly three trillion US dollars. Tourism brings in a large amount of money, as France is the most visited country in the world. The GDP of Russia, which is many times the size of France, is just over half of that amount, which speaks to both political history and stability as well as geography.

France's main trading partners are Germany, Belgium, Spain, the United Kingdom, Italy, the Netherlands, China, and the United States.

France produces most of the agriculture needed to support its population and exports its agricultural products throughout the world. Natural resources are abundant, especially in the northeast. Coal, iron, bauxite, zinc, gypsum, timber, and fish are among its most plentiful resources. One thing that France lacks in abundance is petroleum, which is one reason why the nation has become highly involved (along with its allies) in the Middle East.

France is not the military superpower it once was, but it is part of NATO (the North Atlantic Treaty Organization), which was created as an alliance against the communist Soviet Union after WWII. Today, NATO includes not only most of the western European nations but also a considerable number of eastern European nations, with the unsaid uniting fact being a continued suspicion and fear of Russia and its leadership.

France is one of a handful of nations that possesses nuclear weapons, and its arsenal alone is likely enough to destroy the planet. Its navy and air force are powerful enough to exert France's influence throughout the world, and its military has been and is still involved in many of the world's hotspots. The Middle East and Central Africa, in particular, are two areas in which France had considerable colonial possessions.

France's government is headed by a president, though officially, the position is labeled as the chief of state. The prime minister acts as the head of government (an important but largely ceremonial post). The legislature consists of two houses: the Sénat (Senate) and the Assemblée Nationale (National Assembly), which functions similarly to the United States Senate and House of Representatives. France's national judiciary consists of a large number of judges divided into sections and assignments.

Lastly, though French is the primary language of the nation, a sizable portion of the population speaks French as well as another language or regional dialect. Provencal, Breton, Alsatian/German, Basque, and Arabic are the major language groupings, along with a sizable number of Vietnamese and Spanish/Catalan speakers in the south as well. A significant portion of the population speaks English as a second language, though the journey from French being the language of diplomacy and business to English has not been an easy one, as many English-speaking tourists know!

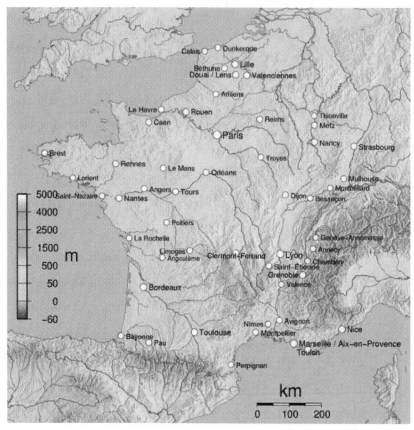

France and its major cities.

Chapter 2 – From the Last Great Ice Age to the Rise of Rome

Prior to the Great Ice Age (beginning about 30,000 years ago and ending about 10,000 years ago), our evolutionary ancestors had moved from eastern Africa into the Middle East and wandered off on four main routes to populate the "Old World." One branch slowly made its way into Asia, another into the steppes of today's Russia and central Asia, one into western Africa, and another into Europe.

Anthropologists believe that the most famous groups of the advanced primate family, Neanderthals and the Cro-Magnon people, reached as far north as modern-day Denmark and Great Britain, which was connected to Europe at the time by an expanse of land known today as Doggerland.

Early human migration, including the later migrations into the Pacific and the Americas.
*AltaileopardSVG by Magasjukur2, CC BY-SA 2.5 <https://creativecommons.org/licenses/by-sa/2.5>,
via Wikimedia Commons https://commons.wikimedia.org/wiki/File:Spreading_homo_sapiens.svg*

Then, with the spreading of the glacial ice, which made most of Europe uninhabitable, our ancestors retreated southward. It's believed that two main areas of habitable land remained in Eurasia: one in the area of modern Ukraine and the other in the borderlands of today's France and Spain. When the weather began to get warmer about 10,000 years ago, our ancestors, both Neanderthals and *Homo sapiens*, moved slowly back into the spaces vacated by the ice.

One of the groups that remained in what is called the "Franco-Cantabrian refugium" (Cantabria being a region of northern Spain), which sheltered our ancestors, were the direct ancestors of today's Basque people, whose language, *Euskara*, is both the oldest and most unique of the European languages. (Actually, most linguists believe that *Euskara* is unrelated to any other European language.)

Over the next 8,000 years, a succession of cultures developed and faded into history in many of the areas of western Europe, including France. Today, these cultural groups are known by the characteristics of their art, tools, and other implements (such as urns, pitchers, etc.)

From about 3100 BCE to around 2350 BCE, the culture known today as the Corded Ware culture populated northern France, southern Scandinavia, southern Germany, and today's Russia. As you can see in the picture below, their pottery shows rough "cords" in their construction and outer design.

Examples of Corded Ware pottery in the Berlin Prehistory Museum dating from circa 2500 BCE.

The peoples of the Corded Ware culture were centered in northwestern Europe and eastward. Toward the end of this cultural period, another group of prehistoric humans, known today as the Bell Beaker culture (named, yet again, for the characteristics of their art and implements), expanded from today's France and Spain and into other parts of Europe. This occurred in roughly 2400 BCE. Generally speaking, the Bell Beaker culture was the last of the Stone Age cultures, for it was followed by what is known as the Atlantic Bronze and Nordic Bronze Ages, which had many commonalities and significant differences as well.

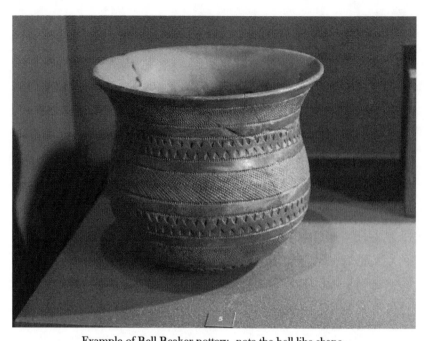

Example of Bell Beaker pottery—note the bell-like shape.

The peoples of today's France, Spain, Switzerland, Italy, Great Britain, Ireland, and Denmark developed the use of bronze in c. 1700 BCE, and they also developed their own cultures with significant trade routes and an advanced economy. At about the same time, the peoples of Scandinavia moved into their own separate bronze age, the so-called Nordic Bronze Age, which developed unique artistic and societal differences from the rest of Europe.

Atlantic Bronze Age exchange products:

Imports:
* Urnfields' crested helmets
* "Elbow" fibulae
* "Cleavage" shields

Exports:
* Tube sickles (Britain)
* Tube and double ring axes (Portugal)

➤ Approx. western limit of Urnfields expansion

Significant archaeological finds of the Atlantic Bronze Age.
Sugaar, CC BY-SA 3.0 <http://creativecommons.org/licenses/by-sa/3.0/>, via Wikimedia Commons https://commons.wikimedia.org/wiki/File:Atlantic_Bronze_Age.gif

Take a good look at the map above. Generally speaking, the extent of the development of the Atlantic Bronze Age indicates the spread of the Celtic peoples, of whom the Gauls were a part. The Gauls and Celts inhabited large parts of central Europe in the time before the rise of Rome. Our story of France begins with the many Gallic tribes of France as the Roman Empire spread into western Europe.

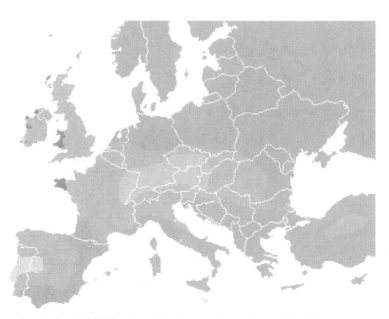

As you can see from the map above, the Celtic culture, whose lineal descendants populate today's Ireland, Scotland, and the French province of Brittany, spread across much of Europe, beginning in the area around today's small and beautiful Austrian town of Hallstatt and its salt mines, which made it rich in the age before coinage. As you can see, the Gauls were just one part of a larger culture, located roughly in the borders of today's modern France.

The Celts were not an empire. There were great commonalities, such as language, religion, and clothing, but the Celtic people were tribal. Occasionally, tribes would make alliances for defensive or aggressive purposes and for economic reasons. Sometimes, a popular or powerful local leader would unite a group of tribes for a time. But overall, the Celtic tribes existed autonomously.

The map above shows you not only the expansion of Celtic culture but also the area of Italy that was controlled by the Roman Republic circa 250 BCE. Over the next 200 years, the Romans would expand into other areas of the Mediterranean, the North African coast, and the Middle East, enveloping the cultures of those areas into the Roman Empire (which, it must be remembered, was not led by an emperor until the ascension of Julius Caesar's nephew Octavian, known more widely as Augustus).

Julius Caesar's dreams of becoming the first Roman emperor became less of a dream and more of a reality in one place—Gaul.

Chapter 3 – Vercingetorix

When Julius Caesar was named the governor of the Roman province of Gaul in 58 BCE, Roman rule in the area hardly amounted to much. Though they claimed much of today's France, the Romans really only controlled the Mediterranean coast and the area along the Rhine River, and that was tenuous at the best of times in 58 BCE.

In many ways, the Romans were an advanced culture compared to the Gauls. They were unified where the Gallic tribes were divided. The Romans' skill at organizing men was unsurpassed in Europe (and perhaps the world) at the time. The Romans excelled at architecture, road-building, and much else. They had a trade network that brought them riches from one end of the known world to the other. Their armies were second to none in Europe and the Middle East.

Generally speaking, when the Romans approached a new people, they gave them a few choices. One was to submit to Roman rule and accept their government and taxation/tribute system. In return, these people had access to the greatest trading network in the world, as well as Roman protection. The other choice was to fight. This was often tantamount to genocide, as happened to Carthage in the Third Punic War in 146 BCE.

The Romans described the Gauls as "barbarians," which was exactly how the Greeks had described the Romans centuries before. The Latin word for "barbarian" is *barbara*, which stems from the Greek *barbaros*. Like the Greeks before them, the Romans used that word to mean anyone who was not a Roman citizen. The Greek and Latin meanings of the word are "foreign," "non-Greek/Roman," or "strange." Yes, it likely was used as a pejorative by Romans and Greeks at times, but the true essence of the word did not mean what we think of as "barbarian" today, though writers, painters, and filmmakers (until recently) have portrayed the tribes of Gaul and other non-Roman parts of Europe as primitive savages living in dark forests, perhaps one step up from cavemen.

That impression of the Gauls (and the tribes of Germany and Great Britain) came from the Romans, whose writings on the subject were extensive and almost the sole source of contemporary information we have on the people of present-day France, Belgium, Holland, Britain, and Germany.

Of course, since Rome was, well, Rome, and there were no competing sources of information (the tribes had very rudimentary alphabets, if any at all), we have a biased vision of what the Gallic tribes were like. For centuries, historians have put together a picture of Gaul based on Roman writings, with the foremost among them being Julius Caesar's recollections of his war in Gaul.

As pointed out above, the Romans had the most advanced civilization in Europe at the time. There was much about Rome that the Gallic tribes could barely comprehend. The size of the Roman Empire alone would have been mystifying for many of the Gauls and other tribes. The architecture and art would have been absolutely stunning, not just in the sense of beauty but stunning enough to be almost magical. Nothing like the statuary and art of Rome existed in Gaul. Nor did the roads, political administration, etc.

Historians of the time were hardly unbiased. From the time of the first great Roman historians, such as Sallust (86 BCE–35 BCE) and Livy (59 BCE–17 CE), Roman historians propped up the Roman Republic or Roman Empire, castigating its enemies and those Romans seen as being on the wrong side of whatever opinion the writer held. One of the more notable things about Roman histories is that they frequently express admiration for enemies or enemy leaders that (at least in Roman eyes) fought and likely died with bravery.

The Roman view of the Gauls was the prevalent view that is still held even today. That view essentially sees the Gauls as living in their tribal areas, almost as nomadic woodsmen. Typically, one thinks of the Gauls as living in the dark forests and hills, following game and living in primitive huts, tents, or even caves.

Most likely, Roman writers (including Caesar) knew this was not the correct picture, but this image of the Gauls served an important purpose. Portraying the Gauls and others as savages gave the Romans "permission" to conquer the "barbarians." After all, the "uncivilized" tribes presented a threat to Rome, or at least this was what the Romans said.

Brennus and His Share of the Spoils, painting by Paul Jamin, 1893. Images like this not only titillated Victorian sensibilities but also spread the image of barbarian Gauls and civilized Romans.

Roman writers, politicians, generals, and the governing upper classes also told themselves that any invasion of Gaul was, in a way, "for the Gauls' own good." In their mind, they were bringing the Gauls "civilization," and they knew that the Gauls would eventually see the error of their ways, much like rebellious children eventually grow into cooperative adults.

We know from recent archaeological discoveries in France and throughout Celtic Europe that the Gauls and the other Celtic tribes of central and western Europe were much more sophisticated than was believed. Rather than being the semi-nomadic forest-dwelling people that the Romans believed (or wanted their public to believe) they were, the Gauls had an extensive trade network that reached from the Atlantic to the Danube. These trade routes consisted of roads (albeit dirt or laid stone, not the paved roads of the Romans) and river systems.

One of the ways we know this is the minted coins the Gauls left behind, as well as images on some pottery. Many times, these images were of horses, which played an obviously large part in Gallic life at the time, not only for travel and transport but also within Celtic mythology. In differing areas of Celtic Europe, horses were portrayed differently. Archaeologists have found Celtic coins with these localized styles in other parts of Europe, indicating both an advanced and extensive trade network. We know from Roman sources and other finds that the Celts traded in salt, grain, skins, meat, timber, wooden goods (wagons, etc.), cloth, and more.

To some Gauls, the Roman way of life had its appeal. By forming alliances with Rome, they had better access to Roman trade routes, knowledge, and military power. Having the Romans as allies meant that certain tribal chiefs could exert inordinate power over their enemies and/or competitors, which, of course, was part of the Roman plan.

Unfortunately for both the Romans and the Gauls, Rome was hard to satisfy. In return for Roman protection and access to more Roman trade, the Gauls were required to pay ever-increasing amounts of tribute to Rome. In return, the Gauls seemed to receive ever-lessening benefits and ever-increasing demands for more. These demands also included demands for slaves, which the Gauls took from each other and presented to the Romans. At times, the Romans required Gallic chieftains to give up their sons for "education" in Rome, which was a way to subvert the Gallic culture.

Of course, much of this was intentional, as the Romans were the masters of the phrase "divide and conquer." Gaul promised untold riches, resources, and men. If they could make Gaul part of the Roman Republic (soon to be Roman Empire), then most of Europe would be theirs, and their position as the world's preeminent power might be assured. Gaul would also act as a stepping stone to other parts of the world, mainly Britain and Germany.

However, the Gauls, like others before them and others afterward, eventually had enough. That's where Vercingetorix (82 BCE–46 BCE) stepped into history.

Vercingetorix was the son of the Arverni tribe's tribe, and he lived in the area of today's southern France, specifically in the Auvergne region around the modern city of Clermont-Ferrand and the Massif Central mountainous region. Vercingetorix's father, Celtillus, had been elected the nominal chieftain of the Gauls in the region, but he was later put to death for trying to establish a Gallic kingdom with himself at its head. The Gauls were known to be fiercely independent, with each tribe existing independently except in times of great danger.

In 58 BCE, Julius Caesar was named the governor of the Roman province of Gallia Narbonensis, today's famous Provence region. The region had been taken by the Romans in 121 BCE after the Gauls staged an uprising against increasing Roman settlement in the area. Over the course of the next few years, Caesar, who was a master not only of military matters but also political ones, instituted a policy of "divide and conquer" in Gaul, which he combined with the "carrot and stick" approach. Some of the Gauls, hypnotized both by Roman power and riches, received positions of power from Caesar and lorded it over their cousins in other tribes. But the weaker the Gauls became, the stronger the

Romans became. Roman settlement and military power in the area increased and expanded away from the coastal areas.

Over the course of Caesar's time in Gaul, many other Gauls were beginning to understand the Romans' intentions—that with the success of Roman ways came the end of the Gallic way of life.

In 52 BCE, a Gallic tribe called the Carnutes, whose territory in central France was beginning to be invaded by Roman settlements, rose up against the foreigners and slaughtered as many of them as they could. Vercingetorix and many of his followers and dependents (he was a prince, after all) were eager to join the revolt. He believed the Romans would only get more powerful over time and that the time was ripe, for events in Rome (chiefly the power struggles between Caesar's followers and Pompey's followers) had Caesar and the Romans in Gaul focused on events at home.

Unfortunately for Vercingetorix, a large number of other Gallic leaders, including his own uncle, believed that the Romans were simply too powerful to be challenged. Vercingetorix was sent into a kind of exile with his followers, but he returned to his tribe's capital city (then called Gergovia, today's Clermont-Ferrand) with an army of poor peasants and younger tribal leaders and took over the city.

By all accounts, Vercingetorix was a charismatic and skillful leader. Like many leaders then and now, he could also be harsh and brutal. He sent out messengers and met with other Gallic tribal leaders from throughout the region and other parts of Gaul, cajoling, convincing, and threatening them to unite against the Romans.

Caesar had spies and well-paid allies among the Gauls, so he was kept apprised of Vercingetorix's plans to unite the tribes. Small battles between Romans and Gauls led by Vercingetorix had resulted in Roman victories, and Caesar was determined to crush the rebellion by seizing a major city and granary, what the Romans called an *oppidum* (a settlement), called Avaricum (present-day

Bourges).

Vercingetorix knew that Caesar was headed toward Avaricum, and he proceeded to burn every single grain he could find for fifteen miles around the town. The residents of Avaricum begged Vercingetorix not to burn their city to the ground, and realizing that the town and area around it was defensible, the Gallic leader left it intact.

Over the next month, the Romans besieged Avaricum. While they were doing so, Vercingetorix's cavalry and other units harassed them endlessly. Combined with their slowly dwindling food supply and growing hunger, the Romans, when they finally breached the city walls, killed virtually every person in Avaricum. According to Caesar's writings, they killed an estimated 40,000 people and left only about 800 alive.

If the Romans believed the slaughter at Avaricum would cow the Gauls, they were wrong. If they wanted to anger the Gallic rebels and draw them into battle, they got their wish. Caesar had about ten legions with him in southern Gaul (around 40,000 to 60,000 soldiers). To prevent the tribes of northern Gaul from joining Vercingetorix, he sent six legions northward to block any northerners from moving south. With his remaining forces, Caesar moved toward Gergovia, the capital of Vercingetorix's tribe, the Arverni. This took place in the late winter of 52 BCE

After a series of maneuvers and counter-moves, Caesar's forces attempted to take control of the town's water supply. When they did, his allies, the Aedui, turned on him, as agreed with Vercingetorix, and a costly battle began. Caesar defeated the Aedui and moved toward the town with the remainder of his forces. As he did, Vercingetorix led a massive cavalry charge into Roman lines, then dismounted and joined the remaining Aedui in attacking the Romans on foot. Caesar recorded his losses at several hundred officers and men, but modern historians think it was much more, closer to perhaps several thousand. Caesar, who was nearly surrounded on the hilltop where Gergovia lay, ordered a retreat.

Gergovia was an important victory for the Gauls, as it resulted in many other tribes joining forces with Vercingetorix. Over the course of the next few months, Vercingetorix and the rulers of the other tribes trained the armies of Gaul for the fight they knew was coming. Vercingetorix was reputedly a harsh leader. He trained his men relentlessly in more modern tactics and punished laziness and insubordination severely, for he knew that defeat at the hands of the Romans likely meant slavery or death for many of his people. At the same time, Caesar summoned 10,000 men from the Teutonic (German) tribes along the Rhine River and recalled his other Roman legions southward.

By September, Vercingetorix's forces numbered about 80,000 men. They had fought a number of smaller battles with the Romans and had been defeated in virtually all of them. The Gauls fell back to the fortified town of Alesia and awaited the Romans' next moves. Caesar, inflating the Gallic forces for his own political purposes, numbered them at 250,000. The Roman forces themselves numbered an estimated 60,000.

Alesia was set on a hillside with rivers on both sides. Around the town, the Gauls had dug trenches and erected a large stone wall. Recognizing its strength, Caesar knew that a frontal attack was doomed to fail and ordered his troops to begin a siege. They dug an amazing eleven miles of trenches around the Alesia *oppidum*, which were connected by twenty-three strong points.

Vercingetorix knew there was only about thirty days' worth of supplies in the town, so he sent his cavalry out through a gap in the Roman lines one moonless night, hoping they would reach the forces of other Gauls in the area to aid the town. Caesar learned of these plans from prisoners his men had taken and set about preparing an additional set of trench and fortifications three miles outside of his lines, facing the town.

Sometime later, Vercingetorix's hopes were achieved when a large relief force of Gauls was sighted in the distance, but on the first day of battle, which lasted from dawn to dusk, the Roman forces and their German allies were able to prevent the Gallic reinforcements from breaking through their lines to relieve Alesia.

On the second day of the battle, the Gauls inside Alesia and those outside assaulted the two Roman lines. While Vercingetorix's forces made a little progress, they received word that their allies had been repulsed again on the Roman lines miles from the town.

The third day of the battle was the key. Both Vercingetorix and Caesar personally took part in combat, leading their men at dangerous moments. The Gauls outside the city broke through a gap in the Roman lines and were threatening to join with Vercingetorix, but in a series of quick-thinking and rapid moves, Caesar succeeded in surrounding this large force of Gauls and almost completely wiped it out. Those men who survived ran in panic to the remainder of their forces outside the town and caused them to flee. That left just Vercingetorix and his dwindling number of men in the town.

That night, Vercingetorix called together all of the Gallic leaders in Alesia and asked them how they wanted to proceed. Did they want to kill him, or did they want him to surrender to Caesar? Hoping to appease Caesar with the surrender of their leader, the Gauls told Vercingetorix to give himself up the next day, which he did.

Vercingetorix surrendering to Caesar. A painting by Lionel Royer, who based the scene on Caesar's description.

Because Caesar respected Vercingetorix and because the Arverni had fought with great bravery, Caesar spared most of the tribe from slavery or death, but many of the other Gallic tribes were not so fortunate. As a lesson to the Gauls and as a concession to his men (whose support he would need for his future plans), Caesar gave many of the survivors to his troops as slaves. Over the next four and a half years, Caesar and the Romans would settle more of their countrymen in Gaul, and most of Gaul would become part of the Roman Republic. Alesia allowed Julius Caesar to become the legend he is today.

As for Vercingetorix, he spent those next five and a half years as a Roman prisoner. In Caesar's triumphal marches on his return home, Vercingetorix was displayed before roaring crowds in Rome, then taken back to prison and strangled, per the Roman custom.

Vercingetorix's image was rehabilitated during the time of Napoleon and his nephew, Napoleon III. His image as a fierce French/Gallic warrior was just what the two 19th-century French emperors needed. Napoleon III had a massive statue of Vercingetorix erected near the town of Clermont-Ferrand, near Vercingetorix's capital, where it still stands today.

Carole Raddato from FRANKFURT, Germany

Chapter 4 – Charlemagne

Some 852 years later, a new Roman emperor would be crowned in Rome. The circumstances of this coronation were vastly different than that which existed at the dawning of the Roman Empire with the naming of Julius Caesar's nephew, Octavian, as the first Roman emperor, Augustus Caesar, but the ritual sent the same message: "I am the most powerful man in Europe."

The man being made emperor was not Roman, and there wasn't truly a "Roman Empire" to rule over, but in 800 CE, the pope and the emperor-to-be decided that the title was fitting and that it was likely needed to bring back some semblance of order to a western Europe that had fallen into darkness since the end of the real Roman Empire centuries before.

That new emperor was Charlemagne or, in Latin, *Karolus*, and he was a Frank, meaning he was neither a Roman nor a Gaul. The Franks were a Germanic tribe that had settled on both sides of the Rhine River sometime in the 3rd century CE, and both France and Germany have claimed Charlemagne's legacy for their own in more recent times.

In the centuries between the Roman conquest of Gaul and the rise of Charlemagne, the population of what is now France, as well as parts of Belgium, Luxembourg, Switzerland, and western Germany, changed almost completely. The Roman conquest of Gaul was so complete that a new culture, "Gallo-Roman," was born. Of course, this meant not only the spread of Roman culture and its incorporation into Gaul but also the spread of Roman DNA and vice versa. Though millennia have passed, even today, traces of Roman influence can be seen in the French population, especially on the southern coast, where, very generally speaking, the people have darker hair and more olive skin than their northern brothers and sisters.

The Gauls who remained outside of the Roman sphere of influence were located as far as possible from the Romans as they could be while still being in Gaul/France. These were, and are, the people of Brittany, which is the French province that borders the English Channel in the northwest and the Atlantic to the south and east. Even the name "Brittany" is Celtic, and it is linguistically related to the words "Britain" and "Britons" (the name for the many tribes of England and Wales that lived there before the Romans arrived in that country). Though the Bretons (the modern French word for the distinct people of Brittany) are French citizens, many still speak a unique language, and you will see road signs throughout the region in both French, Breton, and occasionally Gallo. The last two languages are members of the Celtic language tree that includes Gaelic, the native language of Ireland.

The Germanic tribes known collectively as the Franks made their home in the Lower Rhine area. "Lower" in this case is actually north, not south, as the rivers in western Europe, with the exception of the Danube, which really begins in central Europe, flow from south to north. The Lower Rhine is in the area of today's Belgium, part of Holland, and the part of France known as

Flanders.

For our purposes, the more significant of the four groups above are the Salian Franks (a word that describes their location near the North Sea) and the Ripuarian Franks (*ripuarian* connoting "river," in this case, the Rhine). The location of the Franks' homeland was unfortunate in some ways.

We know that the Romans had contact with them before the 3rd century CE, which was when the name "Frank" began to be used in Roman writings. The Romans had conducted trade with the Franks, and a significant number of Franks were in the Roman army, especially in the later years of the empire.

On their northern borders, both the Salian and Ripuarian Franks were faced with the Saxons, which was a rival and quite warlike Germanic tribe. By the 3rd century, Rome's power was in decline, and those living in the Roman settlements along the Rhine River were frequently the subject of powerful raids from the Saxons and their allies to the east. As a result, the Romans, along with their Frankish allies, relocated farther west, away from the Saxon homeland and into more defensible and populated areas.

As the power of the Romans became even weaker in the 5th century, the Franks began to assert themselves on the left bank of the Rhine River. In 462, the Ripuarian Franks took Cologne, one of the largest Roman cities in Gaul/France.

In the middle of the 5th century, one Frankish family became dominant. This was the Merovingian family, who took their name from a legendary Salian Frankish king named Merovech, who purportedly took part in the Battle of Chalons, also known as the Battle of the Catalaunian Plains, in 451. In this battle, an allied army of Romans, Goths, and Franks defeated the forces of Attila the Hun, preventing them from driving into France.

The grandson of Merovech, Clovis I, was the founder of a united Frankish kingdom after killing most of his powerful rivals. By the 480s/490s, Clovis had conquered most of Gaul with the exception of the powerful Burgundians and the Ripuarian Franks. By 509, he was proclaimed the king of all the Franks when he seized Cologne from the Ripuarians, He died in 511, and he set a poor precedent by dividing his kingdom between his four sons, likely in the hope that they would work together. This was not to be.

After a century of divided rule, the Merovingians united behind Clotaire II to form a single Frankish kingdom. In those one hundred years and after the death of Clotaire's son Dagobert I (r. 629-639), the Merovingian kings, for many reasons (including weak personalities, infighting, and giving more attention to luxury than ruling), saw their power decline in favor of their chancellors, known to history as the mayors of the palace.

Of these mayors of the palace, the most significant were Pepin II, also known as Pepin the Middle or Pepin of Herstal (b. 635-d. 714), and his grandson, Pepin the Short (b. 714-d. 768).

Pepin II came to rule the Franks in all but name after defeating the forces of the other powerful mayors in the divided Merovingian kingdom. He ruled from 687 to his death in 714, and he ceded power to his son, Charles Martel, known to history as Charles the Hammer (*Martel* means "hammer" in the Frankish language). A more apt name would be hard to find in history.

Charles Martel at Tours.

The early Merovingian kings, as well as their mayors of the palace, were known for their ruthlessness. Charles the Hammer might have been the most ruthless of them all. Of course, he needed to be, for throughout his young life, people, including his stepmother, were trying to kill him.

The story of Charles is long, but for our purposes here, he is important for two reasons. The first is his defeat of the Moors at Tours. The Muslim Arab armies, which had stormed out of the Arabian Peninsula after the revelations of the Prophet Muhammad, were referred to as the Moors by contemporary historians. By defeating the Moors at Tours, Martel prevented the spread of Islam into the rest of Europe (the Moors had conquered Spain in 711). Charles also subdued the tribes of Saxony and extended the Frankish Empire into the southern part of modern-day Germany, placing puppet kings in each area. Both of these territories would give Charles's grandson trouble. The second major reason Charles Martel is remembered is that he was the founder of the Carolingian dynasty. His son, Pepin the Short, became the first Carolingian king, and his grandson, the great Charlemagne, followed in his father's footsteps.

By the time of Charlemagne's birth, the Franks had established themselves as the most powerful European dynasty outside of the Byzantine Empire, but it was Charlemagne that would make the Franks a rival to anyone on the Continent. He was born on April 2nd, but his birth year is unclear. Some have it as 742, others 747, and still others 748. He died at the considerable age of sixty-five (if one goes with 742 as his birth year). Back then, the average lifespan was between thirty and thirty-five.

We know very little about Charlemagne's early life, though a great deal can be at least somewhat accurately surmised. Being a prince, he was well educated for his time. He spoke his native language, and he could also speak Latin and understand Greek. He was given as much education about the world outside of Frankish domains as was known. For his entire life, Charlemagne pursued knowledge, bringing in experts on many subjects to study and write at his court. The years between the fall of the Roman Empire (c. 400) and the start of the Renaissance (c. 1300) are often referred to as the Dark Ages, for it was believed that in those centuries, the progress made by the Greeks and Romans had been lost and forgotten. Until the latter part of the 20th century, historians had a tendency to portray this time as a bleak, barbaric, and ignorant time, and in a lot of ways, it was. However, while much of the knowledge of the Greeks and Romans was lost to most of Europe, much of it was kept in the former Roman provinces in the Middle East and Egypt, as well as in the court of the Byzantine Empire. The "rediscovery" of this knowledge by Europeans in the 12th century and its application and expansion led to the Renaissance. But in the vaults of the Catholic Church in Rome and in churches and monasteries throughout Europe, much of that knowledge remained, and the kings and queens of Europe, like Charlemagne, had access to it if they wanted it badly enough. Charlemagne certainly did. By all accounts, his appetite for knowledge was unbounded.

Charlemagne's hunger for knowledge was not limited to the study of languages and the sciences (such as they were at the time), as he also craved to learn of his kingdom. As both king and emperor, Charlemagne spent much of his life traveling to the far reaches of his lands. He did this sometimes out of military necessity, but he often traveled to the courts of his underlings to make sure that things were happening as he was told, to make sure his deputies knew he was watching them, and to find out both the problems and assets of his lands firsthand. Additionally, it has recently been brought to light that Charlemagne had a vast, well-organized, and powerful network of spies and informants throughout both his lands and, in some cases, the lands of his enemies.

Charlemagne was able to keep this network strong in a few ways. Firstly, he was the wealthiest ruler in Europe (excluding the Byzantines, much of whose empire at the time was outside the Continent). He paid handsomely for both information and loyalty. Secondly, he had spies watching his spies, which is a quite modern idea. Thirdly, Charlemagne inspired loyalty, as he was a charismatic and intelligent figure. Fourth, in addition to being charismatic and intelligent, he was also ruthless. In this case, the name "Dark Ages" is apropos. Torture was not the exception in the 8th and 9th centuries—it was the rule.

Charlemagne's Rule

When Pepin the Short died in September 768, his domain was given not to his eldest son Charlemagne but to both Charlemagne and his other son, Carloman. They were to rule as co-equals, though each was to govern specific regions. Generally speaking, Charlemagne governed the outer parts of the kingdom bordering the seas, except in the south. Carloman governed the interior part of modern-day France down to the Mediterranean and bordering on today's northern Italy.

This arrangement must have rankled Charlemagne to a degree, and he spent much of his early reign outwardly accepting the situation but maneuvering behind the scenes to box his brother in both politically and geographically, moving in his own allies to areas ostensibly under his younger brother's control. Not only was Carloman nine years younger than Charlemagne, 'but he was also hardly experienced in all the ways that mattered at the time. Mostly, this meant at war. By the time the brothers came to rule Francia, Charlemagne had been fighting battles throughout the kingdom at his father's side or behest.

For many years, historians suspected that Charlemagne had his brother murdered. We do know that Carloman died shortly after a major disagreement between the two brothers, but it seems that this was a coincidence. Although we don't know for certain what killed Carloman, it was more likely he died from complications from a peptic ulcer than at his brother's hand.

The brothers' disagreement arose over what to do about unrest in the southwest of France, in one of the richest and most fertile areas of the country known as Aquitaine. It was named after an ancient tribe, the Aquitani, who were likely related to today's Basques. It is thought the Basque language and the language spoken by the people in the area, also known as Aquitani, were related. Aquitani is a dead language today.

From 759 to 768, the people of Aquitaine fought a brutal war against Charlemagne and Carloman's father, Pepin the Short. A year later, the Aquitanians invaded Frankish territory, seeking both revenge and attempting to divide Charlemagne and Carloman. The brothers argued over what to do. Charlemagne was in favor of putting down the Aquitanians, which Carloman opposed. Charlemagne led a successful campaign against the Aquitanians, and through a series of negotiations, he allowed their leader, Hunald II, to live out the rest of his life peacefully in a monastery. All of Hunald's men swore allegiance to the Franks, more specifically to Charlemagne. As a result, the territory was finally and irrevocably made part of the Frankish Empire.

Throughout his time as the joint king of the Franks, Charlemagne was advised by his wise and impressive mother, Bertrada of Laon (a city about eighty-five miles northeast of Paris). Bertrada clearly favored Charlemagne over his younger brother and counseled the former in his attempts to nullify Carloman's influence. Bertrada also greatly influenced Charlemagne's love life. Perhaps "love life" is the wrong term. Bertrada instructed Charlemagne on forming political alliances through marriage.

Charlemagne's first wife, Himiltrude, gave him one son, Pepin the Hunchback, who would later lead an abortive revolt against his father. After the birth of Pepin, Bertrada counseled Charlemagne to marry Desiderata, the daughter of the powerful king of the Lombards, Desiderius, in order to gain a powerful ally and further surround Carloman's territories. Apparently, however, Desiderata was not Charlemagne's cup of tea, for he soon divorced her to marry Hildegard, a Frankish princess.

Desiderius was furious at this slight and vowed to make life miserable for Charlemagne. Step one would have been to ally himself with Carloman, but it was at this moment that Carloman passed away, allowing Charlemagne to become the sole ruler of the Franks. And as soon as he had become king in his own right, he was involved in international power politics.

In 772, Adrian I was named the new pope. One of the new pope's first acts was to demand the return of former papal territories near the city of Ravenna and some farther south. These former papal territories had first been seized by armies of the Byzantine Empire and then lost to the Lombards when they moved into northern Italy from their homeland in what is now northern Germany. The Lombards had reached an agreement with the papacy that they would return these territories upon Desiderius's ascension to the throne, but when he became king,

Desiderius instead marched toward Rome, intent on taking much of Italy, including Rome, for himself.

Charlemagne's father, Pepin, had supported the papacy in the negotiations with the Lombards, so Adrian I appealed to Charlemagne to do the same. The Frankish king was a devout Catholic, despite his many wives and concubines, and sent ambassadors to support the pope in negotiations with the Lombards. In the end, Charlemagne demanded the return of the territories, and Desiderius, as you can imagine, adamantly refused.

Charlemagne then conducted a brilliant campaign and besieged the Lombard capital city of Pavia for much of 774. In the end, Charlemagne defeated not only Desiderius but also his son, Adelchis, who attempted to relieve the city. Desiderius was forced into a monastery, and his son escaped to live in exile in Byzantium. This left Charlemagne in control of northern Italy, which was the strongest power in the country. He crowned himself the king of Lombardy and gave control of the disputed cities to the pope. Two years later, he interrupted another campaign in Germany to return to Italy to put down a rebellion, and with that, Charlemagne was the undisputed master of the Italian Peninsula, France, and much of southwestern Germany.

Growth of the Frankish Empire. Charlemagne's additions are in light grey-green.

Sémhur, CC BY-SA 3.0 <https://creativecommons.org/licenses/by-sa/3.0>, via Wikimedia Commons
https://commons.wikimedia.org/wiki/File:Frankish_Empire_481_to_814-en.svg

As you can see from the map above, Charlemagne was at war with the Germanic tribes for decades. The most troublesome and prolonged struggles the king faced throughout his long reign were with the Saxons in northern Germany, and it is there that the deeds of Charlemagne have come under the most scrutiny in recent years.

In the whole of Saxony and in parts of northern Thuringia and the coastal territory of Frisia, the people worshiped the Germanic gods of Odin, Thor, Frey, and Freya, among others. As a devoted and zealous Catholic, Charlemagne was determined not only to add Saxony to his empire but also to stamp out the pagan religion in both territories once and for all.

Charlemagne's armies were large for the time. Contemporary writings and reports numbered his armies at 100,000, but modern historians put it closer to 30,000 or 40,000, which was still large for its time. Charlemagne warred against the Saxons in 772, 785, 792 to 793, and from 798 to 803. As you can see, the struggle against the Saxons was long, and it became extremely brutal. Throughout the campaigns, especially in the last one, Charlemagne and his men forcibly converted the Saxons to Christianity.

In the first years of his war against the Saxons, Charlemagne would be satisfied when Saxon leaders swore allegiance to him and renounced their pagan religion. In some instances, Saxon leaders would remain loyal to Charlemagne, who, in return for loyalty and conversion, could be generous. However, many Saxons who converted at the end of a spear soon turned their backs on Christianity when the Franks left. The Frankish army usually had to fight in other areas of the empire, for instance, against the Muslims on the Spanish border or in central Europe against the Avars, a nomadic tribe that had settled in what is now modern-day Austria, Hungary, and parts of Serbia.

In the later campaigns against the Saxons, Charlemagne was ruthless. In 782, his troops slaughtered over 4,000 Saxons who refused to convert. All throughout Saxony, people were forced to convert. The Franks used the Saxons' loyalty against them, forcing their children into learning a Christian education and encouraging them to report on their parents or anyone else who practiced pagan rituals or espoused pagan beliefs in private. Anyone accused or caught in the act of worshiping pagan gods or conducting pagan rituals was often put to death, sometimes in very slow and painful ways. The last Saxon rebellion against Christianity and Charlemagne's rule was in 804, over thirty years after the Frankish king had first made war against them.

Frankish expansion ended at the modern Danish border. In the latter years of Charlemagne's reign, Danish and Norwegian Vikings had begun small-scale raids of Frankish territory, but the Vikings were a more significant problem for Charlemagne's heirs than the emperor himself.

Holy Roman Emperor

On Christmas Day of the year 800, Pope Leo III crowned Charlemagne as the emperor of the Romans. The title of Holy Roman emperor would live on until 1918, by which time it had long lost any real meaning.

However, in 800, the title was fraught with meaning in a number of ways. Pope Leo was an unpopular pope, and he was almost killed by a Roman mob in 799 after being accused of adultery and perjury by relatives of the former pope, Adrian I. Leo's family was not a noble one, and this, too, made him many enemies, as they believed that only nobility should hold the highest position in the church. Because of Charlemagne's power and his devout Christianity, Leo fled to Charlemagne's court, which was then at Paderborn in today's Germany.

Charlemagne knew that any rift in the Roman Catholic Church was likely to have serious effects through his realm and elsewhere. A divided Catholic Europe would only become weaker, making it an even greater target for the Muslims in Spain and the Eastern Orthodox Christians of the Byzantine Empire. The Byzantine emperors had long laid claim to authority in Rome and considered themselves the heirs of the Roman Empire itself.

Charlemagne called a synod, which is a meeting of clergymen, in Rome, with himself presiding, to determine Leo's innocence or guilt. The long and short of it is that Leo swore an oath to Charlemagne that he was innocent, and Charlemagne accepted it. Since Charlemagne controlled most of Italy with his army, the attending clergy fell into line.

Now seen as dependent on Charlemagne, Pope Leo contrived to raise the office of pope back to its former stature. He then announced his intent to crown Charlemagne as *Imperator Romanum*, or "Emperor of the Romans." Since it was the pope doing the crowning, the intended impression was for Europe to see it as the pope who had the ultimate power, not Charlemagne.

Centuries later, during WWII, British Prime Minister Winston Churchill suggested to Soviet leader Josef Stalin that it might be a good idea to invite the pope to the Tehran Conference of 1943, where issues regarding the war and post-war Europe were to be made. Stalin's reply perfectly fits the situation between Pope Leo and Charlemagne in 800. Stalin replied, "The Pope? How many divisions does he have?"

In 800, as in 1943, everyone knew where the real power lay: Charlemagne. Still, it put the Frankish ruler in a strange position. Firstly, he was in negotiations with the Byzantines, mainly its empress, Irene, who was eligible for marriage. Charlemagne had grand plans for his empire, as he wanted to unite both the Western and Eastern Empires into a renewed Roman Empire with himself at its head. By accepting the crown from the pope, Charlemagne undermined his negotiations by not taking into consideration the position of the Byzantines. Some historians, therefore, believe that had Charlemagne known what the pope was going to do, he would not have entered the hall that day. However, others believe that Charlemagne was well aware of the pope's intentions and knew it would add an extra dimension to his power, as he would become the defender of Western Christendom.

With his ascension to Holy Roman emperor and with his armies in possession of most of western Europe and significant areas of central Europe, Charlemagne is considered by many to be the forefather of the idea of a "United Europe." Today, that idea is represented, for better or worse, by the European Union. But others with less benevolent intent have held Charlemagne up as a role model, including Hitler and a Frenchmen of the late 18th and early 19th centuries that we shall be telling you about later.

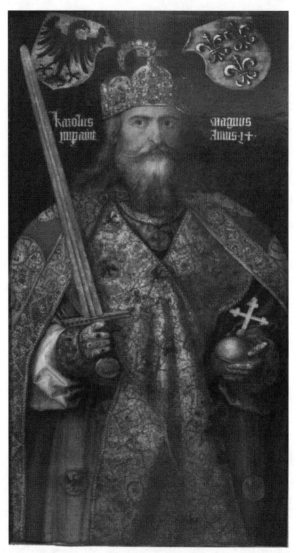

Charlemagne as depicted by Albrecht Durer (1471–1528). In the upper left is the symbol of the Holy Roman Empire, and the upper right depicts the symbol of the kings of France.

Chapter 5 – A Collision of Cultures, 814–1429

As you may have noticed, we are using a number of famous individuals as the foundation for this brief history of France. French history is so rich, so influential, and so detailed that writing a 150-page book can swiftly turn into a 400-page book in the blink of an eye.

However, in order to understand the situation facing France and our next major protagonist, we are going to have to include a chapter covering the years between the death of Charlemagne and the situation facing France in the early 1400s.

Knowing he was dying, Charlemagne named his son Louis (known as Louis the Pious) as the king of the Franks and the co-emperor of the Holy Roman Empire. Louis had also been given charge of Aquitaine in 781, and in that position, he had reclaimed much of northern Spain from the Muslims. By the time of his father's death in early 814, he had considerable experience in both ruling and warfare.

Unfortunately for Louis, he had three sons, each of whom wanted to be king, and much of Louis's later reign was a time of civil war. In fact, there were three great uprisings involving his sons and their allies in their quest for power. Unfortunately for his sons, Louis was a skilled warrior. During the long civil wars, each son allied with his father or at least made peace with him only to wage war on the others.

When Louis the Pious died in 840, the brothers all warred upon each other again for three years, but none of them was able to get the upper hand. Of course, in all of this violence between royal brothers and their allies, the common people suffered.

In 843, the brothers met at the town of Verdun in today's eastern France. There, the brothers hammered out an agreement to divide the empire among them. The eldest of Louis's children, Lothair I, was given control over what is known as Middle Francia, and he was also given the title of Holy Roman emperor, as he had been so designated by their father. This title, however, did not give Lothair any control over his brothers or their lands. On the following page, you will see a map illustrating the division of the empire.

Louis the Pious's middle son, Louis II, is known to history as Louis the German, and you can probably guess why. He was given control of the eastern part of the empire, which encompassed modern-day Germany. In German, "Louis" is "Ludwig," as you will see on the map below.

Lastly, the youngest son, Charles the Bald, was given the largest and perhaps richest portion of the empire: western France, with the exception of Brittany, which was under the control of its own powerful dukes.

contains the following labels:

Treaty of Verdun 843
The division of the Frankish realms

Anglo-Saxons

Independent Territories

Sorbs

Brittany

Ludwig the German's Kingdom

Bohemia

Charles the Bald's Kingdom

Bavaria

Carinthia

Lothair I's Kingdom

Papal State

The Moors

Great Politburo

This division of the Carolingian Empire is regarded by historians as the founding of France and Germany as we have come to know them. Though many similarities remained, it was at this point that new cultural and political customs appeared, as well as two new languages, French and German, though in much different forms than they exist today.

For our purposes here, Charles the Bald is our focus. Firstly, was he bald? It is not likely. Contemporary paintings of him show a man with a full head of hair, and accounts of his person describe someone very hairy indeed. The name may have been a sarcastic reference, or it might refer to an earlier meaning of the root of the word "bald," meaning "without land." As the youngest child of Louis, Charles did indeed have much less land than his brothers, at least for a time.

You might be familiar with Charles the Bald from the TV series *Vikings*. Like much of that series, the writers played fast and loose with the timelines and many of the facts, but they did get some of Charles's story right. He did have a daughter named Gisela or Gisla, but he - did not marry her off to Rollo, who is Ragnar's brother in the series. The real Rollo didn't live until long after Ragnar Lothbrok, and it's still debated whether Ragnar existed at all. In the series, Charles is asked to appeal to his brothers for aid, which he initially refuses to do, then reports that he had but with no results. Whether this was true or not, his brothers likely would not have come to his aid, as they were bitter rivals even after the Treaty of Verdun. Lastly, Charles the Bald fought the Vikings himself, relatively successfully. Charles's grandson was another Charles, this time called "the Simple." Initially, this nickname meant "straightforward"; one later writer called him Charles the Stupid for a battlefield error in 919. Charles the Simple was the man who actually gave Rollo land in western France, and it was Charles the Simple who had a daughter named Gisela or Gisla, whom he married to Rollo.

Rollo is where things get complicated. Rollo's history before he came to France is immaterial here. Let's just say he was a Viking—and a tall one at that. He was known as *Hrolf Gangr*, or "Rollo the Walker," for he is said to have been so tall that when seated on a horse, his legs touched the ground.

What we do know is that Rollo is a pivotal figure in history. He was a Viking chief, and by the time he besieged Paris and the city of Chartres in 911, he must have been a veteran warrior and highly regarded Viking chief. Though Rollo was defeated by Charles the Simple's army at Chartres, the French king decided to reach terms with Rollo to avoid further raids on his territories.

Rollo was given what became known as Normandy, which simply means "Land of the Northmen." In return, he swore loyalty to Charles, meaning he would fight for Charles when requested.

This included fighting other Vikings, but Vikings fought against each other all the time. One of Rollo's first wars as the ruler of Normandy was against another Viking group that sought to take Normandy from him. Additionally, Rollo agreed to be baptized and bring his children up as Christians.

Rollo's great-great-great-grandson was William the Conqueror, although he didn't gain this epithet until later in life. By 1028, around the time William was born, Rollo's descendants had made Normandy the most powerful entity in France. Normandy was essentially a country unto itself. Rollo's descendants (shown below) developed a powerful army that was renowned throughout Europe for its prowess.

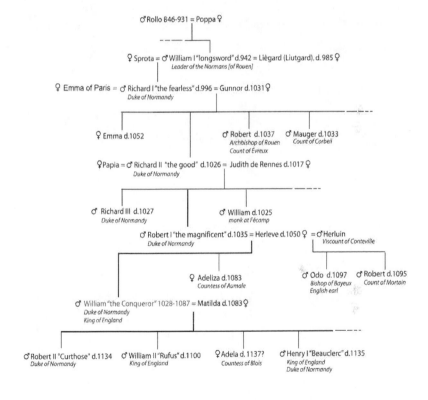

Chronological tree of William I
https://commons.wikimedia.org/wiki/File:Chronological_tree_of_William_I.svg

William, also known as "the Bastard" for his illegitimate birth, would become the duke of Normandy in 1035. In addition to that, he had a claim to the English throne as well. His first cousin once-removed was Edward the Confessor, the English king. A first cousin once-removed may seem a bit distant to be the heir to the English throne, but Edward was childless.

Also in the running to become the English king was Harold Godwinson, whose powerful noble family had been both rival and ally to Edward the Confessor. Harold became Edward's right-hand man later in the king's life and helped him put down numerous rebellions, including one by Harold's own brother. Edward fell into a coma in late 1065, but before he died, he regained consciousness and expressed his wish that Harold "protect" both his kingdom and his soon-to-be-widow. Harold took this as Edward's wish for him to be the next king, so he proceeded to gather the Witan (the Anglo-Saxon king's council), which voted to name him king, and he was crowned on January 6th, 1066.

Harold was immediately beset by problems, namely keeping his throne. Not only did the powerful William of Normandy claim the kingship of England but so did another formidable enemy, the man historians call the "last great Viking king," Harald Hardrada ("Hard-ruler") of Norway.

Harald's adventurous life could fill a book itself. It was he, not Ragnar Lothbrok, who staged his own death in order to help breach a besieged city's walls, and he had fought from Byzantium all across Europe. Now a king in Norway, Harald's claim was tenuous at best. He claimed descent from Cnut the Great, the Scandinavian Viking king who had become king not only of Denmark and Norway but also England and who had ruled from 1016 to 1035. Harald also claimed that Harold Godwinson's brother, Tostig, who had rebelled against his brother and King Edward and fled to Norway, promised him the kingship of England.

Muddying the waters even further, William of Normandy claimed that he had received Harold Godwinson's oath that Harold would support William's claim to the throne. This had allegedly (and probably) happened when Harold had gone across the English Channel in 1064. There are numerous theories as to why Harold went to France, but they are too numerous to discuss here. Suffice it to say that Harold was taken prisoner by the count of Ponthieu, an area south of Normandy, with the count likely hoping for a rich ransom from the Godwin family in England and perhaps the king himself. That was not to be, as William of Normandy personally went to Ponthieu and ordered Harold to be released. And William was not a man to be trifled with.

For the next few weeks, Harold made the acquaintance of William and even accompanied him in battle. He apparently rescued two of William's men from quicksand and generally acquitted himself well, whether it was in battle, drinking, or feasting. However, it was clear that Harold, despite the pleasurable surroundings, was William's prisoner, and what William seemed to want was a promise of Harold's support when it came time for William to claim the throne of England.

For those of you interested in this topic, there are many fascinating books on the subject, as well as the amazing Bayeux Tapestry, which was woven shortly after William's conquest of England and still survives today. Andrew Bridgeford's *1066: The Hidden History in the Bayeux Tapestry* (2009) tells the amazing tale of the tapestry, the story of William and Harold, and many other secrets woven within the cloth.

As you can imagine, when Harold returned to England, he soon forgot, or at least dismissed, his oath to William, which was taken under duress. William, on the other hand, did not forget.

Bayeux Tapestry: Harold gives his oath to William with his hand on two altars.

Upon hearing of Harold's ascent to the kingship, William began preparations to invade England.

Harold Godwinson was between a rock and a hard place, and in September 1066, his kingdom was invaded, but it was not by William. The first to strike was Harald Hardrada, who sailed with a large Viking army and landed in the north of England near York. King Harold of England moved northward with his army to meet the Vikings, despite the many warnings that William and the Normans (the far larger threat) were amassing a fleet on the Norman coast. Harold was convinced he could march north, defeat the Vikings, and then attend to William, if he even came.

Harold and Harald Hardrada met at Stamford Bridge just outside of York. The English defeated the Vikings handily, and Harald Hardrada was killed in the battle. Many consider this the end of the Viking Age.

Unfortunately for Harold of England, word came to him at Stamford Bridge that William had landed on the southern coast of England. He was counseled by some of his aides to rest his army before moving south, but Harold was determined to meet William in battle before the Normans could move too far inland.

As you may know, the two armies met at Hastings in southern England on October 14th, 1066. Though the outcome hung in the balance for some time, William was eventually victorious, Harold took an arrow to the eye and died, and the last successful invasion of England was a reality.

For the next nearly 400 years, the English, whose Anglo-Saxon culture was married (some would say forcibly) to Norman French culture, controlled not only England but a significant portion of France as well, at times controlling almost half of that country either directly or through marriage and alliances, especially with the ruling families of Burgundy. At times, the English kings attempted to assert tenuous claims to the French throne and even included the French royal coat of arms on their standards.

Chapter 6 – Jeanne d'Arc

In August 1346, the English under Edward III, whose grandfather was the famous Edward I Longshanks of *Braveheart* (1995) fame and whose mother, Isabella, was the daughter of King Philip IV of France, defeated the armies of the French king at the famous Battle of Crécy. Crécy was a crushing defeat for the French, and it gave the English a much larger foothold in France, including the important and rich port of Calais.

Before we go any further, remember, *Braveheart* was a drama, and like the aforementioned TV series *Vikings*, and it was based in fact. In *Braveheart*, Edward I arranges a marriage to Isabella of France, but as you can see, she was married to his grandson, and when she came to England, she was only twelve. She also did not grow up into the kind, intelligent woman portrayed in the film but rather as the woman who became known as the She-Wolf of France and who ruled England along with her lover, Roger Mortimer, until Edward III put them in their places. For Isabella, it was a monastery. For Mortimer, it was the noose.

As you can see, the French and English, as well as the Burgundian ruling families, were all connected, which resulted in much confusion for later historians and a war that lasted one hundred years (give or take).

In 1356, the English won another great victory at Poitiers in Aquitaine. At both Crécy and Poitiers, the battle was decided by the English archers with their longbows, as they were deployed in large numbers. These bows, made from the wood of the yew tree, had an effective range of over 300 yards and could punch through almost any armor of the day given the right arrowhead. These defeats, especially Poitiers, were humiliating and decisive defeats for the French, whose political landscape was greatly affected by them. Still, while the English were able to secure favorable terms and either reinforce historical claims or gain more land on the French coast, they were not powerful enough to move into the heartland of France to fully conquer the country and claim the French throne outright.

Fifty-nine years later, in 1415, the French and English were still at war, though they had maintained an uneasy and frequently broken peace for a number of decades after Poitiers. The young warrior Henry V, of Shakespearean fame, was on the throne of England at this time. He and his "band of brothers" were in France to reinforce their claim on the French throne through Henry's great-grandfather, Edward III. Henry had only come to the throne of England two years earlier and was challenged in his rule and power from many different quarters. Asserting his claim in France and winning a military victory would go a long way to cementing his power. Though Henry was fully prepared to go to war, he was also prepared to negotiate with the French for much less than the French throne—he wanted official French acknowledgment of English claims on Aquitaine and a number of other smaller coastal French areas, especially major port cities.

Already having been humiliated enough by the English, the French refused Henry's terms, and the war was on again. This time, as you may know from Kenneth Branagh's *Henry V* (1989) and the excellent 2019 movie *The King,* the French were defeated once more, this time at Agincourt. Of the estimated 6,000 French dead, most were members of the nobility, which further weakened the French kingdom. As part of the peace terms, Henry (who had lost only 600 men) married the youngest daughter of the French king, further complicating already complicated matters of blood, inheritance, and rule.

Still, despite another decisive English victory on the battlefield, Henry was not strong enough to push his claim to the French throne and still remain strong in England, where plots and the Scottish always threatened his power. The war went on, but the tide was about to turn.

The Maid of Orléans

Three years before the English victory at Agincourt, a farmer's daughter was born in the town of Domrémy in the Vosges Mountains of northeastern France. Her father's name was Jacques d'Arc. So, contrary to what some people might think, Joan of Arc was not born in a town called "Arc." The area where Joan was born was caught in between French factions, or rather between the people loyal to the royal family of France and those loyal to the ruling families of the Duchy of Burgundy, which, you can see from the map at the end of the last chapter, retained its independence, had its own claims on the French throne, and was allied with the English.

Joan, like many children in Europe at the time, was no stranger to war. Raids and skirmishes between local lords and between forces loyal to one side and another occurred throughout the area. At one point, her father's farm was burned to the ground.

At about the age of thirteen, Joan reported she had religious visions and heard voices. In her first vision, she saw three figures that she believed were Archangel Michael and the early Christian martyrs and saints Catherine and Margaret. According to Joan's later testimony, these three figures instructed her to drive the English out of France and to support Charles VII of France, the eldest son of Charles VI, who had yet to be crowned.

Historians have debated the nature of Joan's visions. Many believe they were true religious revelations, although this was more so in the past than today. However, hundreds of thousands, if not millions, of Frenchmen and women and many other Catholics still adhere to the idea that Joan was "touched by God." More recently, historians, psychologists, and others believe that Joan may have suffered from schizophrenia, a type of migraine, or epilepsy. Others have posited that she ingested a type of mold known as "ergot" that infects rye grain. Ergot poisoning has been known to cause hallucinations. Some have also put forth the theory that Joan acquired bovine tuberculosis, which can affect the brain, from drinking unpasteurized milk (obviously, since "pasteurization" was developed in the 19th century by famed French scientist Louis Pasteur, all milk prior to this was "unpasteurized" and could possibly lead to some type of sickness). However, if Joan had been sick with this type of tuberculosis, she would not have been able to become the active person she was destined to be.

Whatever the cause of Joan's visions, they were real enough for her to believe and act on. One does not go from peasant girl to hero of the nation unless they are convinced something monumental has happened. Between the ages of thirteen and sixteen, Joan, who referred to herself as Jeanne la Pucelle ("Joan the Maid"), had a number of these religious experiences. At the age of sixteen, she asked a male relative to escort her to the nearest royalist military garrison, where she appeared in front of the post's commander and asked to be taken to the court of the king, some 200 miles away. As you can imagine, she was dismissed with laughter, but a few months later, she returned and spoke with two of the commander's men and convinced them she was telling the truth. These two officers took her once again to the post commander, where she repeated her story about the visions that approached her and predicted that the French and their Scottish allies were about to lose a battle to the English near Orléans. A few days later, word arrived at the post that just such a defeat had happened.

Having already told the commander, a minor noble named Robert de Baudricourt, about her visions and now having told him that she had seen the battle's outcome while tending her fields, he offered to take her to Chinon to see the Dauphin. The eldest son of the French king was called the Dauphin as he had not yet been crowned king; father and son had fought each other, leading to the French court being divided by factions.

Arriving in Chinon, Joan met with Charles and told him of her visions and the voices guiding her to her destiny. Charles VII's father was a man who was mentally ill and reportedly believed at times that he was made of glass and about to break into a thousand pieces at any moment. He had also reported seeing visions or hallucinations, so the young prince was used to people making and acting upon unusual claims. As far as we know, Charles VII and Joan's meeting went so well that she was able to convince him that her appearance at the continuing siege of Orléans would lead to a French victory over the English.

Contrary to Hollywood legend, Joan did not take part in hand-to-hand combat at Orléans or anywhere else for that matter, though she was twice wounded—once by an arrow and once by a crossbow bolt. Joan's role in the siege was to inspire the troops. Backed by the Dauphin, she told her story to the troops and their leaders, wore armor given to her by Charles, and urged the French soldiers on during the battle, convincing them that God had already given them the victory.

Orléans was and still is a major city in the heart of France, 85 miles south of Paris and just over 250 miles from the English Channel. It sits upon the Loire River, one of the key commercial rivers in France then and today. Control of Orléans would give the English a significant advantage over the French in the fight for control of the country.

By the time Joan arrived at Orléans, the English had been there for five months fighting off the French siege, which was seemingly going nowhere. However, at the time of Joan's arrival, the battle had begun to swing in favor of the French, with provincial French troops seizing a number of smaller strongpoints around the city and keeping the English bottled up within.

On May 7th, 1428, Joan, who was dressed in battle armor, arrived on the front lines during the battle for the main British strongpoint. Word of Joan's visions and her confidence that God and his angels were on the side of the French had encouraged the French troops, so her arrival at the scene of combat spurred the French on. It seems that Joan, by waving her banner, which depicted Christ and his angels as well as the symbol of French royalty, the fleur-de-lys, and encouraging the soldiers with assurances that God was watching, may have turned the tide of battle that day. It was then that she took an English arrow between the neck and shoulders. She was taken from the frontlines, treated, and then returned to the area of the fighting to drive the men forward in their final assault on the English position. The English were forced to retreat from Orléans after the capture of their main strongpoint.

Image of Joan from a 1429 French document, though the artist never saw Joan personally. In the Romantic Era of the 19ᵗʰ century, Joan was a much-painted figure, but virtually all of those paintings/sculptures are inaccurate.

https://commons.wikimedia.org/wiki/File:Contemporaine_afb_jeanne_d_arc.png

Before the battle, Joan had promised a sign from God to the French. The victory at Orléans was taken to be that sign, and Joan was elevated to a position of greater influence. Her suggestions for a French attack on the far-off English-held city of Rouen were accepted. Over the course of the next month and a half, Joan and others led the French to a series of astounding victories over the English. Joan was wounded again but again recovered, which was taken as a further sign of God's approval.

On July 16th, 1429, the city of Reims, where French kings were traditionally crowned and blessed, was taken bloodlessly by the French, and Charles VII was officially made the king of France. Joan and the French army then moved toward Paris, which had been occupied by the English for some time, taking a number of towns outside of the city and threatening the English positions. These battles and skirmishes took place in the fall and winter of 1429, which was when Joan was struck by the aforementioned crossbow bolt in the thigh. For her sacrifices and her role in leading the French, Joan and her family were given noble titles. This was the high point of her life, for the rest of it was short and destined to end in the most medieval fashion possible.

Joan had made the war with the English into a sort of holy crusade with her stories of visions and predictions. Of course, in every religious war, there are two sides whose views are interchangeable, depending on who you're talking about or to. In a time when nearly everyone was devoutly religious, those who opposed you were on the side of the devil, and this is how the English saw Joan; to them, she was an agent of Satan.

In the winter and early spring of 1430, the French and English upheld an uneasy truce, but when the weather improved, the fighting began again. On May 23rd, 1430, Joan was with a group of French soldiers attempting to break the English siege of Compiègne, which is north of Paris. (As an interesting side note, this city would play a significant role in the 20th century as the place where the Germans surrendered to the French in WWI and where Hitler forced the French to capitulate to him in 1940.)

Joan and her column of horsemen were ambushed by Burgundians, who were allied with the English. Joan was dragged from her horse and captured. Joan was clearly a charismatic person, and she was also obviously quite brave. In addition to her wounds in battle, she attempted to escape captivity, including once when she jumped some seventy feet out of the tower in which she was held. Luckily, she landed on very soft earth and was relatively unharmed, but she was recaptured.

The English prevailed upon the Burgundians to release Joan to them, which they did so for a price. She was taken to the city of Rouen, halfway between Paris and the English Channel on the Seine River, which was the base of English operations in France. Joan was held there for a year, during which the French attempted a number of abortive rescue attempts. Of course, she was also famously put on trial for heresy.

Heresy, as defined by the Oxford English Dictionary, is "belief or opinion contrary to orthodox religious (especially Christian) doctrine." Of course, the English at the time were Catholic, just like the French, but they wished to prove that Joan was lying about her visions and claiming to "speak for God," which they claimed was a heretical act. Other charges were brought against her, including the very serious charge of dressing like a man. She had done this in battle and in prison, as she had refused to give up her clothes. She felt that pants were more of an obstacle to remove than the simple shift they tried to get her to wear, and she knew that rape was a very real possibility. In other words, the English were trying to do what most accusers do even to this day—throw mud against the wall and see what sticks. At the time, a woman dressing as a man or attempting to pass as a man was a serious offense. Her famous "bobbed" hairstyle, which was similar to that worn by the French king and French soldiers, for both reasons of cleanliness and combat, was also used to accuse her of passing as a man. This was key for the charge of heresy, which was only punishable by death the second time someone was accused. However, when the cross-dressing charge was added, Joan was in real danger.

Her trial was conducted by French and Burgundian clergy who were clearly pro-English, either because they were on the English payroll or were allied with them. English soldiers at the trial were there not only to prevent Joan from being rescued but also to act as an unspoken threat to anyone who voted against punishing Joan.

During the trial, Joan stunned the court with her intelligence, despite the fact that she was illiterate and had no formal education. The trial was recorded for posterity, though many of Joan's statements were altered in the final document. At the end of the trial, Joan was ordered to sign a document, the contents of which she could not possibly know and which she could not sign without help since she could not write. The order was given under threat of death, and Joan signed a document stating that she had never had the visions that she claimed to have had. She also forswore wearing men's clothes. A few days later, Joan changed back into men's clothes while in prison (she had reported rape attempts before the trial). This was clearly a trap and one which was designed to catch her going back on her "signed and sworn testimony before God." A death sentence was pronounced, and on May 30th, 1431, she was burned at the stake in the center of Rouen. The English burned her body again to prevent anyone from getting her bones, as relics of holy or revered figures were important aspects of life in medieval Christendom. Her ashes were dumped in the Seine River. Joan was nineteen at the time of her death.

The Hundred Years' War continued for another twenty-odd years after the death of Joan. The ascension of Henry VI of England, who was a weak king, enabled the French to gain the upper hand and drive the English out of most of France, save a small number of coastal cities on the Channel.

In 1920, Pope Benedict XV canonized Joan, but by that time, she was already a sainted figure in France. Charles VII had also ordered a new investigation and trial of Joan in the 1450s, which, of course, cleared her of all the charges that had been levied against her. To this day, Joan of Arc's spirit has been invoked by the French in times of war and hardship. Statues, mostly Romantic Era creations, showing Joan charging into battle abound throughout the country, especially in Orléans and the other cities that played an important role in her life. There are also numerous statues of Joan in the USA, including in the nation's capital.

Statue of Joan in Orléans, France.
Croquant, CC BY-SA 4.0 <https://creativecommons.org/licenses/by-sa/4.0>, via Wikimedia Commons
https://commons.wikimedia.org/wiki/File:Orl%C3%A9ans_Jeanne_d%27Arc_place_du_Martroi.jpg

Chapter 7 – "L'état, c'est moi" ("I am the state")

"I am the state," declared Louis XIV (1638-1715). Louis XIV was the absolute king of France and one of the most interesting figures in French history. He reigned over France from 1643 to 1715, and during that time, he fashioned France into the most powerful nation in Europe. Louis, for reasons that will be explained, also was the epitome of the phrase "absolute monarch," and many historians consider his reign to be a distant forerunner of the authoritarian regimes of the 20th century.

Due to his power and immense personality, Louis also became *the* trendsetter in Europe. His fashion, his taste, and especially his palace all became the templates for contemporary and later kings and queens, not only in France but also throughout Europe. The most famous portrait of Louis XIV, which was done by Hyacinthe (a French corruption of his Catalan name of Jacint) Rigaud in 1701, shows the aging king resplendent in purple (the color of royalty since the days of the Roman Empire) and white ermine robes, wearing his famous black curly wig, light blue hose with gold high-heel shoes, a broadsword, and his crown and scepter.

Today, Louis might be viewed as a dandified and effeminate figure of ridicule. But then? Louis XIV was the absolute epitome of manhood. In his younger life, he was a notorious womanizer, and he engaged with an innumerable number of concubines, some of whom grew quite rich and influential at his court. Louis was also trained in the art of war, and though his armies were often defeated, he was a capable military leader and also knew how to delegate to his commanders. Lastly, Louis XIV could be absolutely ruthless. Many of his enemies met the ultimate fate, many times suffering the pains of torture before being killed. Anyone questioning Louis's manhood would likely have met a similar fate.

Louis XIV of France
https://commons.wikimedia.org/wiki/File:Louis_XIV_of_France.jpg

Before we delve into Louis's life, let's quickly examine the centuries between the death of Joan of Arc and the rise of Louis XIV.

It is difficult to review in just a few paragraphs the monumental changes that occurred in Europe from the time about fifty years before the birth of St. Joan to the ascension of Louis XIV, but for our purposes here, three historical eras or events concern us: the Renaissance, the Protestant Reformation/St. Bartholomew's Day massacre, and the weakening of the French monarchy before Louis XIV.

The Renaissance, or "Rebirth," refers to the revival of and building upon Greek and Roman ideas in Europe. There is no single date that one can look back on and say, "On this day, the Renaissance began." Rather, it was a gradual process that had actually been taking place quietly for decades before its explosion in the mid-1300s.

There are a number of factors that caused this explosion of study, knowledge, and scientific and cultural reflowering. Among them was the rediscovery of Greek and Roman writings that had long been secured in Christian monasteries and Muslim libraries. In the case of the former, many Greek and Roman writings and ideas lay discarded, remnants of a time when the Catholic Church was still, in many ways, a very "Roman" institution and its doctrine still in flux.

The solidification of Catholic doctrine in the centuries after the fall of the Roman Empire, at a time when authority was generally unquestioned (often because of an illiterate/uneducated populace), meant that whatever did not agree with official church teachings was either forbidden or literally stored and hidden away. The monasteries, which were isolated communities of relatively learned men, were the places where these documents and ideas were stored, sometimes literally in the hopes of more educated times.

Islam, which rose from the sands of Arabia in the 700s and spread rapidly through the Middle East and into Spain, did not become the scientifically stagnant entity that European Christendom became. It's interesting that just as Europe was beginning to experience the beginnings of people questioning religious dogma, much of the Islamic world was heading in the opposite direction. However, in the years between the rise of Islam and the Renaissance, the Islamic world safeguarded many of the great works of the Romans and Greeks, both of whom had great direct or indirect influence in the Middle East and North Africa. While Europe descended into the Dark Ages of ignorance, Muslim scholars rediscovered or built upon the ideas of Plato, Aristotle, and Hippocrates, as well as many of the Roman histories and other works, especially in the realm of architecture and art.

During the 600-odd years of medieval Europe, much trade (along with much war) went on between Europe and the Islamic world, especially that of Muslim Spain. Ideas and sometimes documents were not the only things brought back from the Islamic world, as tales of the amazing architecture and gardens of the caliphs and other Muslim leaders were too. These buildings and sometimes even the gardens were built on mathematical principles discovered by the Greeks, which were then used by the Romans and elaborated upon by the Muslims.

This exposure to ancient and new ideas also led to a rediscovery of the works that were essentially hidden in plain sight in monasteries throughout Europe, especially in the home of the former Roman Empire, the lands of Italy, where the Renaissance can be said to have started. By the time Louis XIV became king in his own right in 1661, after eighteen years of a regency that held power in his stead, Europe had been experiencing a period of scientific and artistic growth that it had not witnessed in more than a thousand years.

This period of cultural and scientific learning had its limits, as it began to encroach on both church power and beliefs. In the years before 1517, before German priest Martin Luther nailed his *Ninety-five Theses* (charges leveled against the Catholic Church of its more questionable practices) to the church door in Wittenberg and began the Protestant Reformation, the Catholic Church had become the dominant feature not only of the Continent's spiritual life but also of its economic, legal, and moral life as well. Anything that went against the beliefs and practices of the church (unless, of course, you were rich and powerful) was liable to be deemed "heresy" and punished severely, as you have seen with Joan of Arc in the prior chapter.

The most famous example of these types of restrictions is the famous case of Galileo Galilei, the Italian astronomer who challenged church beliefs by stating that the earth revolved around the sun, implying that the planet was not the center of God's universe. Galileo's fame and the retraction of his beliefs under threat saved him from being burned at the stake, but it sent a clear message that the church would only put up with so many challenges to its authority.

However, that could only be the case if it was powerful enough to hold the challenges back. Over the centuries, the people of Europe had watched the Catholic Church grow incredibly rich and powerful, all while telling the populace that one sure way of getting to heaven was through the humility that came with poverty. The tipping point for Martin Luther came when he witnessed many of his fellow clergy selling indulgences. Simply put, these were payments made to the church (or a particular churchman) in order to secure one's place in heaven. Essentially, people were buying their way out of sin by "donating" to the church. Of course, this practice had no root in Christian theology, but no one, except for Luther and a few others, was willing to risk their life in challenging the practice.

Luther and the people had also seen priests and monks be married and have concubines and children when the Catholic clergy had been sworn to celibacy since the 11th century. Of course, God only knows the extent of the sexual abuses that must have occurred in the church at a time before any kind of press or free speech. This most likely only added to the resentment felt by the people of Europe.

You can read more about the Protestant Reformation in Captivating History's *The Reformation,* as well as in thousands upon thousands of other books, papers, and articles, but for our purposes here, suffice it to say that by the time of Louis XIV, the Reformation had split western and central Europe into two Christian belief systems, which warred with each other figuratively and literally throughout the 16th and 17th centuries (as a side note, there was a third branch, that of Orthodox Christianity, which primarily remained in the Balkans and Russia). These wars were not limited to national borders—they often took place within nations. The Thirty Years' War took more lives within Germany than it did outside the country, and to this day, Germany is more heavily Protestant in the north of the country and more Catholic in the south.

France was not immune to this religious strife, and one event more than any other illustrates the struggle for religious freedom in the country. This event and those surrounding it may have led to Louis XIV making the greatest decision of his reign, which affected not only France but also set off a chain of events that led to the settlements in the New World and the amazing flowering of freedom and inquiry known as the Enlightenment. These later events, in turn, led directly to the American Revolution, the French Revolution, and the modern world as we know it today.

In France, the Protestant Revolution found some limited success, but, as opposed to the lands of Germany and Italy, the country was not fractured into many different states with its own kings and independent rulers. Thus, the Catholic Church and the monarchy of France were able to more greatly control the effects of the Reformation in the country, with a couple of small exceptions. One of them was the relatively independent Kingdom of Navarre, a small entity in the southwest of France on the Spanish border. In 1572, the king of Navarre was Henry III, who was Protestant and also had a claim to the French throne. His ascension to the French throne is confusing even to professional historians, but suffice it to say that Henry overcame all other claims to the throne, and through his marriage to the impressive Margaret of Valois, he became the king of France, taking the name of Henry IV, in August 1589. However, to take the throne, he was required to do one thing: convert to Catholicism. Henry famously proclaimed, "France is worth a mass."

However, many Frenchmen and women were not convinced his conversion was real, so they harbored great enmity toward any French Protestant, which was returned in kind. Of course, there was criticism to Henry's right to the throne. This culminated in the Saint Bartholomew's Day massacre, which occurred a few days after Henry's marriage to Margaret of Valois in August 1572 (it also coincides with that saint's day). This massacre included the assassinations of some of Henry's friends and allies (mainly Protestants), an attempt on the king's life, and the wholesale slaughter of Protestants, first in Paris and then throughout the country. Modern estimates of the dead number from 10,000 to 40,000. Prior to the massacre and the battles that followed it, the French Protestant population is estimated to have been around 10 percent. Afterward, the estimates sit at around 6 percent.

Henry survived the massacre, and as king, he did his best to quell religious warfare in France with his Edict of Nantes in 1598, which attempted to legalize religious tolerance within his kingdom, give Protestants the right to practice their religious beliefs freely, and remove a number of economic sanctions. But throughout the last part of the 1500s and into the 1600s, France was wracked by not only religious civil wars but also a breakdown of royal authority, with church figures dominating weak kings and with nobles fighting each other for the right to claim the throne, which was not also religious in nature. Among the victims of this strife was Henry IV, who was assassinated in 1610 by a fanatic Catholic. He was Louis XIV's grandfather. Louis XIV was born into this situation in 1638. He was the son of Louis XIII, called Louis the Just. He reigned for thirty-three years, but his rule was marred by palace intrigue, plots, and his inability to rule on his own. Famously, he turned to Cardinal Richelieu, who was depicted in *The Three Musketeers*, to govern the country in his later years. Though one of Louis the Just's accomplishments was to declare that the monarchy, rather than the nobles of the country, had the right to the ultimate use of force, the aristocrats continued to struggle with each other for riches and power, with some plotting to take the throne themselves.

Though Louis XIV was only a boy when his father died, the struggles inside the palace and for power among the nobles left a strong impression on him. When his father died, Louis was only four years old. Despite the last wishes of his father, Louis's mother, Anne of Austria, seized power as the regent, along with her adviser and the former king's right-hand man Cardinal Richelieu. Though Louis was officially the king, he would not have power until he took it for himself at the age of twenty-three in 1661.

Throughout his teens, Louis was given increasing responsibility and was instructed in the arts and sciences that he would need when he became king in his own right, such as warfare, fencing, math, economics, religion, and the classics of Rome and Greece. As he grew older, he chafed against the rule of his mother and Richelieu's successor, Cardinal Mazarin. One incident, in particular, may have determined Louis's later course to take all the power unto himself.

In 1648, a series of uprisings against royal power, collectively known as the Fronde (for the slings used by peasants during the riots), erupted. The main conflict came between the monarchy and the Parlement, a body of nobles and clergy who were eager to seize more power. They were especially eager to bring down Anne of Austria and Cardinal Mazarin, who was Italian, as they were seen as foreign interlopers attempting not only to seize complete power in France but also place her under the thumb of foreign powers.

The Fronde turned quite violent, and at one point, a mob went to the royal palace on rumors that Louis XIV had been killed by those loyal to Anne in an attempt to place her on the throne. The mob marched into the palace, demanding to see the king and threatening to kill anyone who stood in the way. In the middle of the night, they barged into Louis XIV's bedchamber, where he lay in bed, feigning sleep. Satisfied that the king was alive, the mob left. Louis awoke, vowing that when he took power, France would never fall into the hands of a mob again. The Fronde, as well as the Second Fronde, which took place from 1650 to 1653, were put down by Anne and Mazarin.

Rumors of Anne's hunger for personal power were untrue, as her later life's work was dedicated to Louis becoming the unquestioned king of France. When Mazarin died in the spring of 1661, Louis became king in his own right. His first act as king was to abolish the role of chief minister, the position held by Mazarin and Richelieu, instead taking the rule all for himself. When he announced his intention to the court, Louis left no doubt that France was embarking on a new era: "You will assist me with your counsels when I ask for them...You will seal no orders except by my command...I order you to not sign anything, not even a passport without my command...[You will] render account to me each day."

It is hard to overemphasize the effect of Louis's personality on the royal court and on the nation itself. He soon declared himself to be *le Roi Soleil*, the "Sun King," a figure who illuminates France and whom France revolves around. This may be a hard idea to understand in the 21ˢᵗ century, and indeed many French nobles at the time, who were accustomed to ruling almost as virtual kings themselves, chafed at Louis's ideas of power. However, behind Louis's grandiosity was the idea of the divine right of kings, an idea that was not at all unique to France.

Simply put, this divine right is that God, who rules over all things, has a divine plan. Since this was a time of virtually unquestioned religious devotion, people believed that it must be true that God put the king on the throne. And since God himself ordained the kingship, the king was obviously the representative of God on Earth. And, according to Louis XIV, one does not disobey God.

As if that was not enough, the king was essentially considered to be two entities: the person of the king—the man—and the embodiment of France as ordained by God. Louis XIV grasped those ideas, built upon them, and never let them go.

France at the Time of Louis XIV

When Louis became king in his own right, he oversaw a kingdom that was both rich and powerful, and he was determined to increase this wealth and influence. Like the English, Spanish, Portuguese, and Dutch, the French had embarked on voyages of discovery and colonization. Though the French acquired territory and trading rights in various places in the Far East and India, its push for an empire was mainly focused on the Caribbean and North America, where they came into conflict with the British. The major wars between England and France would be something that Louis's successors would have to deal with, but during his reign, Louis not only had his forces occasionally fighting the British in the New World (mainly but not exclusively in the Caribbean and at sea) but also in Europe. Louis engaged in a series of wars (sometimes alongside his ally Catholic Spain, which was the home of his first wife, Maria Theresa) against the Protestant powers of England, Holland, and many of the northern German states. For Louis, who was a devout Catholic despite his incredible womanizing, these wars were both his religious duty and his responsibility to keep France safe and prosperous. In Europe, his main aim was to enlarge the French nation to the north and east, creating a buffer zone between his kingdom and the Protestants, and to seize (or indirectly control) the smaller duchies, baronies, and principalities that made up most of the area bordering eastern France.

Of course, there was one last reason: to glorify himself. Louis was not above going to the frontlines and directing the battle or at least advising his generals. He was brave and was often in range of enemy guns and cannons. The fact that he was never injured added to his own ideas of his superiority and God's favor.

In the end, however, along with Louis's lavish spending on his own court and palace, the wars he began would eventually contribute to the dire economic straits faced by Louis's great-great-great-grandson, Louis XVI, in 1789, the time of the French Revolution. Louis XIV's wars and the wars of his successors eventually ended in defeat, with some exceptions, and resulted in the rise of England as the preeminent power in the world.

However, in 1661, when Louis fully came to the throne, that was all in the future. During Louis's reign, France became one of the richest nations in the world, and Louis was determined to let everyone know it.

Symbol of Louis as the Sun King, featured on the main gate to the Palace of Versailles.
Trizek, CC BY-SA 3.0 <https://creativecommons.org/licenses/by-sa/3.0>, via Wikimedia Commons https://commons.wikimedia.org/wiki/File:DSC_0840_-_Grille_royale_du_ch%C3%A2teau_de_Versailles.JPG

Louis's Personality

Today, we would undoubtedly classify Louis XIV as an egomaniac, possibly a megalomaniac. What you are about to read will sound incredibly strange, and it was, but for those who lived at the time, especially those in the upper classes of France and especially at the royal court at Versailles, it was everyday "normal" life. The rituals developed by the king were, for the most part, followed to the letter, at least when he was at the palace. Sometimes these rituals and Louis's own need to be constantly on display as both the king and God's representative of France weighed on him, and he would, so to speak, "let his hair down" at a smaller residence on the Versailles grounds, one of the other royal palaces, or among intimates, both his lovers and those who under normal circumstances might be called friends.

Aerial view of Versailles today. In Louis's time, the town itself was much smaller and the grounds of the palace larger. There are some 700 rooms in the main building.
ToucanWings, CC BY-SA 3.0 <https://creativecommons.org/licenses/by-sa/3.0>, via Wikimedia Commons
https://commons.wikimedia.org/wiki/File:Vue_a%C3%A9rienne_du_domaine_de_Versailles_par_ToucanWings_002.jpg

Louis developed a curious and brilliant way to maintain control of the French nobles, which was necessary. For many decades before Louis's ascension to the throne, an assortment of nobles had been either attempting to gain the throne of France for themselves or had been trying to weaken the power of the king and gain more control for themselves. Louis had grown up in tumultuous times and was determined that he would be the ultimate power in France. To this end, he forced (mostly in a nice, polite but unmistakably commanding way) many nobles to live at the court of Versailles.

For some nobility, especially as Louis's power and the grandeur of the palace grew, this was an honor. Many became Louis's confidantes or members of his inner circle. This honor was limited to powerful nobles and clergymen. Other nobles, especially if they were from areas far from Versailles or from restive provinces, were asked to take up residence at the court for a time so Louis could keep an eye on them. In the 1660s, the royal court of Louis XIV numbered some 600 to 700 people. Toward the end of Louis's reign, this number was closer to ten thousand. Oftentimes, their daughters gladly offered themselves up to the king, who was a notorious womanizer in his younger and middle years. In many cases, family members were more than happy that the king began to "see" their female relatives, as this brought positive attention to their family and, many times, their pocketbooks, at least indirectly.

However, as time passed, life at the court and palace became ever grander and expensive. Guests were expected to dress accordingly, feed themselves (at least for the most part), and take part in the many ways to gamble at the court (an invitation to play cards or billiards with the king was perhaps the most sought-after invitation of them all). For many lesser nobles, a stay at Versailles, even for a couple of days, was enough to bankrupt them. In some cases, such a visit might cost half a person's lifetime savings or more. But that was part of the point. After all, who could one go to at the palace when they found themselves broke? There wasn't anyone else but the king. Thus, these nobles, many of whom had opposed the king in some way or other, became indebted to him. And, of course, we all know that once someone has you in their debt, they have you in their grasp.

Louis XIV accomplished much during his long reign, but Louis is perhaps best remembered for his palace and court at Versailles, which is open to all today, or at least most of it. By the time Louis XIV's great-great-great-grandson Louis XVI lost the throne of France in the early 1790s, over one-quarter of the expenditures of France was spent on the palace. This included maintenance, further construction, and the expenses of the royal court. From the time of Louis XIV to Louis XVI, France was one of the richest countries on the planet, and a quarter of its expenditures were spent on the king's "house"!

The palace itself consists of some 700 rooms, some of them secret. The grounds are unbelievably elaborate, as you can see from the aerial picture on the prior page. The palace grounds feature perfectly geometric lawns and shrubbery, paths, incredible statues and fountains (some of which are both), and the Grand Canal, a semi-navigable waterway 1,670 meters in length. In addition to the grounds, smaller palaces and residences were built over the years, including smaller residences for the king, his wife, and his mistresses.

Within the palace itself are the famous Hall of Mirrors, which hosted not only the signing of the Treaty of Versailles that ended WWI but also the surrender of France in 1871, Louis's royal chapel, the private and public residences of the king and queen, an opera house, a theater, and an amazing number of salons and meeting rooms for various purposes.

Though each of the rooms at Versailles had a separate purpose, together with the grounds and the splendor of the court, they had one purpose: to overawe those visiting and in living there with Louis's power.

The famous Hall of Mirrors. Much of the palace was destroyed or ruined during the French Revolution of 1789. Since that time, most of Versailles has been restored, with many of the original pieces returned to it.

Throughout the entire palace, paintings and statues portrayed Louis in various roles, such as the king, the intermediary between God and man, the reincarnation of the Greek sun-king Apollo, a knight and/or general, a family man, the father to the country, and much else. Looking about the palace through today's eyes, it is easy to see that Louis was an egomaniac of a scale seldom seen in the world, and in many cases, it is easy to shake one's head or laugh at the scale of his self-centeredness. But one must remember Louis XIV wasn't a king in the 21st century. He was a king in the 17th and 18th centuries, and times were much different. Louis and most of the people of France (both noble and otherwise) believed he was placed on the throne by God himself. Not only did they believe that, but they also believed that Louis was not only Louis but the embodiment of France. A noble or commoner coming into contact with Louis for the first time must have been absolutely overwhelmed.

What is amazing about this is that, by all accounts, Louis could at times (usually behind closed doors) be amazingly personable and real. For the most part, when Louis was with his advisers debating matters of state, he tolerated dissent from his own opinion as long as it was tempered and not overly familiar. Louis was not a stupid, vain man. He was educated in the arts, military affairs, math, science, and much else. He was able to keep up with the most learned men of his day, or at least to the point of being able to ask them important questions, and he allowed artists, scientists, and ministers to disagree with him, even encouraging them to do so. However, there was a limit. If Louis's mind was made up and he gave a command or a strongly worded "suggestion," it had to be followed.

Louis had a small residence built near the town of Marly, which is not far from Versailles. Today, the town is known as Marly-le-Roi ("Marly of the King"). Here, Louis would relax, sometimes even greeting visitors in a bathrobe and skullcap. Louis's hair had fallen out as a young man, and to compensate for this, he began wearing the elaborate wigs for which we know him. It became the fashion, not only in France but also throughout the Western world. These times at Marly were welcome and rare for Louis, for he trapped himself in a world of daily rituals that were followed to the letter at Versailles.

Every day the king was in residence at Versailles and even, with some variation, when he was on campaign with his armies, a strict ritual was followed. The king would be awoken every morning at the same time. While he roused himself, his chamber pot from the night before would be removed and given to his personal physician and his staff. They would examine the king's urine and stool closely, monitoring any change from the days or weeks before. In one case, blood in the king's stool led to the discovery of a fistula in his colon. The king underwent a painful and life-saving operation while conscious.

Once the king had risen from his bed, a retinue of servants and nobles would enter his apartment. Each was assigned a task, whether it was to put on the king's robe or to help with his slippers. Those most in favor with the king attended to these "events." For example, if someone had been the person to hand the king his hat as he left the apartment for some time and then told to hold open the door for the king after he had dressed, that was not a good sign. In that instance, the king and/or his closest advisers had determined that someone else was more important or that this person had displeased the king in some way.

The king often took breakfast and lunch with his intimates or closest advisers, but dinner was a public affair. The king sat at the center of a long table, with his closest relatives and favorites down on either side of him, facing outward. They were not alone. Before the king's table was a small gallery with seating, where nobles and other important personages (artists, mistresses, clergy, wives of nobles, etc.) would sit or stand to watch the king eat. Each course was announced as it was brought to the table. Louis would partake of each dish before anyone else touched it. Once he had eaten what he wanted (he rarely filled up on one dish as there were many to come), that dish was passed to those at the table in order of importance and/or rank. This could go on for literally hours. As one can imagine, seats in the front row meant you were in the king's favor. If you were a "nobody" from the provinces (that is, a baron from miles and miles away), you might bribe a court official for a place to stand during the meal and hope that you somehow caught the king's eye.

If one managed to do that, you might be told to attend the king's promenade, which was Louis's regular walk around the main palace grounds. Of course, the king and the royal family would lead. They would be followed by his advisers, priests, generals in attendance, and so on in importance. They would then be followed by a myriad of minor nobility, some of whom lived at the palace (at least temporarily) and some of whom were visiting. Oftentimes before the royal walk, Louis would be informed of who was in attendance at the palace, and he would decide who joined him. If someone had displeased the king in some way, he might tell those in charge of the walk, "I have never heard of that person." That was a sign that whoever the king was speaking about was in hot water, and it was often a message to that person that the king expected them to change their ways or opinion, to offer the king a gift, or to simply go away. When Louis's coterie joined him for the walk, everyone knew who was where. Any absence or movement toward the rear or closer to the king was noted, as one's well-being might depend on it.

Versailles was the crown jewel of Louis XIV's realm, and it was the symbol of France's power and influence. It was at this time that French really became *the* language of diplomacy, reflecting not only France's power but also its style, culture, and influence. If you are interested in learning more about Versailles, you will find references to a video and website on the building and glory of Versailles, as well as on the life of Louis XIV, at the end of this book. However, Versailles is just part of Louis's story.

For much of Louis's reign, France's economy was healthy. He reorganized the country's tax system and expanded it to increase revenue. The government (meaning Louis) had a monopoly on the mining, cultivation, and sale of salt, which was needed for the curing of meat in a time with no refrigeration, and it also had a monopoly on the creation and sale of matches, which was, again, a needed commodity before gas and electric lighting and heating. On all of the major roads of France, there were tolls. In most instances, these were controlled by a local lord who paid Louis for the right to do so. Everyone expected the locals to take a cut above what they reported collecting, but as long as Louis saw his share, he found it acceptable.

Additionally, France's income rose from increased trade around the world. France imported fine goods, such as porcelain, jewels, and spices, as well as exported them, mainly doing so in the form of textiles. Much of Louis's reign saw good harvests, and in general, most of the people were happy or at least satisfied with Louis's rule.

One group of people who were not at all happy with the rule of Louis XIV were the Protestants of France. As you read earlier, Louis's ancestor, Henry IV, issued the Edict of Nantes in 1598, which gave religious liberty to Protestants who had been severely persecuted, killed, and forced to hold their services in secret or renounce their religion. Henry adopted Catholicism in order to ascend the throne, and though he was a relatively popular king with many achievements to his name, he was assassinated in 1610 by a Catholic fanatic who believed his conversion was disingenuous.

Louis XIV was a devout Catholic and attended Mass frequently. His chapel at Versailles was constructed under his direct instruction and is one of the more beautiful areas of the palace. The king even had a small chapel installed behind a secret wall in one of his apartments so he could worship, pray, and meditate unobserved.

Many reasons have been put forward for Louis XIV's revocation of the Edict of Nantes in 1685. By that time, Louis had been in sole charge of the kingdom for twenty-four years. During that time, he had engaged in numerous wars, put down rebellions, and had many of those opposed to him tortured and/or killed. He also slept with countless women and had many children by them, all while being married to his first wife, Maria Theresa of Spain. Louis also spent much of his energy gathering all of the power in the country around himself and worked tirelessly for what he believed was the "unity" of the country. After all, as you have read, his younger years were somewhat chaotic. A number of historians believe Louis's revocation of the Edict of Nantes was a way for him to atone for his many sins. Many also believe that the revocation was a way for Louis to further his aim of unifying France under one God and one king, who was God's instrument on Earth.

So, on October 18th, 1685, Louis formally revoked the Edict of Nantes and took away all legal protections of Protestants in France. He also instituted a policy that became known as the Dragonnards, which had dragoons (cavalry units) move into Protestant areas, mostly in the southwestern parts of the country, where they were quartered among the families there. These families were responsible for feeding and housing them. Since Protestants no longer enjoyed protection under the law, all kinds of abuse went on, though Louis supposedly forbade the worse types of it, meaning rape and torture. Protestants were also forcibly made to attend Catholic Mass and lectures given by priests or bishops on the evils of Protestantism and the glory of the Catholic Church. At some point, Protestants were made to publicly make an abjuration, a public renunciation of Protestant teachings and acceptance of Catholicism.

Needless to say, many Protestants were killed and abused during this period. In some cases, there were armed uprisings, but these were put down ruthlessly and did not amount to much. Many Protestants abjured, some of them truthfully, as they were convinced that might did indeed make right. Others publicly followed Catholic practice but privately remained Protestant. This could be dangerous, for like the tyrants who followed in the 20th century, Louis knew that "educating" the children would have its uses. It would create new Catholics and spies in the household of many "former" Protestants, and many were indeed turned in by their children, sometimes on purpose and sometimes inadvertently.

The final result of the revocation of the edict was that France's Protestant population was reduced from about 10 percent to somewhere near 5 percent, and many fled the country. Some went to Holland, which had won its freedom from Spain in 1648, and others moved to England, where a form of Protestantism was the state religion. Others fled to Protestant German states, while still others decided to put a much greater distance between themselves by moving to the New World. Of these, many went to Canada, where France had colonies. They also moved to the English colonies in Canada and what would later become the United States.

The area under French control in Canada was called *Acadie,* or "Acadia," and it included what is now New Brunswick, Nova Scotia, and parts of Quebec. Forced from the regions by the Catholic majority, these Acadians fled as far as they could to another French colony, one more loosely controlled and with areas difficult to reach. This colony had been named Louisiana in honor of Louis XIV, and those Acadians slowly developed their own culture and French dialect. In time, the name *Acadien* became "Cajun." And this was all thanks to Louis XIV, at least indirectly.

At home, Louis XIV engaged in a number of wars throughout his reign. He succeeded in expanding French borders in the north to include all of present-day Belgium, and he pushed the influence of various German states back (Germany, as such, did not become a nation until 1871. Prior to that, what is now Germany was a collection of independent or semi-independent kingdoms, principalities, duchies, or bishoprics allied with various European rulers.) Louis saw to it that the states along France's eastern border were allied with him.

However, the other nations of western Europe, mainly England and Holland, were wary of every move that Louis made. France was then, as well as for many years, the largest and most populous nation in Europe, and the English and Dutch saw Louis's ego as an ever-present threat. For most of Louis's reign, France was involved in a war, whether it was large or small. To be a king in the 17th and 18th centuries was also to be a warlord. And one had to be a successful one, as no one respected a king who spent money on immense palaces and lost wars.

Toward the end of Louis's reign, his wars began to bankrupt the nation, along with his lavish expenditures. Worse still, a "grand coalition" had risen up against him in 1701 over questions of who would rise to the throne of Spain. Louis naturally wanted his grandson, Philip of Anjou, to be the Spanish king, and indeed, the dying king Charles (Carlos) II had named him as his successor.

Of course, the idea of Louis on the throne of France "guiding" his grandson in Spain was too much for England, Holland, the Holy Roman Empire, many German states (including the increasingly powerful Prussia), Portugal, and the powerful Italian state of Savoy. The rulers of the Holy Roman Empire were closely related to Louis, but even they knew that this move, which would allow Louis to influence Spanish policies, meant too much power in Louis's hands. The war raged on from 1701 to 1714, one year before Louis's death. One of the turning points of the war occurred in 1704 when Louis's armies were defeated at Blenheim, located northwest of Munich, Germany. Leading the English army was John Churchill, the soon-to-be-duke of Marlborough and the direct ancestor of Winston Churchill, who was born at Blenheim Palace (named for the great victory) in England in 1874.

The War of the Spanish Succession ended in 1714 with Philip on the throne of Spain, but he gave a solemn pledge to remain independent from France, which was enforced by a treaty. France did not lose territory, but it did lose prestige and treasure. England was the big "winner," as it secured the control of a number of ports around the world, trading rights, and the control of Gibraltar.

When Louis XIV died in 1715, France was on the path to bankruptcy. Good fortune would ebb and flow, but by the 1770s, French kings were borrowing huge sums of money to keep their kingdoms and their lavish lifestyles afloat. More wars and inept rulers would accelerate that process in the 1780s.

Louis was the king for seventy-two years—the longest of any monarch in recorded history. Louis XIV left behind Versailles. He also created the notion of an absolute monarchy, and some say he laid the groundwork for the modern "cult of personality" and police states of the 20th century. His crackdown on religious freedom and control of the arts led directly to the Enlightenment of the 1700s, which, in turn, led to both the American and French Revolutions.

Louis XIV

Ten years before his death, Louis XIV commissioned wax sculptor Antoine Benoist to create a likeness of him. It is the only work of Benoist that has survived.

Chapter 8 – The French Revolution

Up to this point, we have been telling the story of France through some of its great personalities: Vercingetorix, Charlemagne, Joan of Arc, Louis XIV. For many years, a preponderance of historians believed that history was shaped by "great men" (and, at times, great women), who took control of destiny and shaped it to their own ends. That view of history is not as popular now as it used to be fifty years ago, but it serves as a good way to tell a story.

Perhaps in a time when kings and queens ruled and nobles and clergy vied for power, great men and women did make history, for the events of the life of everyday people were not recorded or even thought of as consequential. However, beginning in the early 18th century, history began to be made not so much by kings but by writers, thinkers, and the men in the street.

When Louis XIV died, his great-grandson, who became Louis XV, took power. Compared to Louis XIV, Louis XV was weak, corrupt, and relatively ineffectual. Although he was smart, he was shy and often let others speak for him. Like his famous grandson, Louis XVI, who followed him, Louis XV had a penchant for acting just a moment too late. He continued many of his great-grandfather's policies, including the suppression of Protestantism and increased government control of the arts. However, censorship of literature and art became a serious problem during Louis XV's reign.

Worse still, Louis XV had a reputation. Politely speaking, we would say he suffered from sex addiction. In truth, Louis slept with every woman he could, including many girls who had just "come of age." He infamously slept with two sisters, and his two most famous mistresses, Madame de Pompadour, whom he greatly loved, and Madame du Barry, were rumored to be the real powers in France. Madame du Barry was particularly hated by both the public and nobility for her lavish expenditures and supposed "power" over the king. She was beheaded during the French Revolution.

During his fifty-eight-year reign, Louis engaged in many wars, nearly all of them defeats, with some of them being outright disasters, like the Seven Years' War with England, which lost France most of its valuable possessions in the New World. These wars weakened not only France but also the king's reputation and France's finances.

As the French monarchy continued to grow weaker after the death of Louis XIV (who went unmourned for the most part after decades of rule as an autocratic father to the nation), more voices began to be heard criticizing the system. The period from about 1715 (the year Louis XIV died) to 1789 (the year the French Revolution began) is known as the Enlightenment, and while many men and women from around Europe and the American colonies began asserting rights and ideas previously unheard of or forbidden, it is France that is considered the home of the Enlightenment.

Perhaps some of the names of the great Enlightenment thinkers are familiar to you. They should be, as much of the bedrock of modern society, especially of Western democracy, was laid by them. Voltaire, Rousseau, Diderot, Montesquieu, and Buffon are some of the most known names, although there were dozens of other men and women, whether they were thinkers, artists, critics, writers, or politicians, who advanced the cause of human freedom after the death of Louis XIV.

Voltaire (1694–1778), who is credited with the famous saying, "I may not agree with you, but I will defend with my life your right to say it," led the way in the early part of the 18th century. Though this famous saying was a summation of Voltaire's beliefs uttered by a writer sometime after his death, the quote perfectly sums up the beliefs of the great Frenchman.

Voltaire, whose real name was François-Marie Arouet, grew famous from his writings, much of which criticized the French government, the Catholic clergy, and the nobility. This had to be done quite carefully in a hidden and subtle manner, for the regime of Louis XV, combined with the Catholic Church, censored any writing it believed was critical of it or of the Catholic faith. Voltaire was twice forced to flee France for England, where he saw for the first time a nation that enjoyed considerable individual freedoms, such as free speech and religion, which had been won at high cost in the 16th century during the English Civil War and afterward.

Voltaire was a prolific writer. He wrote hundreds of essays, poems, and letters addressing the problems of the day. His most famous work, *Candide*, was not so much a criticism of the French but rather the thinking of German philosopher Leibniz and the wave of relatively metaphysical ideas sweeping the upper and intellectual classes in Europe, the first and foremost one being that the world that exists at any one time must be the best one possible. For Voltaire, who throughout his life would attempt to open the eyes of his countrymen to the superstition and irrationality around them, this idea was simply playing into the hands of the powers that be—settling for your lot in life.

One of Voltaire's targets was the superstition of religion. Many people believe Voltaire was an atheist, but he was not. He believed that there *must* be a God, but that human beings, especially the Catholic Church, had added so much superstition, dogma, and unquestioning loyalty to it that they had perverted religion for their own purposes, mainly power and riches.

One of the most famous events in Voltaire's long life was the defense of Jean Calas, or rather the clearing of his name. Calas was a French Protestant who was accused of murdering his son because, it was believed, the son intended to convert to Catholicism. The trial of Calas was filled with injustice and unbelievable amounts of prejudice and superstition, and he was eventually convicted and tortured to death by authorities. Voltaire originally believing that Calas was guilty, but he looked into the case and found that Calas's son had committed suicide and that the trial was tainted by prejudice and religious intolerance. Though it was too late for Calas, Voltaire successfully argued the case in his writings, which by this time were followed by nearly the entire upper and intellectual classes of France, and he succeeded in having the sentence overturned posthumously. The family was paid a handsome amount by the king of France himself.

Jean-Jacques Rousseau (1712–1778) was born in Switzerland, but he spent most of his life in France. In contrast with Voltaire, who was known for his wit, charm, sophistication, and interest in a variety of subjects from religion to botany, Rousseau became focused early in his life on political philosophy and the injustices of society.

Though one is hesitant to use Wikipedia as a source, occasionally, there is something of great value there. In the article on Rousseau, one sentence sums up his life and two most famous works, *Discourse on Inequality* and *The Social Contract*. The entry reads, in part, "His [Rousseau's] *Discourse on Inequality* and *The Social Contract* are the *cornerstones of modern political and social thought*" (author's italics).

It is exceedingly difficult to sum up Rousseau's works in a paragraph or two, but for our purposes here, suffice it to say that Rousseau believed that political authority came only in a social contract agreed upon by all the citizens in that society. Given free thought, it is unlikely that these citizens would vote for an aristocratic dictatorship or an absolute monarchy. All things being equal, they would likely push forward the idea of some sort of representative democracy. Most importantly, perhaps, Rousseau declared that the state of humankind was freedom. "Man is born free, but he is everywhere in chains." Of course, you can see how this might have influenced certain people by the names of Jefferson, Madison, Franklin, and Adams, and it most certainly did.

Alongside the writings and beliefs of Voltaire and Rousseau came a flowering of art and the beginnings of open political debate. All over France, the more liberal wealthy and increasingly numerous and influential middle classes gathered together in the salons of (usually) upper-class women, who were eager to show off both their connections and their knowledge. Since many of the *salonnières* of the time were women, they found themselves debating on equal footing the merits of one political or scientific idea or another with men.

Of course, most of the people were not titled aristocrats, famous writers, or of the middle class. Most of France was poor, and it had been poor since time immemorial. They did not have the time or luxury of debating one school of philosophical or scientific thought over another over tea (and, increasingly, coffee) in the salons of the rich and famous.

However, in the 1700s, the majority of people became more informed through the increasing growth of the newspaper. Though most people of the time were illiterate, a growing number, especially in cities like Paris, was learning how to read, and they would read the news of the day to their families and friends. Newspapers, which were really nothing more than pamphlets or broadsheets, began having loyal followings, and the vast majority of them were critical of one aspect or another, such as the church, the monarchy, or the aristocracy.

Of course, the popularity of the salons, the writings of the Enlightenment *philosophes,* and the newspapers brought about a backlash. Censorship was increased. Government spies were widespread in cities throughout the country, and many, including Voltaire, were jailed for their thoughts and opinions. In Paris, many of the "enemies of the King" were sent to the infamous Bastille prison (pronounced "Bas-tee").

When Louis XV died in 1774, he left the country on the verge of bankruptcy, and under his successor, Louis XVI, the monarchy and the country would tip over that verge and go broke. In addition to the vast expenditures the kings spent on Versailles and other residences, the wars of Louis XV in North America, the Caribbean, and Europe had severely depleted the treasury.

Louis XV's grandson, Louis XVI, did nothing to contain the spending of the court and nation. Brought up to believe that he (like his predecessors) was God's instrument on Earth, the sixteenth Louis could not see any reason why he should curtail his spending. After all, France was rich, populous, and powerful. And that was true, to a point.

As a nation, France was rich: rich in resources, rich in population, and increasingly rich in bankers. As Europe entered into trade or colonization with the rest of the world, European economies became increasingly complex. To both help handle this complexity and make a profit, the number of banks had multiplied and grown in power and influence.

Both Louis XV and Louis XVI were increasingly less effectual and interested in the running of their kingdoms. When there is a vacuum of power, people or institutions rush to fill it. In the case of Louis XV and XVI, the void left by their illustrious ancestor, Louis XIV, was filled with rich nobles and clergy, a growing middle class, and increasingly powerful banks.

In the mind of both Louises, the surest way to raise money was to increase taxes, and they did this many times. Eventually, however, a number of things can happen. First, there was simply no more money to be gathered—you can't get blood from a stone. Second, oftentimes (and especially in the case of Louis XVI), the reason there was no more money was because, despite being an increasingly modern economy, France was still dependent on agriculture, as were its nobles with their vast lands. When drought or other natural disasters hit, revenue went down, and hunger and frustration went up. Third, for a fee, the king essentially licensed out the right to tax in many areas. For instance, if a farmer was carrying his crops to market, he might have to pay a toll to cross a bridge. Farther on, if he entered the territory of another noble, he might have to pay yet another tax. This could go on ad nauseam. Theoretically, the king was supposed to receive a cut of these taxes, but they often were under-reported. Louis XIV had his own collectors, and they were closely monitored, but this was not so for his descendants. Revenues declined, fees went up, and then taxes went up, which cut into both money for investment and survival. Fourthly, the people, who were hungry, angry, and fed up with paying taxes in a country in which they had virtually no rights, might just stop paying. They might, for example, start a revolution.

In the United States, the first revolutionary slogan of 1776 was "No taxation without representation!" Since they were not represented in the English Parliament, which levied taxes on them, the American colonists insisted they either be listened to or they would start a rebellion. The American Revolution did not go unnoticed in France; it arrived in the form of soldiers returning home and in the now hundreds of newspapers and pamphlets sprouting up all over Paris. In one of the most ironic twists of fate in modern history, the French monarchy of Louis XVI funded, supported, and helped equip the Americans in their revolution. Louis did not do this out of any affinity for the Americans or their ideas. Rather, he supported the Americans to spite the English.

France and England had been either at war or in a tense peace for decades in the 18th century. In the Seven Years' War, known in the American theater as the French and Indian War, the French had suffered a humiliating defeat at the hands of the English and lost their richest colony in the New World, Quebec, along with other territories in the Caribbean and Asia.

Seeing an opportunity for revenge, Louis XVI decided to aid the Americans, especially after the colonists' victory at Saratoga in 1777. Without French aid in the American Revolution, especially at the Battle of Yorktown in 1781, the Americans would have likely lost the war.

Louis XVI got his chance to humiliate England, but he also bankrupted France to do it. Even worse, many of the officers and men in the French Army and Navy were exposed to revolutionary ideas of the Americans, with the most important ones being political freedom and the lack of a king. In the 1780s, a combination of misrule, centuries of oppression, and bad luck combined to turn France into a revolutionary tinderbox.

Lurking behind all of the issues were two inescapable facts. One was that growing seasons had been bad in France for a number of years, creating a food shortage and hunger in many parts of the country, including Paris. Hand in hand with that, the decreasing food supply, plus the taxes levied on it, forced merchants to raise prices, causing inflation to slowly get out of control.

Just after the New Year, 1789, Louis XVI made a fateful decision. He called a meeting of the Estates General, which had not been done in 175 years. The Estates General was an assembly of the three groups comprising the population of France: the nobility, the clergy, and everyone else. Actually, the "everyone else" mostly meant people of note, such as middle-class lawyers or merchants, though there were a number of poorer farmers sent to the meeting by their neighbors.

Louis XVI's primary reason for calling the meeting was to get the people's permission to raise funds—in other words, to get permission to raise taxes yet again, for both he and France were broke and living on borrowed money and financed debt. Actually, the situation for Louis had gotten so bad (not so bad that he didn't enjoy Versailles) that most of his creditors, both foreign and domestic, would not issue him any more loans. Louis also realized that there were serious issues in the country that needed addressing, with the primary ones being an unfair and arbitrary tax system and the lack of political and religious freedoms.

Politically, the big issues were the lack of freedom of speech and the issue of the *Lettres de cachet*, which were warrants of arrest without any charges. These might be levied by the king or by the king's men at court, who frequently whispered the names of their enemies in the king's ear. A person could be arrested for any number of things up to and including personal enmity.

In Paris especially, but in other cities as well, writers, artists, and newspaper publishers were all subject to strict censorship. Sometimes, these people received a warning. Sometimes, they were arrested, then presented with a *lettre de cachet* ("letters of the sign," with "the sign" meaning a royal seal).

In matters of religion, Protestantism was still officially banned, and Jews were discriminated against and made, in many cases, to pay unfair taxes. The Catholic Church owned much of the land and paid no taxes. As happened during the Reformation in other places in Europe, Frenchmen saw bishops and priests, especially in the cities, walk about in ermine robes and jewels, all the while having sworn themselves to poverty. The one exception was many times the village priest, who sometimes needed to literally beg his congregants, who were also poor, for money.

In January 1789, the call went out across France for the people of each estate to put forward delegates to the Estates General. It took until the beginning of May for the delegates to be chosen and make their way to Paris. When gathered, the members of the estates, with the Third Estate making up the greatest number, were hosted for a processional at Versailles, where the meeting would take place.

The members of the Third Estate wore black and gold overcoats, some of them supplied by the king for want of funds. The assembled 1,200 members waited on the grounds while Louis XVI and his wife, the unpopular Marie Antoinette, paraded before them, bejeweled and decked in regal attire. Louis was applauded. Marie Antoinette was not.

Firstly, despite her French-sounding name, Marie Antoinette was Austrian. She was of the royal Habsburg family, and her birth name was "Maria Antonia. The fact that she was a foreigner was held against her from the start. And the fact that Austria had led France into the Seven Years' War was also held against her. When she married fifteen-year-old Louis XVI in 1770, she was fourteen years old. Louis and Marie Antoinette were distant from each other for years. He was shy and suspicious of his foreign queen, and she felt rejected by him for that and by the fact that they did not have sex for seven years after their nuptials. Many in France questioned Louis's "manhood," and others questioned both of the royals' ability to have children. It is believed this problem ended in 1777 after an operation to remedy a painful condition of the king, although that's just one theory. The other is the queen lacked a sexual appetite and that the king was unable to have children.

Regardless, both problems were eventually overcome. They had four children and, in time, husband and wife became devoted to each other.

Marie Antoinette was also disliked for her supposed greed, which was exacerbated by the Affair of the Diamond Necklace. Put simply, the queen was accused of trying to defraud a number of jewelers who had made a necklace for one of Louis XV's mistresses. The necklace was unbelievably lavish, and it was also unpaid for. However, though she admired the necklace, the queen did not order or want it. Someone had forged her signature, and she refused to pay for the end result. The jewelers possessed certain letters of the queen, which they then made public, and the whole of France read of the queen's duplicitous nature, but they weren't true; they had all been signed by a woman named Jeanne de la Motte. The whole affair was a scam, and most of those involved were arrested. Despite this, Marie Antoinette had already established a reputation for extravagance, which was, for the most part, true, and the affair, which took place between 1784 and 1785, further damaged both the monarchy's and the queen's reputation. (As a side note, Marie Antoinette never said, "Let them eat cake." The quote originated with Rousseau about Maria Theresa, Louis XIV's wife, and the quote had nothing to do with cake. When it was published, Marie Antoinette was ten. In actuality, Marie Antoinette, who did indeed love riches, also gave handsomely to the poor, which is much overlooked in history.)

At the Estates General, Louis, like his forebears, expected the members of the various estates to essentially approve his suggestions, many of them having been provided by his popular economics minister, Jacques Necker. However, by the spring of 1789, France was in such dire trouble that things went wrong for Louis from the start.

To begin with, the king was presented with the Cahiers de doléances—a list of complaints—which are summarized in the chart above. This was unusual, especially in regards to the first two estates, the clergy and the nobility. The length of the complaints and the overlapping nature of many of them were also a surprise, although it should be noted that the nobles and clergy had an entirely different view of them, for the most part, when compared to the Third Estate. When it came to voting on the issues, each estate got one vote. So, even though the members representing the Third Estate far outnumbered the others, they only had one vote. And they knew that the nobles and clergy were certain to vote together against the interests of the commoners on almost every issue. After a little less than a month and a half of meetings, arguments, adjournments, and anger, the members of the Third Estate did something extremely radical—they left the hall where the estates met and journeyed to a nearby tennis court (at the time, tennis was more like squash and took place indoors). There, they were joined by a small number of more progressive-minded nobles and clergymen, and they took the famous Tennis Court Oath, swearing not to adjourn until they had written a new constitution for France. They now called themselves the National Assembly.

To France, this meeting is what the meeting of the First Continental Congress is to the United States. The members of the Third Estate were breaking with centuries of history and declaring that it was they who had the power in France, not the nobles or the clergy.

Drawing of the Tennis Court Oath, c. 1790 by Jacques-Louis David, who first became the propagandist for the French Revolution, then Bonaparte. In the center, a member of each estate (with the Third Estate in the middle) leads the oath.
https://commons.wikimedia.org/wiki/File:Jacques-Louis_David_-_The_Oath_of_the_Tennis_Court_-_WGA06111.jpg

The formation of the National Assembly, the Tennis Court Oath, and the writing of a new constitution were not seen by most of the members as an attack on the monarchy. Rather, the king was still revered by many, as they believed he was being manipulated by powerful nobles and clergy. Once he became "educated," many of the Third Estate believed that the beloved king would see that a constitutional monarchy, such as they had in England, was best for the country.

At first, Louis saw which way the wind was blowing and instructed his supporters to join with the Third Estate, agreeing to change the way votes were taken and giving each representative a vote. Soon, however, whispers in the king's ear by his court councilors, perhaps the queen and other powerful nobles and clergy, made him grow suspicious. On July 11th, 1789, Louis fired his economics minister, Necker, who had for some time encouraged the king to stop spending lavishly and to rewrite and strengthen the tax code, things that were supported by many of the Third Estate. With the firing of Necker and rumors circulating of a violent breakup of the National Assembly by the king's troops, events began to spin out of control.

On July 14th, 1789, a large mob formed in Paris, and it was joined by disenchanted members of the army. The crowd marched to the Bastille, the royal prison, where the kings of France had sent their opponents, real and imagined, to languish, be tortured, or wait for execution. Rumor had it that the prison was filled to the rafters with the king's enemies (it wasn't), and the crowd, disenchanted with the slow-moving events in and near Versailles (some fourteen miles outside Paris), were screaming for blood. The powerful symbol of the king's repression, which lay within Paris itself and consisted of thick walls with eight thirty-meter-high towers, was finally broken into by the mob. The people killed a number of soldiers and decapitated the governor (warden) and paraded his head through the streets on a pike.

July 14th (Bastille Day) is a French national holiday today, and with the Storming of the Bastille, the French Revolution began to take on a bloody life of its own.
https://commons.wikimedia.org/wiki/File:Anonymous_-_Prise_de_la_Bastille.jpg

The Storming of the Bastille sent a message not only to the king but also to the members of the National Assembly. The message to the king was clear. The message to the National Assembly was "hurry up."

Louis XVI debated sending troops into Paris, as well as other cities, to quell the violence. Then he turned about and decided to let things play out. He debated this again and again. Indecision was one of Louis's greatest faults. However, by this time, events had already spiraled out of Louis's control, although he didn't know it.

A few days after the Storming of the Bastille, the National Assembly voted for the abolition of the traditional feudal rights of the clergy and nobility. Among other things, this included freedom from many taxes and the right to demand free labor from those living on their land.

On August 26th, 1789, the National Assembly issued the Declaration of the Rights of Man and of the Citizen, which formed the underpinning of the French republics that followed, including the one that is in existence today. The Declaration of the Rights of Man was the embodiment of the ideals of the Enlightenment and the ideas of men such as Rousseau, Voltaire, and Montesquieu. The first article reads, "Men are born free and remain free and equal in rights." The second states, "The goal of any political association is the conservation of the natural and imprescriptible rights of man. These rights are liberty, property, safety and resistance against oppression." The third goes, "The principle of any sovereignty resides essentially in the Nation. No body, no individual may exercise any authority which does not proceed directly from the nation." The remaining fourteen articles include the right of free speech, freedom from arbitrary arrest, giving the power to tax to the people through their representatives, and much else. Essentially, the Declaration of the Rights of Man completely did away with the old system of nobility and privilege based on birth. However, the people still had to organize a government around the declaration and figure out what to do with the king.

Between August and October, rumors swirled throughout France. People spoke about Louis XVI ordering his troops to arrest the leaders of the National Assembly or cracking down on dissent. Some spoke of him even asking foreign powers for assistance in doing so. (It should be noted that there was some truth to these rumors.) These rumors, combined with the already angry mood in the country, the growing hunger, and rising inflation, led to another famous episode in the French Revolution: the Women's March on Versailles, sometimes known as the Wives' March.

Between October 5th and October 6th, 1789, hundreds of women from Paris marched in the rain to the Palace of Versailles. By this point, many of the women had not only become angry about the price and scarcity of food, but they had also been involved in revolutionary politics. When they arrived at the palace, they were somewhat overawed but managed to present their demands to the king. The next morning, after a tense evening, more radical voices took over, and it was determined that they should bring the king and his family to Paris, where someone could keep an eye on them. To do this, they pushed into the palace, killed a number of guards, and threatened even more radical violence, including threatening cannibalism as revenge for the food shortage in France.

The queen, her children, and servants fled in terror through a secret passage, and a number of guards were decapitated. On the grounds, troops of the National Guard, under the command of the famous Marquis de Lafayette, who aided in the American Revolution, began to talk with the remaining members of the Royal Guard, and a truce was established. Louis reluctantly agreed to accompany the women to Paris to take up residence in the Tuileries Palace.

Throughout 1790, the National Assembly passed a variety of radical laws. They abolished the nobility and created the Civil Constitution of the Clergy, which essentially stripped all clergymen of any privilege. In November, under tacit threat of force, the French clergy was instructed to take an oath to France, not the church. Most did. However, many did not, and they suffered various forms of persecution.

In June 1791, Louis and Marie Antoinette, having corresponded in secret (or so they thought) with many of the royals of Europe for aid, decided their time in France should come to an end, at least until they could marshal enough forces to regain their power and defeat the revolutionaries. On the night of June 20th, they fled in rather flimsy disguises and were discovered not far from the French border near Varennes in eastern France. They were led back to Paris, where the crowds, which had already grown hostile to the idea of any monarchy at all, essentially kept them under guard at all times.

In September 1791, a new constitution was passed with the grudging support of Louis. In sum, the Constitution of 1791 placed all the power in France in a legislative assembly. The king was basically a symbol. For the other kings, queens, and nobles of Europe, the events in France were frightening, and many European rulers had begun to hear calls for reform in their own kingdoms, and they were determined to stop them.

The meddling of Austria, the home of Marie Antoinette, in the form of plots, pronouncements, and threats was most egregious, at least in the eyes of France's new leaders. In April 1792, France declared war on Austria. In June, Prussia declared war on France. This war, which was the first of many, went back and forth, but it did cause more economic suffering in France. On August 9th, 1792, the people of Paris established their own government, known as the Commune. They decided not to take direction from the National Assembly because it was not radical enough. The next day, a mob besieged the Tuileries Palace and placed Louis XVI and Marie Antoinette under arrest, charging him with plotting with the foreign enemies of France.

Throughout the spring and summer of 1792, Louis XVI, who still had veto power over the assembly (now called the Legislative Assembly), chose to veto some of their more radical and popular proposals. Tensions within the Legislative Assembly and on the streets of Paris were exceedingly high by late August, which was when the armies of Austria and Prussia threatened mass violence against the population should any harm come to the king and his family. For many of the revolutionaries, this was the breaking point for their relationship with the monarchy. On August 10th, 1792, a large number of members from the National Guard of Paris and the militias of Marseille and Brittany marched through the capital. They attacked the Tuileries Palace, where the royal family was kept under surveillance, and slaughtered hundreds of the Swiss Guard—the king's personal guard, which he had been allowed to retain. An equal number of revolutionary soldiers and citizens were killed as well. The king, Marie Antoinette, their children, and some of their servants were arrested and taken to the Temple, a small prison in Paris.

The revolutionaries from Marseille sang a song on their march to the front, which was written by Claude Joseph Rouget de Lisle, an army captain who was, ironically, a royalist. He composed the song that became the rousing national anthem of France, "La Marseillaise," shortly after France declared war on Austria.

The Revolutionaries

At this point, it is important to identify some of the major players among the revolutionaries before we go further.

Firstly, there was the revolutionary population of Paris. Not all Parisians were revolutionaries or supported it, but by 1792, most did, and those who did not kept a very low profile. Many from the middle and upper classes who had not openly aligned themselves with the revolution early on fled Paris if they could. Many could not do so for reasons of property or business, while others believed that the worst of the revolution had passed—an error in judgment if there ever was one. Many, if not most, in the non-revolutionary middle class "dressed down" when going about in public, trying to appear as "common" as possible. If they were recognized on the street by their clothes or from their past, many were subject to harassment and violence, which only got worse as time went by.

Those doing the harassing were usually members of the working classes or those who were very poor. History has labeled these men and the women sans-culottes, or those without culottes, knee-britches, as this item of clothing was worn by the nobility and the rich. The sans-culottes wore ankle-length pants, as most people do today. Women still wore skirts or dresses, but the term "sans-culottes" is a catch-all phrase. In addition to their long pants, many of the revolutionaries wore a Phrygian cap, which was modeled after the headwear worn by ancient Roman slaves who had been given their freedom (and also many of the peoples of the Balkans and Anatolia/modern-day Turkey).

Many of the writers of the time, within France and without, referred to the sans-culottes as the "revolutionary mob," and the populations of the poorer districts of Paris (and, to a degree, other cities in France) often behaved like one. During the Reign of Terror, which began in September 1793 and continued throughout much of 1794, the sans-culottes served not only as enforcers for revolutionary leaders but also as instigators of much violence.

One of the earliest, well-known, and radical of these revolutionaries was Jean-Paul Marat (1743–1793). A relatively accomplished scientist and physician, Marat traveled Europe as a young man before settling in London for some time, becoming a relatively well-known physician. By the 1770s, he had absorbed much of the thinking of the Enlightenment and began to write tracts on despotism and the rights of man. When he returned to France in 1777, he concentrated on a scientific career and published some papers of note, especially on electricity. He also began writing about the injustices of the criminal law system in France and in much of Europe and was corresponding with Benjamin Franklin, exchanging ideas on liberty. By 1789, Marat had become one of the most radical voices in France, and he had begun publishing one of the most influential revolutionary papers of the time, *L'Ami du Peuple*, or *The Friend of the People.*

By the next year, the focus of much of his work was on plots (both real and imagined) of nobles who had fled France and were working with foreign monarchs to restore the absolute monarchy. In 1790, his writings had become too radical even for the new National Assembly, which sentenced him to a month in prison for inciting violence, but he escaped and went into hiding. By the time he came back out into public, the mood of the country had changed, as it had become more radical than before. Marat was elected to the National Convention, a branch of the Legislative Assembly.

Though he had originally opposed going to war with Austria, he soon supported it and called for a dictatorial committee of revolutionaries to govern France. In the National Convention, Marat was part of a faction called the Mountain, or the Montagnards, named for the place they occupied in the chamber. The Mountain was the more radical subset of the Jacobins, whose name stemmed from the monastery near their headquarters. The Jacobins were radicals, and they sat on the left. Opposed to them were a mixed group of moderates, led by the Girondins, many of whose early members came from the part of France known as the Gironde, and they sat on the right. Ever since that time, the terms "left" and "right" have been associated with liberals/radicals and conservatives/reactionaries, respectfully.

Marat was seen as a loose cannon, so he was kept out of most of the Montagnards' deliberations, but he was used to incite action and distrust against the movement's enemies. In April 1793, Marat was brought up on charges that he had encouraged the murder of political enemies, but he was acquitted. This move spelled the end of the Girondins, which was a more moderate voice in France, and the ascension of the Jacobins and Montagnards.

A month and a half later, in July 1793, Marat was in his bath (which he often was, as he was the victim of a painful skin disease, most likely scrofula) when a visitor called. Her name was Charlotte Corday, and she claimed to have evidence of the activities of Girondins, who had fled the capital after their downfall. Marat interviewed her in his bath and reportedly told her he would see to it that these Girondins and their sympathizers were killed. At hearing that, Charlotte Corday, who was really a Girondist sympathizer whose family had fled France in fear in 1789, stabbed Marat in the chest, killing him almost instantly. The French Revolution had its first real martyr. Corday was beheaded, and the event played a large part in ushering in the infamous Reign of Terror.

The Death of Marat by Jacques-Louis David. This romanticized portrayal became one of the most popular revolutionary images, and it was copied in print, canvas, and marble throughout France.

https://commons.wikimedia.org/wiki/File:Death_of_Marat_by_David.jpg

Danton and Robespierre

On September 20th, 1792, the French defeated the Prussians at Valmy, which seemed to prove the value of the French Revolution and its army. On September 21st, France was proclaimed a republic, and the monarchy was abolished. The king was no longer known as King Louis XVI but rather as Citizen Louis Capet, which the revolutionaries believed was his royal house (he was actually from the House of Bourbon).

With the enemy pushed back, fever for the French Revolution high, and the king's popularity at an all-time low, the revolutionary leadership put Louis XVI on trial. Louis's trial split the revolutionaries in two. The Girondins were for keeping Louis under arrest and as a hostage, which would keep both foreign kings and French nobles who had fled France (known as the *Émigrés*, or "emigrants," though they were more like escapees) in line. The Jacobins, especially the more radical Mountain, pushed for Louis's execution.

There were many impressive personalities among the revolutionaries, but two, in particular, stand out: Georges Danton and Maximilien Robespierre.

Danton was the son of a farmer, and he had an unfortunate early childhood. As an infant, he had been attacked by a bull and run over by a herd of pigs. Making matters (and his looks) worse, Danton also survived a bout of smallpox, a regular and many times deadly scourge in virtually all parts of the world until the widespread development and adoption of vaccination techniques in the late 18th and early 19th centuries. As a result, Danton's face was uneven and disfigured by the pockmarks, which were seen on many faces during that time. Nevertheless, Danton had a reputation as being somewhat of a ladies' man when he grew older (he was widowed twice and married thrice). Danton was a tall, broad man with a deep, booming voice.

As a young man of humble background, the seminary was virtually the only place he could receive an education, and he entered one at the age of thirteen, leaving a few years later to become a clerk in Paris, where he served as a minor functionary in the *Conseil du Roi* ("Council of the King"), which was the office that governed administration throughout France.

In his years on the council and living in Paris, Danton became intimately familiar with the injustice and corruption in the government and with the disenchantment of the people around him in Paris's poorer districts. On July 14th, 1789, Danton took part in the Storming of the Bastille and confronted the troops of the famed Marquis de Lafayette. A few months later, he was elected as the representative of his Paris neighborhood and as a representative to the Paris Commune.

Danton was reportedly an incredibly fiery and charismatic figure and speaker, and his appetite for food, wine, and coarse words made him popular among the people. He also gathered about him other influential revolutionaries, such as Marat and revolutionary publisher Camille Desmoulins (a man—Camille (pronounced "Cam-ee") serves as both a male and female first name in France).

Danton soon grew to be a power to be reckoned with, protecting the less powerful and becoming the president of a political club known as the Cordeliers, formally known as the Society of the Friends of the Rights of Man and of the Citizen. He was also one of the prominent members of the Jacobins.

In the summer of 1791, Danton had to flee Paris in the aftermath of a massacre of revolutionaries, which had followed a riot near the center of the city over the future of Louis XVI after his attempted escape. Many prominent revolutionaries went into hiding for some time. Danton went to London for a few weeks.

Danton returned shortly before another revolutionary mob stormed the Tuileries Palace and put the royal family under arrest in 1792. That day, he was made the minister of justice in the Paris Commune. Danton and his associates often get overlooked in the use of terror during the revolution (Robespierre has the more infamous name in that regard), but over the next few weeks, somewhere in the neighborhood of 1,000 people were arrested without warrants and some without cause in the hunt for counter-revolutionaries. That September, Danton's Ministry of Justice, the revolutionary mood in Paris, and rumors of plots against the revolution caused an outburst of violence known as the September massacres, in which nearly 2,000 people were killed. Danton bears some of the responsibility, for he declared in a speech that anyone who was not in service of the revolution or aided it should be considered an enemy, calling for their death.

During his time as a prominent man, Danton apparently became quite wealthy. Some believed he illegally profited off the dissolution of the French East India Company, procured favorable loans for friends, and bought/sold land near his birthplace in Champagne at an exorbitant discount or profit. He also suffered the loss of two wives and children in childbirth during this period.

In March 1793, Danton and others pushed for the creation of the Revolutionary Tribunal, a special court that would deal with "enemies of the people." In April, the soon-to-be-infamous Committee of Public Safety was formed, with Danton as one of the members, though he often missed meetings, preferring to "act as a spur to action." These frequent absences may have contributed to him not being elected as a member in the July elections. A few days later, Maximilien Robespierre was elected to the Committee of Public Safety, and Danton's power slowly began to decline, though it was not obvious at the time.

In late winter/early spring of 1793, a revolt against the revolution occurred in the Vendée region of western France. The revolt was made up of royalist nobles, devout Catholics who saw the French Revolution as an attack on their faith, and many poor farmers (France, as a whole, had suffered yet another poor crop system and further inflation). Also contributing to the revolt was an order from the revolutionary government for a military draft (*levée' en masse*), which had never been done before. The Vendée revolt lasted for some months before being brutally put down. At this time, the Vendée, another rebellion in Brittany, and the population's unrest resulted in both violence and the expansion of the revolutionary government's power. The Committee of Public Safety and the Revolutionary Tribunal were both reactions to open revolt and the less violent but growing grumblings in the country.

During the summer of 1793, a power struggle between the Girondins and the Jacobins came to a head. The main issue was the arrest of Marat by the Girondins and his acquittal by the

Revolutionary Tribunal. Marat was protected by both Danton and the sans-culottes, and the loss of the case put the Girondins on the defensive. The final straw was the murder of Marat by Charlotte Corday in July 1793. It was at this point that the Reign of Terror began.

During the late summer and fall of 1793, the Committee of Public Safety declared terror to be "the order of the day"—literally. Throughout France, both real and imagined "enemies of the Revolution" or "enemies of the people" were arrested and many times executed. In the winter of 1793, the "Revolutionary Razor," the guillotine, was invented by Dr. Joseph-Ignace Guillotin as a "humane" method of execution.

During the winter, Danton was at the center of events in Paris. He began calling for a slowdown of the Terror, and he also had to deal with the aforementioned accusations of financial impropriety. By February, Danton was the target of many of the more radical members of the Jacobins, and he was growing frustrated with Robespierre, who had climbed to the top position of power within the Committee of Public Safety.

During February, Danton, Robespierre, and their supporters jockeyed for the top position within Paris and France. Since Danton no longer had a seat on the Committee of Public Safety, he was in a weaker position, and his growing calls for moderation put him in Robespierre's sights. Robespierre will be discussed in a moment, but for now, suffice it to say that while he and Danton were friendly, they were never close. They were complete opposites: Danton was coarse, while Robespierre was fastidious and prim.

Convinced by his henchmen that Danton was both corrupt and working to take power for himself and his more "moderate" friends, Robespierre ordered Danton's arrest. The trial of Danton (along with many of his friends, most notably the publisher Camille Desmoulins) was a farce, devolving from charges of financial impropriety to anti-revolutionary activity and even Danton's love of food and wine as a sign of his lack of "revolutionary fervor and solidarity." Danton was not allowed to speak in his defense, though he managed to make his voice heard. However, laws preventing him from being heard and other points of procedure were rushed through the assembly to make the outcome certain. Even those who had most vocally and openly supported Danton in the past were silenced, afraid for their lives. Before he was beheaded with a group of fourteen others on April 5ᵗʰ, 1794, Danton predicted that "Robespierre will follow me; he is dragged down by me."

A contemporary engraving of Danton's final moments.
https://commons.wikimedia.org/wiki/File:Ex%C3%A9cution_de_Danton.jpg

Maximilien Robespierre did follow Danton to the guillotine, as the execution of Danton caused people to wonder if the revolution had gone too far. They started to believe that Robespierre, in particular, and his followers were beginning to act like dictators. And though he would likely have denied it, Robespierre had long let power go to his head.

Robespierre's nickname was "the Incorruptible," and honestly, if a nickname ever fit, this one did. Throughout his rise and time in power, Robespierre had more than ample opportunity to enrich himself, but he never did. Up to his death, he lived in the same simple apartment that he had lived in before the revolution began, preaching the ways of what he called "revolutionary virtue" and encouraging others to do the same.

As was mentioned above, Robespierre was the exact opposite in personality from Danton. He was prim (probably because of the example he set in his everyday life, he continued to wear an upper-class wig when many others were hiding or burning theirs), fastidious, and spoke quietly. When he did speak, though, people listened. Later in his relatively short life, they listened often from fear, but there was no doubt that Robespierre was a brilliant and well-spoken man.

Maximilien Robespierre was born in 1758 in Arras, central France. He came from a family whose occupation had been the law since at least his grandfather and likely before. Robespierre was to follow in these footsteps. His family life was disrupted when his mother died in childbirth, taking an infant girl with her. Robespierre's father was devastated by the loss, and he fled Arras and disappeared into history. Maximilien's two younger sisters were taken in by his father's sisters, and he and his brother were raised by their mother's parents. Perhaps Robespierre took refuge in books, for he was already fully literate and reading advanced works by the ages of eight and ten, respectively. Like Danton, he attended a seminary school, as it was the only choice for the very few gifted poor and the sons of the middle class. There were no public schools, which was something that Robespierre and other revolutionaries pushed for in later years. One of his fellow pupils was Camille Desmoulins, who Robespierre later had executed along with Danton.

At school, Robespierre was fascinated with the Roman Republic (not the Empire), and he studied the works of the great Roman orators Brutus the Elder, Cato, and Cicero. In combination with the study of their oratory, Robespierre also became fascinated with the idea of Roman virtues: bravery, the incorruptibility of the mind and body, piety, and the like. Like many others of his time, he also read Rousseau's *The Social Contract*, and among the many things he gleaned from Rousseau, it was the idea of the "citizen-soldier" acting on behalf of those less fortunate that appealed to him the most.

Robespierre, however, was not a friendly person, though he had long-time acquaintances. From an early age, he seems to have interpreted these and other readings to seem to require the "virtuous man" to stand aloof above the crowd as an example, which he did until he took it too far. Some say part of the reason for Danton's break with Robespierre was Danton's impatience and boredom with Robespierre's constant preaching of "virtue."

Like other revolutionaries in both France and the United States, Robespierre believed in the theories espoused by many of the Enlightenment's great thinkers: direct democracy, the "will of the people," and equal rights under the law. He studied law for three years was after being admitted to the prestigious Sorbonne, also known as the University of Paris. He graduated among the top in his class, and immediately after, in 1782, he was given a position as a judge in the criminal court of his hometown of Arras. Interestingly enough, Robespierre resigned from that position over his opposition to the death penalty.

Over the next few years, Robespierre made a name for himself as an intellectual and writer, winning a number of prestigious prizes for essays written on criminal justice reform and the like. During this time, he became acquainted with some of the people who would make names for themselves during the French Revolution.

Robespierre was elected as one of the representatives to the Estates General from his region in 1789 after he had written an influential tract about governmental reform. During the Estates General, Robespierre began to gain his reputation as a speaker, despite his quiet voice. Some said it was the evident fervor with which he spoke that gained him adherents rather than his logic. Either way, he soon developed a coterie of followers and critics. His critics managed to keep him out of positions of power; at the time, everyone was afraid of one man standing out among the many revolutionaries. After all, they had weakened (and would soon kill) the king, and they did not want to replace him with a dictator.

Robespierre was, however, the presiding member of the Jacobin Club, the political group that would become progressively more radical and powerful as time went by. Though Robespierre has a bad name in history today, his work early on in the French Revolution should be recognized and applauded. As part of the group that worked on writing the new constitution of France, he championed universal suffrage and admission to public office and to the officer corps of the army for all who deserved it, regardless of birth or status. He also argued against religious and racial intolerance and the absolute veto of the king. In many ways, Robespierre was ahead of his time, even among revolutionaries. For example, laws mandating equality for women were reversed after his demise.

Like Danton, Robespierre called for the king's trial after the escape attempt to Varennes, and he was present at the massacre at the Champs de Mars, for which he had to go into hiding for a time. While in hiding, he kept the Jacobin Club alive, and when the danger had passed, he was greeted with a hero's welcome by the sans-culottes of Paris.

Between this time and the convening of the National Convention, which governed France from September 1792 to October 1795, Robespierre moved in and out of positions of power, sometimes being acclaimed as a hero and sometimes as a villain with the goal of dictatorship. The National Convention was the body that outlawed the monarchy and declared France a republic.

The Trial and Death of Louis XVI

In December 1792, after the shedding of much blood, the king was put on trial. Among the most prominent of those calling for the king's execution was Robespierre. During the trial, Robespierre and others accused the king of many crimes, including the murder of innocents, torture, the abuse of the law, conspiring with foreign governments to overthrow the revolution, and much more.

Still, at the beginning of the trial, many were hesitant to sentence Louis to death or even a long prison term. The power of the French monarchy went back centuries, and the French populace had been inculcated with the notion that the king was not only above the law but also a representative of God on Earth. However, in the decade and a half of Louis XVI's rule, things had gotten so bad in France that the ideas that had once sustained the French monarchy for centuries had begun to rapidly break down.

For the first part of the trial, Robespierre took ill, and his place was taken by who many considered his radical lap-dog, Louis Antoine Léon Saint-Just (simply known as Saint-Just to history), who became one of the most bloodthirsty men of the Reign of Terror. Robespierre, Saint-Just, and others argued that the king had not only conspired against the inherent rights of the people but had also plotted with foreign kings and agents, which he had. Louis was confronted with over 700 letters signed by him that asked foreign powers for aid; these had been intercepted by the revolutionaries. The king somewhat clumsily denied the letters were his, but everyone, including himself, knew this was a lie.

The king's vain arguments and a powerful speech by a recovered Robespierre on December 3rd, 1792, convinced many that the king was a danger to the revolution and its ideals if left alive. By January 1793, the trial came to an end, with the National Convention declaring the king guilty of conspiracy and endangering the public safety and good. By mid-January, the National Convention was debating the sentence, with many Girondins and other moderates arguing for clemency and a long prison sentence. Robespierre, who was by now the acknowledged leader of the radicals of Paris and France, and the Jacobins argued for the death sentence. By a close majority, those calling for immediate execution won the day. Three days later, on January 21st, 1793, Citizen Louis Capet, formerly Louis XVI of France, was led to the guillotine and killed. His wife, Marie Antoinette, would be put on trial and executed in the same manner that October. Only their daughter, Marie-Thérèse Charlotte, would live into adulthood, as the others succumbed to illness before and shortly after the French Revolution.

Orléans (Égalité) holds out by the hair the decollated head of Louis XVI, while he waves his cap in his right hand

Even before the king's execution, the revolutionaries had begun to change France and its culture. They had already abolished the monarchy and nobility, and they had also weakened the clergy's power through the Civil Constitution of the Clergy, which forced the Catholic Church in France to give up much of its land, privileges, and wealth. It also forced priests and other clergymen to swear obedience to the constitution over the church. Most did so, and those who did not were often punished or sent to out-of-the-way parishes. Churchgoers who attended services by these refractory clergy were often persecuted.

The revolutionaries had declared equal rights for Protestants and Jews (at the time, there were virtually no Muslims in France), but as the French Revolution entered a new era under the influence of Robespierre, the whole idea of a Judeo-Christian deity came under attack.

When Robespierre entered the Sorbonne and began his rise to notability through his writings, he was an advocate of religious tolerance, like many of the later revolutionaries and much of the educated populace of France, especially in Paris. This continued when the revolution first began in 1789. However, as time went by and he saw how entrenched the ideas of the Catholic Church were in France, both in regard to spiritual matters and earthly ones, that position began to change.

Among the many things the Protestant Reformation had changed in much of Europe, including pockets of France, was to make the Bible available in local languages, not just Latin, as it had been for centuries. With this move, literate people began to read the Bible for themselves and develop ideas that were different than those held by the church. Many of those who could not read were read to or instructed in the Bible by men and women who had read the text themselves. Sometimes, they came up with radically different conclusions than those held by the pope and the Catholic hierarchy.

In those parts of Europe that had turned to Protestantism, such as England, much of northern Germany, Scandinavia, the Netherlands, and much of Switzerland, new ideas about Christ and Christian doctrine arose. During the period of tolerance between Henry IV's rule Louis XIV's revocation of religious rights, a sizable Protestant minority had grown in France, but it was forced underground under Louis XIV. In the time leading up to the French Revolution, some Protestants felt a bit more freedom to practice their religious convictions, but there was hardly religious freedom as we know it in the West today.

In 1793, as the Reign of Terror began, the radicals among the Jacobins and others promoted the Cult of Reason, and it was actually supported by the state as an "atheistic religion" devoted to the idea that human reason and scientific knowledge could solve most or all of the world's mysteries and/or problems. Among historians, the Age of Enlightenment was preceded by the Age of Reason, which was made famous by the works of Isaac Newton, René Descartes, Francis Bacon, Gottfried Leibniz, and many others. Thus, "reason" gave way to "enlightenment," and for the revolutionaries in Paris, Christianity (in particular, Catholic Christianity) was a superstitious cult created by the few for their enrichment and the oppression of the masses. Many Protestant sects, particularly the sects that had arisen in Switzerland and eastern France that incorporated the idea of predestination, were another way of elites holding the masses down. To counter the thousands of years of religious oppression in France, the Cult of Reason was formed by two prominent revolutionaries, Joseph Fouché and Antoine-François Momoro.

The Cult of Reason stressed the idea of civic duty according to the ideas of the Enlightenment philosophers, such as Voltaire and Rousseau, and refused to allow "reason" as an idea to be personified as a god, meaning they didn't want abstract statues or paintings of "reason" to be created for purposes of worship. The Cult of Reason and adherence to it became a trademark of many of the revolutionaries, especially of the sans-culottes, who had become the most violent supporters of the revolution and the Reign of Terror. One of the more interesting people of the period, a Prussian who adopted French citizenship, Anacharsis Cloots (he took the French name Jean-Baptiste du Val-de-Grâce), declared that there would be only one god—the people. He was later guillotined by Robespierre.

After Robespierre rose to the top of the Committee of Public Safety, he rejected the Cult of Reason and replaced it with something he had developed himself: the Cult of the Supreme Being. This happened for many reasons. Firstly, many of the Enlightenment greats in both Europe and North America were not atheists; they were Deists, meaning they believed in a supreme being that gave rise and order to the universe and life on Earth but did not truly involve itself in the everyday lives of people and especially did not call for the giving of money to a church for the forgiveness of sins.

Robespierre was a Deist as well, as were many of his friends and other revolutionaries throughout France. He believed that the masses of people were eager to be free of the oppression of the Catholic Church but not willing to give up the idea of a god. His Cult of the Supreme Being supplanted the Cult of Reason and became the official religion of France for a very short time.

Robespierre also believed that the idea of a god was necessary for social order, as people needed to answer to a higher power or authority for human society to remain orderly. He often quoted Voltaire: "If God did not exist, it would be necessary to invent him." For Robespierre, "the Incorruptible," religion was the path to the virtues he had believed in and extolled since he was a child.

At this point in time (around the summer of 1794), Robespierre had risen to control not only Paris but also France through the Committee of Public Safety and its offices and agents throughout the country. He had begun to strike at his enemies in the fall of 1793, and this continued into the spring and summer of 1794. This was the infamous Reign of Terror, and some of its first victims were not only political foes of Robespierre and the Jacobins but also men who had pushed the Cult of Reason, such as Fouché, Momoro, and Cloots.

On the twentieth day of Prairial in the Year II (the revolutionaries created a new calendar to mark the departure from the old ways), the Festival of the Supreme Being was held in Paris, as well as smaller ones in towns throughout France. The festival was designed by Jacques-Louis David, who painted the famous *Death of Marat* and would soon immortalize Napoleon, and it was similar to a Roman-style event, with some actually wearing togas and olive wreaths. A man-made mountain was erected in the Champs-de-Mars (the "Field of Mars") in Paris, and many weren't exactly sure what to do and sort of just milled around, waiting. The worst part was a long, dry speech by Robespierre, who came down the mountain in the style of Moses. To many, the Festival of the Supreme Being was a sign that the revolution had gotten out of hand and that a small group of people, led by Robespierre, was setting themselves up as dictators.

By the summer of 1794, the people of France and Paris, in particular, had grown weary of the Reign of Terror. Initially, they supported the Terror as a way to either eliminate or cow the enemies of the revolution. These are the times depicted in Dickens's famous *Tale of Two Cities*, with its revolutionary crowds screaming for blood, egged on by sans-culottes and revolutionary women, such as the fictional Madame Defarge.

The Reign of Terror lasted from early September 1793 to the end of July 1794, which was when Robespierre and his supporters went to the guillotine themselves. During these ten months or so, it is estimated that some 20,000 or more people were executed by official decree. Many others were killed without record. During the Terror, revolts took place throughout France, and many of those opposing the Terror or the French Revolution were killed. It is important to note that the Terror didn't just abruptly end; it slowly petered out as people grew weary and moved on to another form of revolutionary government.

Throughout France, people turned on neighbors, rushing to report them for "anti-revolutionary activities" or as "enemies of the people." This allowed them to get revenge for old arguments, fights over property and businesses, and even love affairs. Once a person was accused, it was very hard to find innocence, especially since most cases were "tried" by People's Tribunals that met either every day, in the case of Paris and other large cities, or irregularly, in the case of smaller towns. Either way, a lack of harsh prison sentences or executions showed a "lack of revolutionary vigor" and could often get those on the tribunals in hot water themselves. As Danton had reportedly said, "The Revolution, like Saturn, devours its own children."

The total dead through officially sanctioned executions, of which many were signed off by Robespierre, may never be known. Estimates run from a low 20,000 to over 100,000 or more. What is known is that the Reign of Terror and the rule of the Committee of Public Safety was in many ways the precursor to the multitude of totalitarian governments of the 20th century.

In the end, Robespierre, who had begun as a relatively tolerant man, gradually became convinced that he could lead France into a life of incorruptible "virtue." The problem was, as he neared the end of his life, Robespierre and those around him began to see enemies everywhere. Not that he didn't have them—he just thought that there were many more than there were. Making things worse, there had been assassination attempts on Robespierre and others close to him. Robespierre pushed through laws on dissent that rankled other revolutionaries and made them think about the reasons the revolution had begun in the first place.

Robespierre and his cronies also spread lies about people who dared speak against them or the Terror. Toward the end of the Terror, the violence of the Committee of Public Safety actually increased, with the mobs of sans-culottes, who Robespierre and others secretly despised, being set upon their enemies.

By late July, many of those in power had had enough of Robespierre, Saint-Just, and the Committee of Public Safety. Robespierre had made many enemies throughout the revolutionary ranks, accusing them of leniency, corruption, and much else. Some of this was true, but much of it was false. On July 27th, 1794, the National Convention met in Paris. News came from the frontlines that the French had defeated the Austrians yet again, and many in the National Convention supported an easing of the Terror as the war wound down. Knowing that this would lead to a decrease in his power, Robespierre and his adherents protested, but many outside of his circle began to openly accuse him of wanting to be a dictator.

Robespierre and Saint-Just had made speeches in the Jacobin Club earlier in the week, accusing many in the National Convention of being traitors and working against the revolution. They planned to give the same speeches in the convention hall, but as they attempted to do so, they were shouted down every time they tried to speak. Member after member rose to speak against them, including a leading revolutionary named Jean-Lambert Tallien, the commissioner of the National Convention. Tallien's wife was an influential critic of Robespierre, as well as an early friend of Joséphine de Beauharnais, who would become the wife of Napoleon, and Robespierre had her arrested.

Robespierre's attack on the wife of the commissioner of the National Convention was the last straw. Tallien, as commissioner, made a passionate speech against Robespierre and called for a vote against him and his followers. Subsequently, Robespierre, Saint-Just, and a number of others were arrested. These men escaped to the Hôtel de Ville (city hall), where, that night, a mob besieged them and wounded Robespierre in the jaw, allowing curiosity seekers to gawk at him in agony. The next day, "the Incorruptible" and about twenty others were executed on the Place de la Concorde, the same place where Louis XVI and Danton had lost their lives.

History knows this episode as both the end of the Reign of Terror and the Thermidorian Reaction, named for the month of the French Revolutionary calendar in which it took place.

The Thermidorian Reaction against Robespierre in the National Convention.
https://commons.wikimedia.org/wiki/File:Max_Adamo_Sturz_Robespierres.JPG

After the death of Robespierre, the Terror was halted, and the revolution headed in a slightly more conservative direction. A new form of government and yet another constitution were formed. The executive branch of this government was called the Directory, and it lasted four years, from November 1795 to November 1799. The Directors were five men in an attempt to prevent the rise of another Robespierre, and a bicameral legislature, similar to the American system, picked the Directors.

The Directors were equipped with weak executive powers, which meant the power devolved to the two legislative houses, so not a lot got done. Corruption was rampant, though. Since the Directors did not have the "power of the purse" and the legislative branch consisted of some 600 members from two houses, with competing interests keeping things at a virtual standstill legally, many turned to bribery. Naturally, citizens who had just been through literal hell asked themselves if they had gotten rid of a corrupt monarchy for a corrupt Directory.

However, one of the lasting achievements of the Directory cannot be overstated. They established the first modern public school system, which was open to virtually everyone. Within a generation or two, France had the highest literacy rate on the planet, and in the late 1800s, it was home to some of the world's greatest scientists, especially in the fields of chemistry, medicine, and biology.

Unfortunately, this was outweighed by corruption, and though many of the actions of the Directory were attempts to cement the gains of the revolution in perpetuity, some of the rules, both said and unsaid, on wealth and personal privilege were relaxed. Many noble emigrants returned, and many sons of the upper-middle classes began to take on noble airs. In fact, in Paris and some of the largest cities, gangs of what became known as the Muscadin ("musk wearers"—expensive perfume for men) or the Gilded Youth roamed the streets looking for trouble, attacking whom they deemed as radicals and attempting to reestablish their life of privilege. For many of these Gilded Youth, these attacks were revenge for the attacks made on them or their families during the Terror.

Additionally, and we will discuss this further in the following chapter, France had been at war for a great deal of the revolutionary period and had made enemies across Europe and the English Channel. This had happened not only because of the losses accrued on the battlefield but also because French revolutionary ideas had begun to spring up within many European territories. Monarchs, nobles, and the burgeoning middle classes in these countries believed their positions and possibly their heads were threatened by revolutionaries motivated by the events in France. There was even trouble in the United States, where the

French ambassador threatened George Washington with mob violence in an attempt to strongarm the American president in supporting French ambitions in the New World and against England.

So, as the 19th century approached, France was still in a period of tremendous change, and its people were beginning to tire of it. After a decade of revolution, terror, wars both domestic and foreign, and great change, many of the people in France wanted a period of peace and stability.

The French Revolution was so radical, so involved, and so politically intricate that it is hard to cover them all in an introductory history such as this. At the end of this book, you will find a number of excellent titles that will both broaden and deepen your knowledge of this earth-shaking event—and it was earth-shaking, for nothing in Europe would ever be the same afterward.

Before we move forward into the next chapter, it is important to examine the lasting effects of the French Revolution.

Perhaps first and foremost, it ended feudalism in France and, for a time, the idea of hereditary privilege. No longer were nobles and the clergy, which accounted for about 3 percent of the population, the holders of almost 97 percent of the land and most of the country's wealth. Though the French monarchy would return after the fall of Napoleon, the idea of advancement through merit rather than birth became more established in France and later in most of western Europe.

The French Revolution also removed the Catholic Church from its place of dominance in French society. Though a civil war of sorts would continue to simmer between devout Catholics and secularists in France into the 20th century, the revolution removed Catholicism from its position of power and influence in much of French life. It also moved religious toleration forward—no longer, at least on paper, were Protestants and Jews discriminated against.

Though France would be shaken by a major scandal in the late 19th century regarding religious and ethnic discrimination, the revolutionaries took the first steps toward broad religious toleration in Europe.

As was previously mentioned, a system of public schools was established, leading France to become one of the most educated nations on the planet. Although the words "nation" and "country" have been used throughout this book to describe France and other territories, it was not until the French Revolution that France and many of the areas of Europe affected by the French Revolution were identified as a "nation" and not a "kingdom." Now, France would be recognized as not only an area of land but also a region of ideals, a specific culture, and equality under the law.

In the United States during the 1780s and most of the 1790s, the idea of political parties and specific ideologies were relatively unknown. It was in revolutionary France that political ideology (the notion that a set or competing sets of political ideals should shape society) was born. The ideas of a liberal "Left," a conservative "Right," and "moderates" were developed in France in the 1790s.

Though many of the French revolutionaries were inspired by the events of the American Revolution, the Americans did not specifically set out to spread their political ideals to other nations in order to "liberate" them from monarchies or other elites. The French revolutionaries most certainly did. The French Revolution ushered in what historians call the Age of Revolution, which swept Europe, as well as South and Central America, for most of the 19th century.

In combination with the above, the French Revolution, though it had its tyrannical Reign of Terror, helped spread democratic and liberal ideals throughout Europe and the world. Today, in the United States, in particular, the word "liberal" has taken on a different meaning in some quarters, but historically, the words "liberal" or "liberalism" meant the spread of ideas, such as equality under the law, mass education, and the freedom of speech, religious tolerance, and much more. Though the French Revolution reached its extremes, today's democratic societies around the world owe the French revolutionaries a huge debt.

Lastly, the impact of the changes wrought by the revolution was such that historians use the period as the dividing line for a new era: the modern era.

Though the painting Liberty Leading the People was created in 1830 by Eugène Delacroix to commemorate another revolution in France in that year, the image perfectly captures both the ideals and events of the earlier 1789 French Revolution.
https://commons.wikimedia.org/wiki/File:Eug%C3%A8ne_Delacroix_-_Le_28_Juillet._La_Libert%C3%A9_guidant_le_peuple.jpg

Chapter 9 – Vive l'Empereur!

One of the many things that students in introductory history classes are always astounded by is how the French Revolution, with its rejection of Louis XVI, morphed into an even grander form of monarchy at the start of the 19th century under Napoleon Bonaparte.

In actuality, the evolution from the radical French Revolution to Napoleon's government is not all that surprising, at least to us today. To the men and women of France and Europe at the time, it certainly was. The cycle of the French Revolution, from localized revolts to violent unplanned uprisings to organized revolution and so on, is familiar to us now and has played itself out many times since 1789, albeit in slightly different forms. In most cases, whether it's an emperor or some other stabilizing force, the revolution is scaled back, though not to the point where its necessary changes are done away with. Since the French Revolution was the first truly modern revolution, this cycle was unfamiliar at the time (the American version began with a revolt against a "foreign" king and then developed or solidified its revolutionary ideas after the conflict was over).

Napoleon declared himself the emperor of the French in 1804. He had ruled the country as the first consul since 1799/1800, and he was the leader of the state in all but name by the time he took his imperial title. During the run-up to his coronation, from 1799 to 1804, there were some royalists (supporters of the Bourbon family, of which Louis XVI was a part) that thought Napoleon would use his power (meaning the army) to install and protect Louis XVIII (Louis XVI's brother) after restoring some sort of order to France.

Napoleon told the would-be king's representatives in no uncertain terms that the only way that the Bourbons would regain the throne was "over 100,000 corpses." And that went for the rest of the nobility's and clergy's feudal rights and former lands. No, Napoleon would be an emperor, but he would be a revolutionary one, and when he could not be that, he would make his own rules. This was even more astounding, for in the eyes of many Frenchmen, Napoleon Bonaparte was a foreigner. He came from the newly acquired Italian-speaking island of Corsica, which was the former possession of the Republic of Genoa.

Corsica

Napoleon was born in Ajaccio, Corsica's capital city, in 1769. That year was an auspicious one in many ways, at least for France, Napoleon, and Corsica. Corsica is a large island that lies about halfway between southern France and northern Italy in the Mediterranean Sea. From 1559 to 1755, the island had been a possession of the Republic of Genoa, a province in northern Italy. In 1729, the Corsicans began a decades-long struggle for independence, which was led by Pasquale Paoli and his family. By 1755, the Corsicans had established control over most of the island with the exception of two Genoese fortresses, and they established a republic with a constitution written for them by Enlightenment philosophe Jean-Jacques Rousseau.

Unfortunately for the Corsicans, their republic was not recognized by any significant power in Europe, and in 1769, the King Louis XV of France purchased Corsica from a cash-strapped Genoa.

Corsica
Francisco Welter-Schultes, CC0, via Wikimedia Commons
https://commons.wikimedia.org/wiki/File:Cyrnotheba-corsica-map-eur-nm-moll.jpg

The Bonaparte family (the name was actually spelled "Buonaparte") had emigrated to Corsica in the 1500s from Tuscany, the region that includes Genoa. Initially, the Buonapartes and other immigrants from the mainland were looked upon as foreigners and strangers by the native Corsicans, who had their own language and culture. However, over the centuries, families like the Buonapartes integrated into Corsican culture, and by the late 18th century, they had no real roots in mainland Europe. Still, for many years, Napoleon considered himself Tuscan or Italian rather than Corsican. (One must remember that Italy did not become a united nation until the late 1860s, though).

Napoleon's parents, Carlo and Letizia, had two children die in infancy before having Joseph, Napoleon, Lucien, Elisa, Louis, Pauline, Caroline, and Jerome. Later in his career, Napoleon placed his brothers on the thrones of various European countries, but they were all relative failures. For instance, his brother Joseph fled Spain after his unpopular term as king, settling in the United States, with a home in Bordentown, New Jersey, near the site of Washington's crossing of the Delaware.

The Buonapartes were descended from minor Tuscan nobility, and like many immigrant families on Corsica, they lived as such. They took on upper-class styles (wigs, culottes for men, stockings, etc.) and considered themselves the elite of the island. Napoleon's father, Carlo, was a lawyer and diplomat, which put him near the top of Corsican society. Carlo also took part in the war of resistance against the French when they first came to the island. However, when that resistance was finally quelled, Carlo became the island's representative to the court of Louis XVI at Versailles.

Naturally, this meant that Napoleon and his siblings (especially his brothers) were afforded a privileged life and access to education, which most Corsicans did not have. It was evident to virtually everyone that Napoleon was gifted. He read books far beyond what most children his age were capable of and excelled in math. History, especially military history, was his favorite subject, and he read voraciously, especially on his hero, Alexander the Great, and the history of Rome. One of his favorite activities was to recreate famous battles with his collection of lead soldiers. Virtually everyone that came into contact with him recognized that he was on a different level from most boys his age and even many adults. Napoleon was also known for being rowdy, independent-minded, and rebellious. His mother, to whom he was devoted, kept him in line.

In January 1779, at the age of nine, Napoleon was sent to the mainland French city of Autun in northeastern France to attend a religious academy. In May of that year, he transferred to a military academy in roughly the same area.

For almost any nine-year-old boy, being over 600 miles away from home is traumatic. For Napoleon, it was hell.

It wasn't until he was ten that Napoleon began to really understand French. Prior to his going to school in France, there had been no reason to learn it. His family had spoken Italian at home, and he spoke Corsu (Corsica's native language) as well. At school, he was bullied incessantly for his bad French, as it had an Italian/Corsican accent. He was seen as a rustic farm boy even though his father had been the Corsican delegate to the court of Louis XVI. In pre-revolutionary France, virtually all of the boys and young men in attendance at schools were of noble families, and they looked down on Frenchmen without titles. It is no surprise that they would look down on a foreigner.

Napoleon at the School of Brienne.
(From the painting by M. R. Dumas.)

Bonaparte the Novice by Maurice Realier-Dumas
https://commons.wikimedia.org/wiki/File:The_boy_life_of_Napoleon,_afterwards_emper
or_of_the_French_(1895)_(14778572322).jpg

It was not only his poor (but rapidly improving) French skills that made Bonaparte stand out like a sore thumb. In a time when people were, on average, much shorter than they are today, he was on the shorter side—at about 5'4" tall. Napoleon did not help his case much either. He withdrew into himself when he could, but among others, he sometimes acted arrogantly, as if he knew more than they. Still worse, he did, and he never tired of letting anyone forget it. Because of his social exile, Bonaparte devoted himself utterly to his studies, especially math, history, and cartography.

If you had asked most of his fellow students at the military school at Brienne what Napoleon was destined for, the vast majority would have likely said that he would've been sent to a far-flung post, likely in the West Indies, where he would remain a low-level officer for the rest of his life.

However, to a few of his fellow students and quite a number of his instructors, Bonaparte stood out. His leadership and skill showed during the now-famous snowball fights, where he would rally his side to victory (often the snowballs were loaded with rocks), and to the discerning and mature eye, Napoleon was impressive in every way. He seemed to think faster than his fellows, he was more decisive, and he had an uncanny ability with artillery. From Brienne, he went to the military academy (the École Militaire) in Paris in 1784 for a two-year officer course. He graduated in one year and was sent to Valence in the south of France as a lieutenant in the artillery.

From about 1787 to about the time of the French Revolution, Napoleon became enamored with two things: republicanism, as advocated by writers such as Rousseau, and Corsican politics. It was unusual, but Napoleon somehow seemed to be able to negotiate or wrangle his way into an extraordinary amount of leave, and he spent most of the years between 1789 and 1792 in Corsica, though he did travel back and forth between France and the island often.

In the days before the revolution, Napoleon was aligned with one of his childhood heroes, Pasquale Paoli, who had fought for Corsican independence from Genoa and was now agitating for the island's independence from France. Napoleon at first supported Paoli's cause, as he still saw himself as a Corsican, not a Frenchman or an Italian. However, as the French Revolution grew nigh, Napoleon began to become more and more supportive of the republican cause and less supportive of Paoli's. While men and women in France were giving up their lives to change the system of absolute monarchy in France, Paoli seemed to be moving in the opposite direction and setting himself up as the power in Corsica. Over time, Napoleon and Paoli became estranged, which was made worse when Napoleon's father, Carlo, who had fought and supported Paoli in the war against Genoa, aligned himself against Paoli's faction in the Corsican Assembly and against Corsican independence.

Napoleon eventually became an adherent of the radical beliefs of the Jacobins in the initial days of the revolution, and he was promoted to a captain in the Republic of France's new army, despite having taken part in a riot against the French in his initial days back in Corsica. His repeated visits and extended stays on the island, sometimes without leave, did not seem to count against him either.

In 1793, Napoleon's support of the revolution led to his final split with Paoli. He supported a French attack on a smaller Corsican-held island, and both he and his family were forced to flee Corsica for France in 1793. Up to this point, Napoleon had considered himself a Corsican, not a Frenchman. Napoleon's birth name was Napoleone di Buonaparte, which was an Italian name. From the time of the split, he began calling himself Napoléon ("Nah-poh-lay-ohn") Bonaparte—the French version.

Napoleon was a relatively well-known man in Corsica, but in France, he was just another junior officer in a rapidly growing army. Historians have debated for centuries over which of Napoleon's personal characteristics was the most dominant. Some say his audacity, others his intelligence, but no matter what they believe, one of the most dominant features was his ambition. From his earliest days at school, when he realized that he was far beyond his fellow students in ability, Napoleon was ambitious. To us, that is no surprise. We know that he rose from relative obscurity to become the emperor of much of Europe. He may be the most widely written-about personality of all time today, but in the 1790s, France was full of ambitious young men. Now, because of the French Revolution and the Declaration of the Rights of Man, these young men were free to exercise their intelligence and abilities, even if they were not born nobles.

Napoleon was present when the revolutionary mob attacked the Tuileries Palace, which held the king and queen. This attack, the first real move toward putting the monarchs on trial and executing them, was a bloody affair, and Napoleon witnessed it firsthand from his apartment window. During the attack, the Royal Guard that Louis had been allowed to keep were essentially torn apart limb from limb, with some of them having their head mounted on pikes and paraded through the streets of Paris. The fury of the uncontrollable mob frightened Napoleon to his core, and he vowed to never allow such violent anarchy if he was in a position to stop it, which he later was.

In 1793, Bonaparte was stationed in the south of France, near the important port city of Toulon. Toulon itself was in the hands of royalist Frenchmen, and they had committed not only the "sin" of supporting the old regime (the Bourbon family and the nobility) but also of inviting the troops and ships of France's most hated enemy, the English, into the city.

Napoleon was given command of the artillery on the hills surrounding Toulon. The heights were a great advantage, for the British ships were not able to elevate their guns to reach Napoleon's position. For most of his career, Napoleon's men loved him. They learned that, in his eyes, they always came first. He made sure, to the best of his amazing abilities, that they were fed, clothed, and well-cared for. He also knew, especially as a younger junior officer, that if he did those things, his men would follow him almost anywhere.

The Siege of Toulon had been going on for some months when Napoleon was given charge of the French guns. He soon had new emplacements dug and secured more ammunition and weapons from nearby French posts. Within a relatively short amount of time, he had reduced the city's defenses to the point where republican troops could assault the city with some degree of surety that they would succeed. And they did succeed. On December 19th, 1793, the British and French royalists in the city surrendered. In the assault on the city, Napoleon, leading from the front, was wounded in the leg. Many of the royalist soldiers, who had either surrendered or were captured in the battle, were executed en masse by firing squad or bayonet. However, this was not at Napoleon's command. He neither had the authority to countermand this order, which came from the powerful revolutionary figure Paul Barras, nor was he even in the city, for he was elsewhere being treated for his wounds.

Not only did his role in the victory at Toulon come to the attention of the leading revolutionaries in Paris, but in his time in the south of France, Napoleon had also authored a pamphlet entitled *Le souper de Beaucaire* (*The Supper at Beaucaire*). In it, Napoleon recounted a dinner he had held for some of the leading citizens in the area in which he was stationed before the Siege of Toulon. Napoleon's goal at the dinner was to allay the fears his dinner guests had of the revolution and the changes it brought in its wake. The other purpose of the pamphlet, the more important of the two to Napoleon, was to illustrate to the powers that be, whether in the south of France or in Paris, that he was a tried and true revolutionary, an officer they could count on. He likely succeeded more in the second purpose than the first, for along with his victory, *The Supper at Beaucaire* reassured the men in Paris that they had a new bright star in the military that they could trust.

Painted after Napoleon's rise, *The Supper at Beaucaire*, by Jean Lecomte du Nouÿ, depicts not only the event but also adds symbolism. Napoleon (standing) tells his guests about the glories of the revolution—he is literally bringing them "into the light," as shown by the candlelight beaming in their faces.

During the Siege of Toulon, Napoleon had risen in rank from captain to major to adjutant general (a staff officer). After his victory at Toulon, Napoleon was named brigadier general—and all this by the age of twenty-four. This was both a testament to his ability and a symbol of the new order in France, that a man could rise as high as his ability, not birth, would take him.

In Paris, Maximilien Robespierre's brother, Augustin, the government's commissioner to the army, wrote to his powerful brother at the beginning of 1794 and told him of the "transcendent merit" of the man from Corsica. In February of that year, Napoleon was given command of the artillery of the French Army of Italy. The French had been fighting there, as well as in the Rhine River area, hoping to both repel Austrian invaders and spread the ideals of the French Revolution.

Even today, any ambitious man is going to make enemies or at least arouse suspicion and jealousy. And it was no secret that Robespierre and the radicals on the Committee of Public Safety had placed Napoleon in his position. He arrived in February 1793, about halfway into the Reign of Terror. Four and a half months later, Robespierre, his brother, and many other leading figures of the Reign of Terror were beheaded. As a result, Napoleon, whom Augustin had referred to as "Robespierre on horseback," fell under suspicion and was charged with conspiracy and treason. He was put under house arrest in Nice for a time.

His connections and his lack of participation in the government or the Reign of Terror led to his release after two weeks. Napoleon took part in an abortive attempt by the French to take Corsica's southern island neighbor Sardinia from the British and the province of Savoy from their Italian allies. He was then given an infantry position in the west of France to help put down the royalist rebellion in the Vendée, but at the time, the artillery branch was the elite branch of the army. To get out of the assignment, Napoleon pulled an old children's trick: he faked an illness. He was then assigned a dreary job as a military cartographer.

Many believe these assignments came to him for two reasons. He had been close to Robespierre, and his ambition was becoming very well known. In Paris, Napoleon began to move in exclusive circles, especially among the salons of the wealthy middle class. This gave him an opportunity to meet some of the leading figures of the time, as well as their wives, whom he knew could influence their husbands. It also made himself and his ambitions known. The salons might have engaged in gossip and rumors, but they also led to important and influential connections.

During this time, he became engaged to Désirée Clary, the daughter of a rich businessman from Marseille. Napoleon's older brother Joseph was already married to Désirée's older sister, Julie. For a time, Napoleon was passionately in love with Désirée, and he even wrote a short novel, *Clisson et Eugénie*, based on their story. However, Napoleon met the widow Joséphine de Beauharnais at one of the Paris salons and fell almost instantly head over heels in love. The engagement to Désirée was off, and Napoleon and Joséphine, who was six years older than the general, which displeased his family greatly, married in 1796. Désirée went on to marry one of the men who became a marshal under Napoleon, Jean Bernadotte, who later became the king of Sweden and Norway. Désirée became a queen, and their descendants are on the throne of Sweden to this day.

It can be said with relative confidence that Napoleon and Joséphine loved each other to the end of their days, though he divorced her in 1810 for the younger, and, more importantly, more fertile and politically well-connected, Marie Louise, the princess of Austria. He had a son with her, Napoleon François Joseph Charles Bonaparte. Napoleon II was born in 1811 and given the title "King of Rome." He lived a short life—he died in 1832 of tuberculosis, which was made worse by pneumonia.

Napoleon and Joséphine are remembered for a number of reasons. First, he was madly in love with her. She seemed to love him as well but not with the same fervor. She was also six years older than him and a widow, which caused a bit of a scandal. When they divorced, Napoleon let her keep her titles, income, and home at Malmaison. Most importantly, throughout their marriage, he occasionally took her advice, which was often good. This usually came in the form of political or politically social advice: how he related to people, how he should present himself, reports of events at home while he was on campaign, etc. Much of the time, she was correct. She died suddenly while walking with the visiting Tsar Alexander I of Russia in 1814. At the time, Napoleon was in exile on Elba, and he went into a fit of grieving for two days. When he died in 1821, again in exile (this time on Saint Helena), her name was the last word he ever spoke.

In October 1795, a little over a year after the Thermidorian Reaction, which had overthrown Robespierre and the Committee of Public Safety, a mob of royalists, believing the time was ripe to push for a return of the monarchy now that the more radical revolutionaries had been put down, stormed the National Convention. At this time, the members of the convention had been meeting in the same Tuileries Palace where Napoleon had witnessed the mob kill so many of the Royal Guard three years before. Back then, Napoleon was convinced that if the Royal Guard had opened fire with their available artillery, the mob would have dispersed. In 1795, Director Paul Barras ordered Napoleon to put down the royalists. Along with a cavalry officer named Joachim Murat, who would go on to become one of Napoleon's favorite marshals, Napoleon gathered together several large artillery pieces and opened fire on the crowd. An estimated 1,400 people were killed, and the rest of the mob fled. Asked later how he repelled the mob supposedly, Napoleon said, "I gave them a whiff of grapeshot." Grapeshot was essentially smaller cannonballs chained together and piled into the cannon's barrel—think of a *very* large shotgun. Napoleon indeed used grapeshot, but he didn't utter those famous words—they were the words of a later British biographer.

If Napoleon had pulled this stunt a few years earlier, he would, at the very least, have been removed from command and/or sent to a distant post, never to be heard from again. However, he had saved the government of the Directory, suppressed the still unpopular royalists, and, most importantly, after years and years of street violence, had stopped yet another riot before it really started.

The suppression of the royalists propelled Napoleon to national fame. Within days, he was given a promotion to the position of commander of the Interior, a handsome reward and salary, and the protection of the government against any jealous competitors in the army. Soon after, he was given command of the Army of Italy, as the French were embroiled in their efforts to spread revolutionary ideas there. France had also been fighting with the armies of Savoy, Piedmont, and, more importantly, the Empire of Austria, which had great influence in Italy, especially in the northern provinces.

Napoleon's Military Exploits

It is literally no exaggeration to say that more books have been written about Napoleon in the almost two centuries since he lived than almost any other figure in history. There are volumes alone on his relationships with Joséphine, his marshals, his family, his effect on the future of France, his relations with a variety of countries, and more. In all likelihood, most of the books on Napoleon have to do with his military campaigns, victories, and defeats. Books on his defeat at Waterloo in 1815 could fill the libraries of large towns. All that to say that this book is a broad history of France, covering from the time of the earliest cavemen at Lascaux to the post-WWII years. The campaigns and the intricacies of Napoleon's battles would take up the rest of this volume and many more. The people fascinated by Napoleon's battles are, in fact, numberless and exceedingly knowledgeable (and there are also literally thousands of reenactors as well). If you're one of those incredibly knowledgeable people, feel free to skim through this chapter, as you most likely have already learned what's to come next. For those of you who are just getting interested in French history and Napoleon, here is your introduction to the man that many believe is still the greatest general in the history of mankind.

Napoleon certainly was the greatest general of his time. His campaigns were marked by meticulous preparation. When he could, he trained and retrained his troops when others at the time were simply putting men in uniforms and pointing them at the enemy, perhaps giving the men a smattering of practice in formation maneuvers and how to load and care for a musket. That was to change after Napoleon's enemies saw how the fruits of his labor paid off, but in the last years of the 18th century and the first years of the 19th century, the French Army under Napoleon was the best drilled, most practiced, and best led in Europe.

In American football, sometimes a coach comes along that simply "throws away the playbook," meaning he does something completely different than what is expected or is traditional. Napoleon threw away the playbook and wrote his own at the same time. It's as if the Green Bay Packers of the early/mid-1960s had to play against the 49ers of the 80s or the Patriots of the 2000s. They would simply not be in the same league, and that was the case with Napoleon's foes throughout most of his career.

Napoleon's campaigns were marked by speed, surprise, and the uncanny ability to predict his opponent's reactions. He often divided his forces when he was about to face the enemy, something that was seemingly against the unwritten rules of warfare of the time, especially since artillery was just coming into its own. Napoleon played with his enemies after a fashion in this manner, as he realized the importance of keeping one's enemies off-balance.

"The Little Corporal," as enemies often pejoratively referred to him and his men occasionally with fondness, drove his men hard. At first, they resented him for it, but when they realized that it paid off with victory after victory, they realized the importance not only of his hard training but also of speed. Napoleon was often at a place days before his enemies expected him to be there. He would know where his enemy was going to march seemingly before they did. Since he arrived before his enemy, he could choose the most advantageous positions at his leisure. Napoleon himself would often comment that the battle is "often won before the fighting even begins."

Napoleon's rise to fame within France began with Toulon and Tuileries. His fame throughout Europe spread after his first Italian campaign, which lasted from 1796 to 1797. In the late spring of

1796, Napoleon was sent to northern Italy to prevent the Austrians from cementing their power and advancing into France. For almost exactly a year, Napoleon and his generals fought the Austrians in some twenty-six battles. Many of these battles were led by Napoleon himself. In others, his generals, who had been molded to fight according to his ideas, fought to great victories. The French were only held or brought to a stalemate on a couple of occasions. Worse for the Austrians, they frequently outnumbered the French, but they were almost always outmaneuvered and outfought by the forces under Bonaparte.

There are two important points to be made here. Firstly, since the French Revolution, the officer corps of the French Army was made up of men who, for the most part, had talent. During the time of the absolute monarchy, generals were always members of the nobility, as were virtually all the officers. A few were excellent, some were good, and many were awful. With the changes brought about by the revolution, officers were promoted, for the most part, on talent. This was accelerated under Napoleon, as a number of his commanders had begun their military careers as non-commissioned officers (corporals and sergeants). It was made clear in Italy that Napoleon earned the loyalty of his men. This was particularly true at the Battle of Lodi ("loh-dee") in northern Italy. At Lodi, the French were forced to cross a bridge under heavy fire from the Austrians holding it and the opposite bank. It was a bloody affair, and it cost the French dearly, but after a number of attacks, bravely led by highly ranked French officers, the Austrians were forced to retreat. It is said that Napoleon himself directed the fire of the French guns near the bridge, assuming the role of corporal for himself and placing himself in danger. From then on, many of his veterans referred to him as the "Little Corporal" with great fondness, for it was apparent that he would not refuse to do what he asked of his soldiers.

During this time, Napoleon set up the Ligurian Republic and the Cisalpine Republic in northern Italy, basing them on French revolutionary ideas. Though he did set up representative assemblies in these territories, for a time, Napoleon ruled behind the scenes, alarming many in the Directory who asked themselves if they had created a monster that might do away with them.

In October 1797, Napoleon and the Austrians signed the Treaty of Campo Formio. According to the terms, France would receive the Austrian Netherlands (today's Belgium), and Austria would recognize the Cisalpine and Ligurian Republics. The Cisalpine Republic would control all of Lombardy (most of northwestern Italy), and the French would also be given Austrian territory east of the Rhine River and a number of Greek islands under Austrian control. Austria would, in turn, receive control of the Italian lands on the east coast of the Adriatic, which makes up much of today's Croatia.

By taking control of the Austrian Netherlands and the left bank of the Rhine, the French, thanks to Napoleon Bonaparte, had regained what had always been believed to be the "natural borders" of France, what they had been first under Charlemagne and then under Louis XIV.

Egypt

When Napoleon returned to France, he received a hero's welcome, but there were many, both in power and on the street, who were becoming wary of the Corsican general. He had an army that was seemingly only loyal to him, and he had exceeded his authority in both forming and running the Cisalpine and Ligurian Republics. Though in the end, the establishment of these lands was good for France (or so it was thought), and the Treaty of Campo Formio had "restored" France's "natural borders." However, Napoleon had also acquired tremendous wealth. Both he and his troops enriched themselves on the lands they conquered. For his troops, it was food, whatever riches they could seize, and the age-old terror of rape and thuggery without consequence. For Napoleon, it was much more. He did send large amounts of treasure back to France (this was how France financed its wars, which meant that, in order to keep the people happy at home, more wars and more plunder were needed), but he also enriched himself at the same time. Banks, local governments, art, and much more were added to Napoleon's personal coffers.

The combination of intelligence and charisma, a loyal army, and wealth made Napoleon a dangerous man for those in power. The Directory itself owed its survival to Napoleon for destroying the royalist mob that was bent on restoring the old order in 1795. He and other generals also sent troops to aid the Directors in removing royalists from the two legislative houses of government in September 1797, which added to his influence. Napoleon was growing in power, and everyone knew it. And if they didn't, they could find out in the two newspapers he established.

However, in October 1797, when the Treaty of Campo Formio was signed, Napoleon was not prepared to seize power, nor is it exactly clear when he began to think of placing himself at the head of the French state. For now, he was satisfied with a new task: planning the invasion of England.

Though England had a relatively small (but growing) army, its navy was second to none. Ever since the defeat of the Spanish Armada in 1588, England's navy continued to grow, bringing English power, influence, commerce, and colonists to almost every corner of the globe. Worse yet, England's position across the English Channel (there's a reason it's called the "English Channel" and not the "French Channel") made her a direct threat to France's coastal cities, its commerce, and any potential navy it might develop. The Directors, like the radical revolutionaries and the long list of French kings before them, were determined to do something about it.

However, after two months of careful study, Napoleon reported to the government that in its current state, neither the government, its treasury, and its forces were in a position to undertake a cross-Channel invasion of the British Isles. The best the French could do was to harass the British wherever possible until they were able to launch an invasion. The French sent money and arms to rebels in Ireland, and it fought a series of naval battles with the English in the West Indies, most of which did not go well.

The Directory was in agreement with Napoleon's conclusions and then supported his idea to harass the English at another point: Egypt. Napoleon's goal was to seize Egypt, which was then ruled by the Muslim Mamluk dynasty, and prevent English trade from going across land to the Red Sea and then to India by ship, where the English were establishing themselves as a power. He also hoped to defeat the Mamluks and, like his hero Alexander the Great, push on to India and take British possessions and influence for himself. This would also serve as a way to get Napoleon far from the center of power in France.

Though Napoleon won great victories over the Mamluks and took control over the richest part of Egypt, in doing so, his troops suffered tremendously from heat, disease, and thirst. Many literally lost their minds and wandered off to their deaths in the desert. The French fleet that had transported Napoleon and his army was also defeated by the man who would become one of England's greatest heroes and Napoleon's nemesis, Admiral Horatio Nelson. Nelson's fleet almost completely destroyed the French at the Battle of the Nile in August 1798, leaving but a handful of French ships afloat.

The Egyptian campaign was a disaster for Napoleon, even though he did not lose a battle on land. His army was decimated mostly from heat and disease, especially from the plague, and the British had destroyed his lifeline to Europe and any additional supplies. In July 1799, Napoleon left Egypt, bringing back some wounded men but leaving most of his army behind. The survivors were repatriated to France in 1801 by agreement with the English, who had defeated the remnants of Napoleon's army there.

Coup of 18 Brumaire, Year VIII

Napoleon returned to France without permission, but the Directory had already sent orders for him to return, which he never received. While Napoleon was away, the situation in France was dire, as France's enemies, which at this point consisted of England, Austria, Russia, and a smattering of lesser powers, including Portugal, Sweden, and a number of German states, had won victory after victory from 1798 to 1799. When Bonaparte returned to Paris, the military situation had stabilized, but the political one was in flux.

The Directory was hated. It was seen as corrupt, which it was, and ineffective, which it was to a great degree, especially in dealing with economic problems. Inflation was perhaps the biggest issue, which terrified both the French people and the government, as inflation had been one of the prime movers behind the French Revolution in 1789.

When Napoleon returned, he was given a hero's welcome. Although the campaign was a failure, he successfully played up his own victories and blamed the campaign's defeats and problems on others. At the same time, Napoleon also entered into a plot with a number of influential politicians to overthrow the government of the Directory. Napoleon was involved with the famous Abbé Sieyès, who had been a powerful clergyman and early supporter of the revolution); Sieyès's brother, Lucien, the speaker of the lower house of the French assembly (the Council of the Five Hundred); another Director named Joseph Fouché; and Charles-Maurice de Talleyrand (better known as just "Talleyrand"), who was the ultimate survivor, as he had gone from royalist to revolutionary to supporter. He later became the foreign minister under Napoleon and then served the succeeding French government after

Bonaparte was gone. These men formed a group bent on overthrowing the Directory and installing themselves as the new power.

This coup occurred on November 9th, 1799 (18th Brumaire by the revolutionary calendar, which is how the event is known to history and historians). Napoleon and the others arranged for the two assemblies (the Council of the Five Hundred and the Council of Ancients) to be moved to another location because of a supposed threat from royalists. Napoleon gave a speech to the assembled representatives in which he poorly attempted to explain what was going on. Many of the men began to heckle and shout him down, and the coup was on the verge of failing when Napoleon's friend and deputy, General Murat, showed up with a contingent of troops. Under threat, the legislators agreed on a new constitution, which was presented to them the next morning and which called for a new form of government known as the Consulate.

General Bonaparte in the Council of the Five Hundred, at Saint-Cloud, 10 November 1799, by François Bouchot, 1840.
https://commons.wikimedia.org/wiki/File:Bouchot_-_Le_general_Bonaparte_au_Conseil_des_Cinq-Cents.jpg

Surprising his fellow plotters, Napoleon named himself the first consul. Abbé Sieyès and the others had to accept this; after all, Napoleon had control of the troops in Paris. As the first consul, Napoleon had the power to appoint the *Conseil d'État* (the "Council of State"), which was given the power to draft laws and appoint army officers, judges, ambassadors, and ministers of state. The three new (mostly "rubber-stamp") legislative chambers were the Tribunat, the Corps législatif, and the Sénat.

What did the people of France think of this radical new change? Generally speaking, the change was welcome. The Directory, as stated, was corrupt and unpopular. The people had been through over ten years of revolution marked by political violence, civil war, and war with enemies outside of France. They wanted stability and order, and Napoleon and his fellow consuls promised both.

The years of the Consulate saw a great change in France and the continued rise of Napoleon's popularity. Napoleon oversaw tremendous changes in the way France was governed, much of which remains in place today. Administratively, France was organized as departments, which were large administrative bodies akin to American states but more closely tied to the central government. Napoleon handpicked *préfets* ("prefects") as regional governors, who were answerable to him, and reformed the civil service. Famously, he instituted France's highest honor, the *Légion d'honneur* ("Legion of Honor"), for both civilians and military, stating that both had an important role to play in the life of the state. Both of these Napoleonic changes are in place today, albeit with some minor changes.

Napoleon also undertook a new program of infrastructure, improving roads, canals, and tunnels for improved and faster transportation, as well as improvements in sewage and public health. The changes were immensely popular in France, and as the period of the Consulate went on (1799–1804), people clearly saw that it was Napoleon who was responsible for the changes.

Perhaps Napoleon's most famous non-military achievement was also installed at this time. This was the *Code Napoléon* ("Napoleonic Code"), the system of laws which bears his name and which he had a great deal of influence over. Many people believe that the Napoleonic Code was actually written by Bonaparte himself—it was not. He formed a commission that met some eighty times to complete the project. Napoleon was present at over half of them.

The *Code Napoléon* codified many of the existing laws of varying regions of France in one place and eliminated those thought to be ineffective, unjust, or outdated. It broke the law down into branches—commercial, criminal, and civil—and further broke down civil law into property and family law.

One of the more unpopular parts of the code, at least among the progressive and revolutionary-minded women of Paris, was its return to the old laws under the monarchs regarding the role of women. The right of women to vote was taken away, and it also took away many of their individual rights, especially in regards to marriage.

Equally distressing from the point of view of the radical revolutionaries of the 1790s was the reintroduction of slavery in France's colonies in the New World, which gave rise to revolts of all kinds, especially and most famously in Haiti.

On the positive side, the equality of all men under the law was recognized. During this time, the majority of European countries still counted the word and deeds of noblemen far above those of commoners, so this was groundbreaking. Religious freedom and the freedom to dissent were also guaranteed.

As you can imagine, the actions of Napoleon and his co-conspirators did not go completely unopposed. Both ends of the political spectrum, royalists on the right, who saw Napoleon attempting to create a new type of monarchy and replacing the old Bourbon royal family, and radicals on the left, who saw exactly the same thing but were opposed to it for far different reasons.

On Christmas Eve, 1800, Napoleon and Joséphine were on their way to the Paris opera house. Because of scheduling, they were riding in different carriages, but they were not far from each other as they rode down the crowded boulevard. As they neared the opera house, a wagon loaded with barrels of gunpowder was pushed down the road and glided in between them. The distance between the carriages of Napoleon, Joséphine, and crude but powerful "infernal machine" (as Napoleon would later call it) was enough so that when the explosives went off, the intended target and his wife were unharmed. However, fifty-two people were killed or wounded, including Joséphine's step-daughter, who was wounded in the wrist. After surveying the scene, Napoleon insisted on going to the opera, where he was greeted with a standing ovation.

The perpetrators of the Plot of the rue Saint-Nicaise, named for the street where the bomb exploded, was the job of staunchly Catholic royalist supporters who wanted a return of the old monarchy and the former preeminence of the Catholic Church.

Amazingly, Napoleon blamed the attempt on his life on the remains of the radical Jacobins. Though his co-consul Joseph Fouché knew that the plot was the product of royalists, he went along with Bonaparte's thoughts, and the two staged an elaborate trial of 130 Jacobins, who were exiled from France. Four of the actual perpetrators (those who constructed and provided materials for the bomb) were guillotined, and their ties to royalist financiers were downplayed. Napoleon believed the radical left was a greater danger to his rule than the royalists, whom he planned to deal with in another way. Another result of the assassination attempt was the further development of the secret police and informer system, which had begun during the Terror and were increased by

Napoleon until France became as close to a police state as possible with the limited technology of the 1800s.

Italian Campaign Part II

France's two prime enemies, Austria and England, were not prepared to make peace with a new type of French revolutionary government headed by a man who clearly had aspirations of grandiosity. France was still the largest, most populous, and richest country on the Continent, complete with the biggest army.

England's goal was not necessarily the complete defeat of France but rather making sure that she was not so powerful as to threaten England's dominance of the sea and commercial interests on land. If Napoleon and France were defeated, so be it, but from this time until the dawn of WWII, the British would seek a "balance of power" in Europe to prevent the dominance of one nation or nations over the others.

The Austrians, on the other hand, were still stung from the many defeats that Napoleon had inflicted upon them in his first Italian campaign (1796–1797), so they were eager to both defeat him and regain their influence in Italy and in Europe in general. Joining the Austrians was a sizable Russian force, which inflicted a defeat on the French at Novi in the Piedmont region of Italy. However, after this, the Russians were diverted to face the French Army threatening Switzerland, and they didn't play another significant role in the campaign.

Napoleon Crossing the Alps or Napoleon at the Saint-Bernard Pass (1801) by Jacques-Louis David. This is perhaps the most famous painting of Bonaparte and an early example of political propaganda. There were five versions of the painting done by the artist with various changes in colors. Note the names engraved on the rocks at the bottom: Hannibal and Caesar.

Napoleon's second Italian campaign (also known as the War of the Second Coalition to historians) went much as the first did, with Napoleon thoroughly dominating the Austrians on land, despite them receiving British aid in the form of naval blockades and coastal attacks. There were many battles and sieges, both large and small, in this campaign, which lasted from 1799 to 1800, but the most significant was at Marengo, Italy, in June 1800. Marengo was a close call for Napoleon, whose outnumbered forces were almost defeated. The late arrival of French cavalry, which had been sent to reconnoiter another part of the area, saved Napoleon's forces from a major loss.

With their arrival and quick thinking and maneuvering by Bonaparte, Marengo and one final French victory at Hohenlinden in southern Germany forced the Austrians to make peace with Napoleon once again. The Treaty of Lunéville gave more Italian territory to France and forced Austria out of the war. Within a year, Britain signed a peace treaty with Bonaparte, and for one year, Europe enjoyed peace. It was to be the only period of peace in Europe from 1793 to 1814.

The Concordat

In 1801, Napoleon reached out to Pope Pius VII in an attempt to reconcile France with the Catholic Church. Ever since the French Revolution, the church had watched its power, wealth, and influence over the French wane. Despite its waning power and influence, the church was still an important institution in France, and despite the attempts of the revolutionaries to remove it from French life, the hold of the Catholic Church on the people's hearts was still strong everywhere but Paris and some of the other larger cities. At times and in some places, devout Catholics and clergy had to hold their services in secret and be very circumspect about their beliefs, but the people still held on to their traditions, feast days, and saints. Napoleon knew this, and he also knew that if he could come to an arrangement with the pope, he might gain even more support in the country.

This proved true. With the Concordat of 1801, France and the Catholic Church reconciled. The agreement was extremely one-sided. Napoleon controlled the outcome from the start, and he essentially dictated the terms of the document to the pope's representatives. The pope wanted, or perhaps hoped is a better word, that the church might gain back most or at least some of the lands and tax privileges it had lost in the early days of the revolution. This was not to be. Napoleon wanted the support of the

French Catholics, who had not supported him up to this point, but he was never going to give the church back the power, wealth, and privilege it had enjoyed before 1789. That would not only threaten his position but also infuriate the people who had given so much since 1789 to reduce the power of the church and nobility.

Napoleon also retained the right to name or approve French bishops. Of course, Napoleon would appoint people who were loyal to him, not to Rome. The government would pay the clergy, not the church. Napoleon announced that the government recognized that most French people were Catholic, but he did not name Catholicism the state religion as it had once been and as the pope wanted. He also asserted the rights of minority religions, expressly Protestantism and Judaism.

For its part, the church could name priests and other clergymen, and holy days, such as Easter, were recognized as festival days in France once again.

As you can see, Napoleon got much while the church received little, but it was enough for the pope at the time, whose alternative was nothing. For his part, Napoleon kept control of the church in government hands while at the same time pleasing most of the French Catholics, who could now worship without worry and be recognized as the majority in France.

In January 1804, another assassination plot against Napoleon was uncovered by the secret police, which was supposed to have been headed by the Bourbon family, which was represented by the duke of Enghien (Louis XVI's godson), who resided in Baden, Germany. Theoretically, he was out of Bonaparte's reach, but he soon found out that he wasn't as safe as he thought. Napoleon had the duke kidnapped and brought to France, where he was held incommunicado for two months. He was then supposedly brought to trial and executed on Napoleon's orders. This action alarmed the crowned heads of Europe, especially Tsar Alexander I of Russia, who, at least for a while, was determined to remove

Napoleon from power.

This plot, along with others, assured Napoleon that he needed to take the final step to solidify his power. Back in 1802, he had held an election. On it was one question: "Should Napoleon Bonaparte be made Consul for Life?" He won 99 percent of the non-secret ballot, but he likely would have won a secret ballot as well. In November 1804, another open plebiscite (a vote on one issue) cemented Napoleon as the emperor of the French.

The Coronation of Napoleon by Jacques-Louis David (1805–1807).
https://en.wikipedia.org/wiki/File:Jacques-Louis_David_-
_The_Coronation_of_Napoleon_(1805-1807).jpg

In the painting above, it appears that Napoleon is about to crown himself, and indeed he did. He already had a Roman-style olive-leaf crown upon his head, which he then removed and crowned himself with, parting with the tradition of French kings, all of whom had been crowned by the pope. It was very obvious that Bonaparte was signaling that, at least in France and its empire, he, not the pope, was the ultimate power. The date was December 2nd, 1804. Some months later, he was also crowned as the king of Italy. Within a short time, he had begun establishing a new nobility, lavishing titles and properties on those loyal to him or to those he thought useful.

Throughout Europe, rulers were alarmed. First came the French Revolution, then the Reign of Terror, and now Napoleon was the emperor of the French and anointed by the pope. Since 1789, many of the kingdoms of Europe had experienced upheavals of varying degrees by those who were inspired by revolutionary ideals. Napoleon establishing himself as an emperor, which is greater than a king, did not calm things. He had shown that certain Enlightenment ideals could exist at least somewhat peacefully with a new type of royalty. Worse still, perhaps, was the idea that no matter under what name or guise, the crowned heads of Europe could be replaced. And a seemingly invincible military genius was the one to test the waters.

1805 and the Third Coalition

The story of Napoleon Bonaparte is long and remarkable. He had risen from a bullied foreigner to the emperor of France. He crowned himself at the age of thirty-five. He had won every battle where he was present. He even changed the course of American history by selling French possessions on the North American continent to the United States in the famed Louisiana Purchase. In 1804, he was back at war with England and much of Europe. In 1805, he would win his greatest victory at Austerlitz.

In the spring of 1803, the British broke the Treaty of Amiens, which had been signed in 1802 to bring an end to the wars of the revolutionary period and redraw boundaries, and once again declared war on a France that was gaining too much power in Europe. By 1805, the kingdoms of Sweden, Russia, and Austria formed the Third Coalition against France.

England had ample reason for declaring war on Napoleon, prime of which was his building up of an invasion force on the French side of the Channel. The story of Napoleon's *Armée d'Angleterre* ("Army of England") is a huge and interesting topic in and of itself, but suffice it to say that Bonaparte assembled over 200,000 men and began building a huge fleet of transports to move his men, horses, and cannons to England to eliminate what he rightly perceived as the greatest threat to his power.

Between May and July of 1805, Napoleon seriously planned for the invasion of England. His plan hinged on a bold idea for part of his navy to break out of their English-blockaded ports and threaten England's valuable possessions in the West Indies. At the same time, another group of French vessels, combined with an allied fleet of Spanish warships, would break into the English Channel and escort his invasion fleet across the Channel.

The idea collapsed for two reasons. Firstly, the main Franco-Spanish fleet was defeated at the Battle of Cape Finisterre in July. Secondly, though a brilliant general on land, Napoleon was forced to cede command to his naval commanders, and both they and the French fleet were nowhere near capable of challenging or defeating the British Royal Navy. Most historians believe that even had the French fleet been able to move into the Channel, they would have been able to only cover the invasion force for all of about two minutes—that's how powerful the Royal Navy was at the time. And even had they been able to move troops swiftly across the Channel, the Royal Navy would have swiftly taken control of that body of water, and the French troops in England would've been stranded and defeated.

Not only had the French Navy been defeated and hemmed in, but by late summer, Napoleon's European enemies were marching westward. One great advantage that came out of his troops' time on the coast was the amazing amount of training they received while waiting for the word to invade. By the summer, the veteran officers and sergeants had whipped his new army into a fighting force that was more highly trained and motivated than any he had commanded before. La Grande Armée of 1805 was the greatest fighting force in the world, and it was led by the best general the world may have ever seen. He was joined by commanders who had, due to the changes brought about by the revolution, risen by ability rather than birth or connections.

At the beginning of September, Napoleon began marching his army toward the Rhine River, where he expected to meet the enemy's forces. At a time when troops traveled mainly on foot, Bonaparte's forces traveled both quickly and with relative secrecy toward France's natural border with the German states.

The resulting Ulm campaign showed Napoleon at his most brilliant. He outmaneuvered a massive Austrian force at the city of Ulm, and in a series of battles, he both defeated and outmaneuvered them back toward their capital of Vienna. In November, he captured the famed and beautiful Austrian capital.

Among the residents of the city was Ludwig van Beethoven, who, in 1803, had begun his Third Symphony and named it "Bonaparte" for the ideals of equality and religious freedom that he believed Napoleon symbolized. By the time the composer was finished with the work, he had changed both its dedication and its name, for Napoleon had named himself emperor in what Beethoven and many other liberals in Europe saw as a betrayal. The Third Symphony has borne the name *Eroica* (*Heroic*) since that time.

The capture of Vienna not only conferred glory and riches on Napoleon and his army but also supplied him with massive numbers of captured cannons, muskets, and ammunition. Both Emperor Francis II of Austria and Tsar Alexander I of Russia were eager to retrieve Vienna from the French. Despite counsel from many of their generals that fighting Napoleon in winter when their armies were still stunned from prior defeats was a mistake, the Austrians and Russians moved to engage Napoleon, and the armies came together at Austerlitz, in today's Czech Republic, on December 2nd, 1805.

Even Napoleon, who had an incredible self-regard about his abilities and performance on the battlefield, later said that the Battle of Austerlitz was his "finest" moment, and most military historians agree with him. The battle was a masterpiece of maneuver, feint, speed, and decisive action. Napoleon rightly gets most of the credit for the outcome of the battle, but his marshals performed perfectly as well.

Out of a force of roughly 85,000 to 95,000 men, the Austrians and Russians lost perhaps 16,000 killed and wounded. Twenty thousand were likely captured. More than a third of their armies were eliminated in one way or another. The French lost comparatively few: just over 1,000 men killed, 7,000 wounded, and under 600 captured. The Austrians and Russians were forced to sue for peace, and in the Peace of Pressburg, Napoleon once again confirmed his control of former Austrian lands in Italy. The Austrian-controlled states in Germany were given to both France and Napoleon's German allies (prime of which was Bavaria). Most importantly, Napoleon gained an indemnity of *forty million* gold francs (likely more than one billion in today's US dollars). In return, Russian troops were allowed free passage back to Russia. (If you are interested in learning more about Austerlitz, there is an outstanding and highly detailed history of the battle in the reference section at the end of this book.)

Only one thing prevented Napoleon from his greatest prize, which was total victory over his enemies, especially Great Britain. This was the French Navy's defeat at the Battle of Trafalgar on October 21st, 1805, during which time he was involved in the Ulm campaign. The British defeat of the French fleet off the coast of Spain meant that Napoleon would never again dream of being able to challenge the British at sea, even with the death of its greatest hero, Admiral Horatio Nelson, who died at Trafalgar. Napoleon would have to find another way to bring England to the negotiating table or, more preferably, to its knees.

The Continental System and the Peninsular War

In 1806 and again in 1807, Napoleon announced that none of his allies or subject countries were to trade with England and its colonies or in English goods. Failure to follow this, what he called the Continental System, would result in greater taxation, looting, and the possible installation of more France-friendly governments.

On the surface of it, it appeared that the Continental System might actually work. Napoleon had the troops guard much of western Europe's coasts and a fleet big enough to challenge unescorted trading vessels or smaller English naval groups. However, Europe is a large continent. By this time, England had established a worldwide trading network. England also had three distinct advantages: its huge navy, the demand for English goods in Europe (England was at the forefront of the Industrial Revolution, turning out massive quantities of refined goods and raw materials from its colonies, especially coffee and spices), and Portugal.

Portugal had been an English ally since the early 1700s. This was primarily because English ships could protect Portugal's large overseas trade from Spain and protect its territory from the Spanish Army. This overseas trade was established in the 1500s/1600s in the Age of Discovery when Portugal had a powerful fleet. Portugal also had a long coastline, which allowed British goods to enter Europe. These goods could (and were) smuggled through Spain into Europe and the Mediterranean.

By 1807, Napoleon had had enough. Convinced that the Spanish were tacitly allowing British goods through their country, Napoleon sent an army of nearly 100,000 men into Spain. By the next year, through a series of political maneuvers that only angered the Spanish more, Napoleon first displaced the mentally ill Spanish king with a noble loyal to Bonaparte, then replaced him with his own brother, Joseph Bonaparte, who became the king of Spain.

Spain had been a divided country. Many supported the king even though he was seriously deranged. Spain was not France, so the Catholic Church played a regular and, some might say, oppressive role in the ruling and life of the country. The Spanish Catholic Church, which had been somewhat independent of Rome for centuries, hated Napoleon and the French revolutionary ideals he brought with his armies. And then, of course, there were the French armies, which soon began to treat Spain as their own bank, farm, and other unpleasant things.

Over the course of the next few years, Napoleon's troops were not able to gain control of the country. This was due to British armies arriving in Spain, the British navy making it impossible to travel quickly from France to Spain by sea (they had to take the overland route across the rugged Pyrenees Mountains instead), and, probably most decisively, the Spanish, many of whom formed into the first "guerrilla" bands in history. "Guerrilla" means "little war," and the Spanish, knowing they could not engage the French in open battle, harassed French troops whenever they could. They participated in assassinations, attacked French supply columns when the advantage was theirs, isolated French bases, and poisoned wells. Everything that typified guerrilla warfare in the 20th century, in places like Vietnam, essentially began in Spain in the early 1800s.

Francisco Goya's famous *The Third of May 1808* depicts the massacre of Spanish civilians at the hands of frustrated and enraged French troops during the beginning of the guerrilla war.

The war in Spain was made worse with the intervention of relatively large numbers of British troops, which were still far fewer than the French. In precisely chosen battles to taken advantage of the French having to occupy most of the country, the British and Portuguese, led by a soon-to-be-famous English general named Arthur Wellesley (or, as he is known to history for the role he played in finally defeating Napoleon, Lord Wellington), inflicted defeats on the French. Eventually, Napoleon himself arrived after securing his rear flank in Europe with negotiations with Austria, which was in no shape to fight again, though they were rapidly retraining their troops, and Russia, with which Napoleon agreed he would do nothing if they took over Finland. Once there, Napoleon pushed the English out of the Spanish Peninsula in 1808 by winning the Battle of Corunna.

However, Napoleon could not remain on a campaign in Spain indefinitely. In 1808, the British sent another army to Spain, where they, their Spanish guerrilla allies, and the Portuguese waged a long, drawn-out conflict with the French, whose troops eventually numbered over 300,000 in Spain. After Napoleon's defeat in Russia in 1812, that number declined rapidly. Some historians believe that if Napoleon had not been bogged down in Spain, he might have had the extra troops he needed to fend off the Russians in 1812.

1809 – Austria, Again, and Tilsit

In April 1809, the newly trained and equipped Austrian army marched out to do battle with Napoleon yet again. This campaign, Bonaparte's fourth against the Austrians, was the hardest fought of them all. He suffered a stunning defeat at Essling (a case of over-confidence and a rare lack of tactical thinking on Napoleon's part), but he was able to impose a harsh peace on the Austrians after a bloody victory at Wagram in late May. Austria lost its territories in Poland, the Adriatic Coast opposite Italy, and other territories.

Back in 1806, Napoleon had defeated the forces of the strongest German state, Prussia, and had inflicted defeat on the Russians at Friedland in 1807. Alexander I decided to make the best of a bad situation and came to an agreement with France to take advantage of Austria's weakness while it had the chance.

At Tilsit (in today's small Russian possession of Kaliningrad on the Baltic Coast), the two emperors met on an elaborate raft in the middle of the Niemen River. Over the course of several days in July 1807, the two men talked on a variety of subjects. Alexander I was apparently in awe of Napoleon, and for his part, Napoleon seemed to like the Russian. The result of the talks was the creation of several French satellite kingdoms in Germany and Poland (some of which were ruled by Napoleon's brothers). In return, Russia received the rest of Austria's possessions in Poland, agreed to join the Continental System, and agreed to hand over some Russian-controlled territories in the Balkans. For that, Napoleon granted safety to the tsar's cousins, who ruled various smaller German states.

Personal Life

In December 1809, Napoleon divorced the love of his life, Joséphine. The reason? She was unable to bear him children. He was in love with her to the end of his days, but by this point, he was becoming concerned with the continuation of his dynasty. He cast about the royal families of Europe, looking for an eligible princess. He even talked with Alexander I about marrying one of his sisters. Alexander was all for this, hoping the marriage might forestall or prevent war between Russia and France, but this fell through to Alexander's consternation. Napoleon ended up marrying the Austrian princess Marie Louise of the Habsburg family, daughter of Francis I, Emperor of Austria and Bonaparte's arch-enemy. It was hoped the marriage would secure peace between the two powers.

Marie Louise gave Napoleon one son, Napoléon François Joseph Charles Bonaparte, who was given the title "King of Rome" at birth. The marriage was not popular in France—if you remember, King Louis XVI's wife, Marie Antoinette, was Austrian and the new empress's great-aunt. Joséphine remained popular in France, however, and kept her estates. She was given the title "Empress Dowager."

Russia

In the years between the Treaty of Tilsit (1807) and 1810, Russia aligned itself, to a degree, with Napoleon. It adhered, at least officially, to the Continental System against England and refrained from military activities outside of its borders. One reason for this was Napoleon's power. Another was the position of England, which was allied with Sweden. Sweden and Russia were long-time enemies, and in this case, the saying "the enemy of my enemy is my friend" held true.

However, at the Congress of Erfurt in 1808, Napoleon and his satellite nations, along with Russia, met to pound out a European foreign policy. Though Russia was a mighty power itself, with the largest land empire in the world, it was, at the time, second fiddle to Napoleon militarily, especially in Europe. As a result, Napoleon treated it and its tsar as such.

Between 1808 and 1810, the Russians began to slowly move away from Napoleon, and in 1810, Tsar Alexander I broke with Napoleon and announced that he would be dealing economically with England once again. The reasons were many, but primarily, any nation that had joined the economic embargo with France against England was subject to English naval blockade, seizure, or even action. Since the majority of Russian trade went through the Baltic Sea and out into the North Sea/Atlantic Ocean, where the Royal Navy was strongest, its agreement with France began to take an economic toll on Russia. In addition, England was in the beginning stages of its second period of colonialism, which would see it carve out the largest empire in the history of man. Already, the countries bordering Russia, such as Persia, Afghanistan, and nearby India, were feeling English pressure, as were the Ottoman Turks in the Middle East. Russia was being hemmed in, and it was partially doing it to itself.

Napoleon, for both personal and political reasons, could not let Russia back out of the Continental System. For one, his image would be tarnished in France and Europe. Personally, Napoleon was not the kind of person one said "no" to, and he could not accept that someone had. Politically and economically, allowing goods into Russia would strengthen England and possibly encourage others to join or at least trade with the British.

Sometime after Alexander I's announcement, Napoleon decided to invade Russia. This was no simple proposition, at least logistically. It would involve over a thousand miles (more if you consider detours) and an amazing number of men, horses, food, cannons, ammunition, clothing, etc. As we have seen, Napoleon was a mathematical genius. Napoleon was going to bring his largest army yet (500,000 men) to Russia, and he knew almost to a "T" exactly what they would need, at least under perfect circumstances.

Interestingly enough, though, while Napoleon was thinking about war with Russia, Russia and its leader were acting on the idea of a war with France. Aside from the issue of the Continental System, Russia had deep concerns about Napoleon's division of the Duchy of Warsaw (most of modern-day Poland) and his placement of Frederick Augustus I of Saxony as the head of the duchy. Poland and Russia had been enemies for centuries, and in 1772, Austria, Prussia, and Russia divided the country between themselves in a local "balance of power." Lastly, the Russians were upset at the French emperor's annexation of the German Duchy of Oldenburg, which contained a major port on the North Sea. Though this was just a pretext, Alexander I used the French move as an excuse to declare war on France.

The problem with Russia was that it was not western or even eastern Europe. Settlements, towns, and cities were far apart, and the lands between them were sometimes just open plains that were exposed to the worst of the weather. Even at that time, the road system in mainland Europe, especially in France, Germany, Belgium, and Austria, was relatively good. In and near large cities, they were many times paved with cobblestones. Even outside the main cities, many of the roads were cared for and were passable except in the absolute worst weather.

This was not so in Russia. Aside from the obvious issues in winter, in both fall and spring, there is a time called the *Rasputitsa* ("the sea of mud"). In the fall, rain causes it, and in the spring, the thaw causes it. A literal "sea of mud" is what it is, as you can see in the picture below of German soldiers experiencing it more than a century later.

This is 1941. In 1812, there were horses to help pull through the mud. It is certainly unpleasant either way.

Historians or TV pundits on bad history documentaries will sometimes say that neither Napoleon nor Hitler knew it could get cold in Russia. But, of course, they knew, at least theoretically. The problem wasn't that they didn't know as much as they didn't care. Both dictators also expected a quick victory. Hitler expected the Soviets to fold completely in 1941 and cede most of the western part of the country to him. Napoleon, on the other hand, did not have illusions about occupying Russia. He would move into the country and inflict a decisive defeat or two on the Russians, who would then sue for peace, pay a large indemnity, and then toe the Napoleonic line. The problem is he didn't inflict that decisive defeat, which means the Russians didn't sue for peace.

Napoleon moved into Russia in June 1812, two months after the Russian declaration of war. As they would more than a century later against Hitler, the Russians traded space for time. They would not engage Napoleon in any sort of decisive way. This was done for a number of reasons. First, they knew they could not match Napoleon on equal terms or on the ground of his choosing, as they were aware that Napoleon was a master of maneuvering his opponents into just the position he wanted them to be. Second, the Russian army was really no match for the French forces, at least not the majority of it. Many of the French soldiers were well-trained veterans, while many Russians were untrained peasants.

However, Alexander and his marshals (the most famous being Mikhail Kutuzov) knew that Napoleon would not likely do the smart thing and leave Russia once he realized the Russians were giving ground. He would move onto the capital, which was, at this time, Moscow, and hope the tsar would sue for peace then.

The Russians were not going to give their ancient capital to Napoleon without a fight, and in the savage battle of Borodino outside the city, the two sides fought to a bloody stalemate. The Russians eventually left Napoleon in charge of the field. He entered Moscow during the second week of September when there was already a nip in the air. The French hoped that Moscow would provide them with enough supplies and shelter to last through the winter, but soon after entering the city, Moscow went up in flames.

The Russians had not only stripped virtually anything of use from the city, such as food, fuel, ammunition, horses, wagons, and clothing, but they had also set it on fire after removing many of the most valuable items of the royal family. The entire city did not burn as many believe, but enough of it did to present a real problem for the French.

By the middle of October, Napoleon knew he had to leave. His marshals had been pressing him to leave earlier, but he held out until he could no longer reasonably hope to remain any longer. The weather had already turned, and it was going to get worse. By the time Napoleon's army reached the Berezina River in today's Belarus a month later, the troops were starving, their clothes were falling apart, and the breeches on their guns and remaining cannons were freezing solid. Worse still, the Russian army, especially its Cossack cavalry, attacked the edges of the main French force incessantly and then retreated before a counterattack could be organized. On top of this, peasant guerillas began to prey on the French. Illness and starvation killed thousands, as did frostbite. Horses were eaten along with anything found in the abandoned homes along the way.

As they entered the Polish frontier, Napoleon received word of a possible coup d'état in Paris and rode on ahead with his personal guard. The rest of his army froze and starved. Of the 500,000 men he brought with him, only *20,000* returned to France. The Russians had defeated Napoleon, but they were not led by any cunning man. Instead, their victory was due to the famous "General Winter," who made it the worst winter in one hundred years. "He" would do the same in 1941.

Russian pre-WWI cartoon of "General Winter," the Russian weather that protects the homeland from invaders.

Napoleon faced unrest when he returned to France, but the force of his personality, his glorious past, and his police kept him in power. But by 1813, the Spanish and English had driven the French out of Spain, from which Napoleon had taken 100,000 troops for Russia. Also, in 1813, his other enemies, especially the English and Austrians, who were now joined by the Prussians,

Swedes, and Russians, engaged his depleted veterans and ill-trained new recruits in the Battle of Leipzig in Germany, sometimes known as the Battle of the Nations. This defeat forced Napoleon to return to France, and in March 1814, the forces of his many enemies entered Paris.

Napoleon's marshals and others came to him, telling him that he had to abdicate or there would be wholesale slaughter or a popular revolt against him. Napoleon conceded to their wishes and, by the Treaty of Fontainebleau, agreed to live in exile on the island of Elba, off the Mediterranean coast of Italy. He was actually given the right to rule the island, which he set himself to almost as soon as he got there. However, his Austrian wife and his only son left for Austria, and he never saw them again.

For the Allies, the problem of Napoleon was over—at least the man himself. They still had to decide what would happen to his former empire, and they set about doing this at the famous Congress of Vienna (November 1814-June 1815). One of their first decisions was to restore the Bourbon monarchy to France. Louis XVI's brother, now Louis XVIII, was put on the throne. There were grumblings, but after two decades of war and a promise that France would be a constitutional monarchy, things returned to something approaching normal.

While the European powers began to decide on a new conservative order in Europe and to limit the power of France, Napoleon was making plans.

The Hundred Days

Of all the comebacks in history, Napoleon's may have been the greatest, though it was short-lived. On March 1st, 1815, Napoleon secretly boarded a small ship with his staff and the small contingent of soldiers he was allowed to retain. His destination was the southern French coast. He slowly moved toward the city of Grenoble and awaited a force under his former officer, Marshal

Michel Ney, who commanded 20,000 troops under the king. Napoleon was not sure whether Ney would arrest him or join him, but when Ney and his men saw their emperor, spontaneous cheering took place. "Vive l'Empereur!"

With Ney's 20,000 men, Napoleon began to move northward toward Paris. Before he even arrived, King Louis XVIII, who was a seriously dim, disagreeable, and unpopular man, fled France after hearing that troops and men flocked to Napoleon's banner wherever he went. On March 20th, Napoleon entered Paris and took possession of the Tuileries Palace.

Over the next month and a half, Napoleon reformed his army. It was not the army of 1805 or even the army of 1812, but he led it, and he was joined by most of his marshals. There was also still a core of veterans to provide the recruits with some training. By June 16th, when he defeated the able Prussian Army at Ligny, Belgium, Bonaparte had formed an army of over 130,000 men. Napoleon knew that virtually every army in Europe would be coming for him, and he was determined to move his armies fast enough that he might defeat them one by one before they could unite.

This was not to be, as you likely know. On June 18th, 1815, Napoleon was defeated at Waterloo, Belgium. His marshals had committed uncharacteristic mistakes and allowed the Prussian Army to unite with a sizable English force under Wellington. Though it was close, Napoleon was beaten and forced once again to abdicate and go into exile. This time, the English were taking no chances. Napoleon's new home was the English possession of Saint Helena, an island in the South Atlantic, halfway between Brazil and Africa. There would be no escape this time.

From 1815 until he died in 1821, Napoleon lived in a small villa in Saint Helena. In actuality, he was lucky. He could easily have been executed, but his enemies did not want to make him a martyr to the French. He lived out his days in comfortable surroundings, albeit with an English guard detachment on the grounds at all times. He spent his time gardening, conversing with the daughter of the governor, and writing his memoirs.

His Legacy

The French Revolution and the Napoleonic era made a lasting impact on Europe and the Western world. The Age of Absolutism was dead or dying. In both Europe and the Americas, the ideas of the Enlightenment spread and grew. The idea of equality under the law rather than privilege by birth began to be seen as the norm, and slowly, religious freedom began to spread in Europe, though in fits and starts. Democratic ideals and political bodies rose up in places outside of England, the United States, and France. And though it would take more than a hundred years, at least in the West, women began to move toward some equality as well, winning the right to vote in the early 20th century (or regaining, as in the case of France, which had given the vote to women at the beginning of the revolution).

Napoleon's legacy has stretched throughout history. Winston Churchill kept three statues on his desk at all times: his ancestor Marlborough, who defeated Louis XIV's armies; Admiral Nelson, who defeated the French at Trafalgar; and Napoleon, whom many regard as the greatest commander in history. It has also become traditional for orchestras to play the *1812 Overture* by the Russian composer Tchaikovsky at American Fourth of July festivities. This is a bit odd, as the piece depicts Napoleon's attack on Russia and Russia's victory over him.

Napoleon on the HMS Bellerophon, depicting Napoleon on his way to exile on Saint Helena. An awed group of British officers looks on.
https://commons.wikimedia.org/wiki/File:Napoleon_on_Board_the_Bellerophon_-_Sir_William_Quiller_Orchardson.jpg

Chapter 10 – The 19th Century

The First French Republic ended with the ascent of Napoleon. His empire ended with his defeat at Waterloo and exile to Saint Helena. From 1815 to 1830, France returned to the Bourbons. King Louis XVIII, who had quickly fled to avoid Napoleon's return in 1815, then returned and ruled until his death in 1824. He was followed by Charles X, the younger brother of both Louis XVI and Louis XVIII, who was then succeeded by Louis Philippe I (r. 1830–1848).

Neither Louis XVIII and Charles X were popular except among royalists, who returned to the country in droves. Both kings attempted to reinstate many of the lost privileges of both the monarchy and the nobility, though Louis XVIII was a bit more cautious out of necessity, as the revolution was still very much alive in the minds of many.

One of the major issues of the reigns of both Louis and Charles was the position of the church. Ultra-conservative Catholics in France and in Rome were eager to see ancient holdings returned to the church, but this was not going to happen. Firstly, there was too much popular support for limiting the power and influence of the church. Secondly, most of the old church lands had gone to a new rising middle class and to the Napoleonic nobility. Neither group was willing to give up such a rich prize. To attempt to do so would have united conservative middle-class businessmen with Napoleonic nobility and radical revolutionaries, who were still alive and well in Paris and other major cities, and the attempt would have resulted in utter failure.

The church was allowed to reopen seminaries and a limited number of parochial schools, but during the revolutionary and Napoleonic eras, France had built one of the first state-supported school systems in the world, and it was open to all, regardless of class, birth, or wealth.

Lastly, as had been the case with Napoleon, the bishops of France (the pope's direct representatives throughout the country) held no political power whatsoever.

Economically, France made a remarkable comeback considering the costs of the wars of the late 18th and early 19th centuries. Not only had France itself spent great treasure on these wars, but much of this treasure had belonged to other kingdoms and regions—Napoleon was as good a looter as he was a general. When the Bourbon Restoration occurred, France was made to pay a great sum to those who had finally defeated her, though it was much less than would've been expected. The European diplomats at the Congress of Vienna (also known as the Concert of Europe, meaning the nations were acting "in concert" with one another and not against each other) were determined to reestablish a conservative, balanced, and peaceful Europe after Napoleon. Welcoming France back into that circle would go some way to lessening hard feelings and resentments on all sides. Until about halfway through the century, it did, which was a remarkably long period of peace, all things considered.

French workers, both in agriculture and in France's burgeoning industries, began to enjoy greater rights and protections, though these were many times given grudgingly. Still, with these reforms, French workers slowly began to enjoy shorter hours, a six-day workweek, better pay, and, in some rare cases, compensation for injuries sustained on the job. Unemployment benefits and a social safety net would come to France before many other countries, but this did not occur until the late 19th and early 20th centuries.

The revolution that followed the French Revolution was no less important, but it did not begin in France. The Industrial Revolution, which truly began in the last quarter of the 19th century, started in Great Britain. Britain had massive coal reserves, which powered the Industrial Revolution and still powers much of our economic life today. In addition, England had iron reserves far beyond what you would think for its size. England's iron and coal reserves allowed it to rocket ahead of the other countries of Europe. Better yet, they didn't "rocket"—they "steamed ahead," for in the early part of the 19th century, steam began to power everything. Machines, ships, and the newest invention of trains were all powered by steam. Within a couple of decades, England was covered in railroads, rapidly transporting goods, raw materials, and people rapidly from place to place. One must also factor in England's worldwide empire, which supplied raw materials the English did not have and purchased finished goods. By the middle of the 19th century, England, which had a population of under twenty million people (about the population of the city of Tokyo today), dominated much of the world both economically and militarily, and it was rapidly trying to dominate the rest.

The French kings Louis XVIII and Charles X owed their thrones to England, among other countries, so they were not openly hostile to it; however, even if they wished to be, they were not equipped or prepared enough to do so. France needed a period of peace in which to reestablish herself and her power in Europe and the world. Not to say that either Louis XVIII or Charles X had any special fondness for the English. Remember, until the second decade of the 20th century, France and England had been mortal enemies for literally centuries. Old hatreds die hard.

Still, everyone recognized that peace was needed after twenty-odd years of war, so the French began their entry into the industrial world. A number of factors, a couple of which we will touch on here, kept France lagging behind other nations in Europe in terms of economic and industrial output.

Before we do that, one should be aware that the word "nation" in reference to any monarchy of Europe, no matter how small, is a misnomer, but it is an easy way for us in the 21st century to understand borders, peoples, and interests. However, aside from the United States, there really were no "nations" in the Western world at the time of the French Revolution. Oxford Languages defines the word "nation" as "a large body of people united by common descent, history, culture, or language, inhabiting a particular country or territory." Many historians, anthropologists, and sociologists might add a further definition: "A nation has also been defined as a cultural-political community that has become conscious of its autonomy, unity and particular interests."

Under the Bourbons, France was not a nation—it was the property of the king, given to him by God. The people did not feel a loyalty to the country but rather to the king, their local region, and/or a *seigneur*, or local lord. A person might think of themselves as a "subject of His Most Glorious Highness, His Excellency Louis XIV, anointed by God." But he or she might also consider themself a Norman, a Breton, or Provencal. Very rarely did these people consider themselves Frenchmen or Frenchwoman. That came with the French Revolution, and that is why the revolution is so exceedingly important—it started giving everyone a stake in the country. One of the things that Louis XVIII realized was that he was not talking to "subjects" but to "citizens." Charles X did not, and he narrowly escaped a mob bent on tearing him apart before he left the country for good in 1830.

Great Britain, which had a more liberal constitutional monarchy, was a nation, and the people of the island saw themselves that way. However, in that peculiar British way, they also saw themselves as loyal subjects of the king or queen.

The other regions of Europe, with the exception of Switzerland, were still governed by crowned heads. Some of these were more liberal than others, but all wanted to keep both their throne and their heads. They were very careful to suppress "revolutionary" ideas such as those espoused by the thinkers of the Enlightenment and the French Revolution. They succeeded or failed in varying degrees in this endeavor, with waves of revolution breaking out across the Continent once again in 1830 and again, in a more determined way, in 1848.

Although France had already experienced its revolutionary throes, the Industrial Revolution had a hard time taking root compared to England. France was a much larger country than England, and it had more large rivers, thick forests, and four mountain ranges on its borders (the Alps, Pyrenees, Vosges, and the Massif Central). This meant that the terrain of France was harder to navigate. However, France did have large quantities of wood and coal, especially in the northeast, which is where most of the French industries eventually located. By doing this, though, much of the country remained agricultural, and it depended on one small and often distant section of the nation for its industrial goods.

A couple of often overlooked factors contributed to the slowness of the French Industrial Revolution, which, despite lagging behind England, was still developing faster than many of the Italian states, eastern Europe, and Russia. The first was that, for centuries, the economic system of France meant the people were tied to the land. Peasants did not have the right to move unless it was specifically given by their *seigneur*. This meant that, in most cases, those working the land were working the same exact land that their ancestors might have. That's a strong tie. It also meant that for many, moving far from the family home was a daunting task, and many people had never been farther than a day's ride (if that) from their homes. Most of these people traveled maybe twenty miles in their entire lives.

Now, people were needed for industry, and word went out all over France. However, building and populating the factories and housing the workers was a slow process in France. Aside from the fact that many had never left their homes, there was, for many, a sort of unspoken notion that one was tied to the land. Even today, in countries from the United States to Africa, farmers find it extremely hard to leave their land and give up a long heritage and way of life.

There was also another subtle difference: religion. In the United States, many have for years been bored to tears by history professors droning on about the "Protestant work ethic" as one of the primary reasons for the United States' success. Just because it's boring doesn't mean it isn't true, though. The spread of Protestantism, beginning with the Reformation, also brought with it a change in work habits. Very generally speaking, the ideas of hard work and thrift became part of the Protestant belief system, especially among Calvinists, but one could find these ideas within all Protestant sects. Hard work and thriftiness, as opposed to sloth and luxury, which were seen as "Catholic" traits, especially among the higher-ranked bishops, were signs that one was worthy of eternal salvation. Hand in hand with this went the supplication from James 2:20 in the Bible, which is usually shortened to "Faith without works is dead," as opposed to the more Catholic idea of redemption through faith alone.

A look at the statistics of the early and middle Industrial eras will clearly show that areas that were more highly Protestant advanced faster economically during the 19th century than the Catholic areas of Europe and the United States. Of course, there were many other factors, but it definitely played an underlying role, especially in the cases of Great Britain and the United States.

1830

In the six years that Charles X ruled France, he managed to alienate nearly everyone. He attempted to restore property to *émigré* families, but the country would not support that, so he compensated them monetarily. He also always seemed to be maneuvering to bring back some form of the so-called Ancien Régime (the "Ancient Regime" of the Bourbons). The problem was, he was not a very smart man nor a good negotiator. He angered not only a large number of republican-minded people in France but also the very people he was trying to help. In addition, he was arrogant and without charm. In July 1830, he attempted to install an ultra-monarchist former prince to the position of prime minister. People saw the writing on the wall—Charles X was attempting to rule as Louis XIV had. After three days of insurrection in Paris, Charles X was chased from the city. The famous painting *Liberty Leading the People* shown earlier depicts the spirit of this event.

In Charles's place, the parliament of the people placed Louis Phillippe, a prince from a different branch of the family. He had the good fortune of being the son of the revolutionary noble Philippe Égalité, Louis XVI's cousin. Philippe Égalité voted to execute his own cousin in 1793. The three days that led to Charles X's abdication and Louis Philippe's rule are known to history as the July Days. The French people hoped that a balance might be struck between the revolutionary ideals of 1789 and the strong but controlled executive branch of the new king. The first part of Louis Philippe's reign was a relief to most Frenchmen. Yes, there were still some of the original revolutionary generation clamoring for a more radical government, but the Reign of Terror and Napoleon had made it impossible for them and their younger followers to do much other than complain.

Still, the threat of revolution kept Louis Philippe and any royalist sympathizers somewhat in check. It helped that the new king took the title "King of the French" and not "King of France"— a semantic trick that seemed to satisfy most. In his first years as king, he was actually quite popular, and he gained the nicknames of Citizen King and the Bourgeois (middle-class) King.

However, those who supported him were from both the very wealthy new middle class and the old noble families. Louis Philippe was dependent on their funds to a large degree, and as time wore on, he was pressured to move in a more conservative direction, and it seemed that he wished to move that way himself.

The changes brought about by the Industrial Revolution created new problems and confusion for both the populace and those in government. Louis Philippe and his advisers handled these problems very clumsily, and the gap between the rich and poor, which had always been wide in France, grew by leaps and bounds. This was not helped by the two years of agricultural and industrial depression. And, as we have seen, hunger is the quickest way to revolution.

In February 1848, Louis Philippe was overthrown and forced to flee to England under the name Mr. Smith. Louis Philippe named his grandson Philippe as his successor, but by this time, the French had had enough of kings. Later on, Philippe actually went to the United States for a time and fought in the US Civil War on Union General McClellan's staff. Despite other attempts by royalists to put Philippe on the throne, he never became king.

On February 26th, 1848, the National Assembly proclaimed the Second French Republic. In December of that year, a president was elected: Charles Louis Napoléon Bonaparte, the former emperor's nephew.

One of the reasons for naming Louis-Napoléon Bonaparte, who came to be known as Napoleon III, as the president was the unrest that roiled both France and much of Europe in 1848. Much like the Arab Spring of 2011, spontaneous uprisings took place in the states of Italy, the Austrian Empire, and the German states. In selecting Louis-Napoléon, the French were attempting to walk a fine line between revolutionary ideas and Napoleon's solidity and conservatism, as he was still a revered figure for many French.

Louis-Napoléon Bonaparte was not his uncle. He was not an original thinker, but he was solid, approachable, and seemed to have a wide knowledge of many subjects. Within a few months of his becoming president, things in France began to improve. They improved so much that, in 1851, after being barred legally from running for president again, he overthrew the National Assembly and proclaimed himself "President for Life." As he had in his first run for president, Louis-Napoléon used his name and his uncle's legacy as a propaganda tool, telling the French what they wanted to hear: a return to stability and glory. For the other countries of Europe, which grew alarmed at the thought of another Bonapartist army running wild over Europe, Louis promised that he would defend France but not attempt to enlarge it, at least in regards to Europe. After all, this was the beginning of the Age of Imperialism, and France, like England, was looking for new colonies in Africa and other parts of the world.

Louis-Napoléon used every power given to him by the constitution to expand his powers. He began placing men loyal to him in the administrative departments of the national and regional government apparatuses. He did the same with the army. He also successfully helped the pope regain his home in Rome after being forced from the Vatican by revolutionaries in 1848. This appealed to conservatives at home and reassured many of the other European nations, as they saw the Vatican as a stabilizing force, regardless of whether they were Protestant, Catholic, or Eastern

Orthodox.

Louis's move to "President for Life" did not go unopposed, but the Republicans who fought against his regime in street battles in Paris and other major cities were outgunned and defeated. Thousands were jailed, sent to the prison camp on Devil's Island off the coast of South America, or forced overseas.

Louis-Napoléon was not completely reactionary. One of the first things he did upon becoming "President for Life" was to declare universal suffrage, allowing the vote for women to be reinstated. In November 1852, once he was secure in his position and relatively popular, Louis-Napoléon held another plebiscite. The question put to the voters was, "Should Louis-Napoléon Bonaparte be made the emperor of the French?" The results were resoundingly in favor, with 97 percent approving of the new title. Most of these votes were completely fabricated. Louis-Napoléon Bonaparte then became Napoleon III, Emperor of the French, on December 2nd, 1852.

Napoleon III toward the end of his reign.
https://commons.wikimedia.org/wiki/File:Napoleon_III.jpg

Napoleon III's rule as emperor lasted for eighteen years, seven years longer than his more famous uncle, but he remains less known. For most of his almost two decades in power, France enjoyed relative peace. There were expeditions to Mexico in an attempt to place a pro-French government in power. (Believe it or not, this is one of the main reasons why traditional Mexican music has that famous "oom-pah" band flavor. This was patterned on popular French military marches, which were about the only thing popular about the French in Mexico). France also began its colonial expansion into Africa and the Middle East during this time. Though France remained at peace with its European neighbors until the final years of Napoleon III's rule, the race for an empire brought it into fierce competition with England. This competition remained peaceful, though later in the century, this competition almost led France and England into war once again.

Under Napoleon III, France grew into Europe's largest military power once again, at least on paper and in the minds of its people and its leader. Fortunately, Louis understood that the place of France in Europe and in the world could easily be lost if he attempted to recreate his uncle's European empire.

Generally speaking, France's economy grew at a great pace throughout the Second French Empire. When Louis came to power, the nation had just over 2,000 miles of railway. When the Second French Empire fell, that number exceeded 12,000 miles, which greatly contributed to the growth of France's economy, especially in coal and steel. However, it still lagged behind Great Britain, and it would soon fall behind a new nation and powerhouse in Europe: Germany.

The Germans are an ancient people, but as a nation, Germany is ninety-five years younger than the United States. Much like ancient Gaul, the lands that comprise Germany (in all of its forms since 1870) were broken up into tribal kingdoms, which then grew into part of Charlemagne's empire and then broke up into hundreds of individual duchies, baronies, kingdoms, and bishoprics. This condition lasted until 1870, of course with many changes in borders and rulers in between.

Additionally, these different regions were often under the control or influence of foreign powers. For the most part, the states in the western part of what is now Germany were dominated by France to varying degrees. For quite some time, the smaller states in the north contended with the influence of the sometimes powerful Kingdoms of Denmark and Sweden. In the south and southeast, regions like Bavaria and others were often under Austrian sway or control.

However, beginning in the 17th century and increasing up to the time of Napoleon III, the Duchy (later Kingdom) of Prussia began its rise. This ascent was not continual, and at times, Prussia's power waned, but beginning in 1740 with the reign of Frederick II, also known as Frederick the Great (r. 1740–1786), Napoleon I's hero, Prussia became a power to be reckoned with. Initially, the growth of Prussian strength was a concern solely for the kingdoms of eastern and central Europe (Russia and Austria), but when Otto von Bismarck became the chancellor of Prussia in 1862 under King Wilhelm I (later Kaiser Wilhelm I; r.1861–1888), this new Germanic power became a direct threat to France.

The reasons are simple. First, the Prussian Army was fast becoming the best trained, best equipped, and best led in the world, though that fact remained a relative secret until 1870. Second, Otto von Bismarck was a once-in-a-generation statesman, and he knew that for the German-speaking states to become a unified nation, he would have to challenge the European powers that still held great influence over many of the German states. Specifically, these were Denmark, Austria, and France.

In 1864, Bismarck led Prussia into a war with Denmark over the succession to the Danish throne, as Bismarck wanted to have a Danish king who would be on good terms with Prussia. He also wanted to answer the question of Prussia's borders with and Denmark, specifically the German-speaking states of Schleswig and Holstein, much of which were ruled directly by Denmark. Though no one knew the true extent of Prussian military development at the time, the outcome of the war surprised no one. The swift Prussian victory was followed by another one in 1866 against Austria, and with these moves, Prussia gained control of most of modern northern Germany, with its important ports on both the Baltic and North Seas.

In the 1864 war between Prussia and Denmark, the Prussians had been joined by the Austrians, who also had direct influence and interests in the states of Schleswig and Holstein and a number of other German states in the north near Denmark. Bismarck knew that when the war with Denmark was over, he could easily provoke a war with Austria about the power-sharing agreement the two kingdoms had reached. With increasing intensity through 1865 and the first half of 1866, the Prussians under Bismarck (with Wilhelm I's approval) began voicing "concerns" about supposed Austrian violations of their agreements. The Prussian press was tightly controlled by the government, and Bismarck, while engaging in diplomatic arguments with Austria, also stirred up Prussian popular opinion against it.

In the Seven Weeks' War of 1866, Prussia inflicted a humiliating defeat on the Austrian Empire. Until that point, Austria was thought to be one of the greatest powers of Europe, and many considered its army to be far superior to the Prussian Army in almost every way. The exact opposite was true, but even after having defeated both Denmark and Austria in two years, many in Europe, particularly France, did not understand exactly how advanced and well-trained the Prussians were.

France and Napoleon III were to realize it in 1870. Napoleon III was not his uncle, neither militarily nor politically, but he was not a stupid man. He just wasn't Bismarck, who played him like a violin. Bismarck began a series of diplomatic and political moves designed to provoke France into declaring war on Prussia. The call for war slowly built to a crescendo, starting in 1867 and continuing until July 19th, 1870, the day France finally declared war.

The diplomacy and maneuvering between France and Prussia in the run-up to the Franco-Prussian War is fascinating in and of itself, and it has filled volumes (one of which you can find at the end of this book). Suffice it to say that after about three years of provoking France in almost every way possible and making it look as if it was France and Napoleon III doing the provoking, Bismarck pulled off a diplomatic trick that left Napoleon III virtually no choice but to declare war on Prussia. If Napoleon had chosen not to do so, he might have lost his throne due to a loss of honor and influence.

In June 1870, a new king ascended to the throne of Spain. This king, Leopold, was related to the ruling house of Prussia. Napoleon III, seeing Prussian influence growing to France's east, did not want a Prussian-allied Spanish king to its south and west. After some diplomatic wrangling, Bismarck withdrew Prussian support of Leopold, which he had planned to do all along, and a new king Amadeo I, who was more acceptable to France, was put on the Spanish throne. The sticking point came when the French demanded that Prussia never again allow or put forward Leopold to be the king of Spain (at the time, Spain was an exceedingly unstable country, undergoing one coup after another since the time of Napoleon I, meaning it was likely to need a new king again). King Wilhelm, with guidance from Bismarck, refused to make this promise.

What's more, Bismarck allowed the publication of a diplomatic telegram (the Ems Telegram) describing Wilhelm's talks with French Ambassador Benedetti at the city of Ems in what is now modern-day Germany. However, the version that Bismarck sent to the Prussian newspapers, which were widely read in French diplomatic circles and newspapers, was doctored to make it seem as if Wilhelm and Benedetti had insulted each other, with the French ambassador getting the worst of it. The actual meeting was cordial, but Wilhelm refused Benedetti's demand that Prussia never back Leopold again.

Within days, French public opinion was boiling over. Combined with the growth of Prussian power on its borders and Bismarck's carefully calculated provocations over the last three years, the French and Napoleon III, who felt he needed one thing to cement his legacy—a military victory rivaling his uncle's, felt they had no choice and declared war on Prussia on July 19th.

Prussia and its aligned states in red, German states aligned with France (Bavaria being the largest).

The Franco-Prussian War lasted roughly six months and ended with a Prussian victory. In actuality, the Prussians had the war won essentially before it even began. New rapid-firing rifles and artillery, a better trained professional army with innovative tactics and strategies, and better leadership assured a Prussian victory. The key victory came at Sedan in September, after which Louis-Napoléon surrendered much but not all of his army and abdicated. The war continued until January 1871 and ended when Paris endured a siege that included much suffering and an early socialist revolution within it.

France and the world were stunned by the Prussian victory and its swiftness. The war ended all foreign influence in the German-speaking states, which now became absorbed by Prussia in the new nation of Germany with the Treaty of Frankfurt. Among the terms of the French surrender was the ceding of the provinces of Alsace and Lorraine, which included both German- and French-speaking populations, to Germany.

The fall of Napoleon III ushered in the Third French Republic, and it gave birth to a grudge that would almost cause a military dictatorship in France and a deadly rivalry with the newest and seemingly strongest European power: Germany. An entire political movement came to life in France known as "revanchism" ("revenge-ism"), and the defeat sat heavily on the hearts of Frenchmen until 1918. Léon Gambetta, a French politician who helped organize the defense of Paris, spoke for all Frenchmen about the humiliation of 1871: "Think of it always, speak of it never." The truth of this feeling among the French truly cannot be overstated.

Europe after 1871. A new power in the center of the Continent, Germany, was born, and it soon challenged France, England, and Russia for dominance. (Courtesy Alex Altendorf)

Alexander Altenhof, CC BY-SA 4.0 <https://creativecommons.org/licenses/by-sa/4.0>, via Wikimedia Commons https://commons.wikimedia.org/wiki/File:Europe_1871_map_en.png

Chapter 11 – The Road to WWI

The Third French Republic lasted from 1870 to 1940, when Hitler's forces marched into Paris. It was as close to the ideals of the French Revolution as any government since that tumultuous time. Since 1940, republican France has been rebuilt twice: once after WWII and another that's lasted from 1958 to this day. This means, at least as of this writing, that the Third Republic was the longest-lasting form of representative government in French history.

The Third and Fourth Republics were experiments in parliamentary rule. Though the leader of the majority party in parliament was ostensibly the leader of the country, especially in the eyes of other nations, his power was relatively weak, which was understandable after centuries of the monarchy and two emperors in less than one hundred years.

This period of stability is known, for many reasons other than its politics, as La Belle Époque, or "The Beautiful Age." It was a time when French culture rose again to lead the world, especially in the visual arts of painting and sculpture. This was the time when the names of men and women such as Monet, Manet, Degas, Gauguin, Seurat, Rodin, Toulouse-Lautrec, Mary Cassatt, and the pianist Satie became household words.

Woman with a Parasol by Claude Monet, 1875.
https://commons.wikimedia.org/wiki/File:Claude_Monet_-_Woman_with_a_Parasol_-_Madame_Monet_and_Her_Son_-_Google_Art_Project.jpg

Much of what people around the world revere about French culture today had its beginnings in La Belle Époque. Two of the most recognizable icons of the world, the Eiffel Tower and the Statue of Liberty, were born in this era. French food and culture spread around the Western world in the later 19th century, a time when trains and steamships brought the world closer together.

In Russia, the language of the court of the later tsars was French, and the language continued its role as the dominant one in international diplomacy, though it would be rapidly replaced by English following WWI. You may occasionally see the term "lingua franca," as in "The Swedes and the Germans use English as their lingua franca." The term seems like a misnomer, but French was so pervasive in Europe that the term, which in Latin literally means "the language of the Franks," now means a common language between people who speak two different languages.

Though French art and culture stood on their own because of their beauty and sophistication, the spread of that culture was "helped" by French participation in the second great age of European imperialism in the latter half of the 19th century.

Most of France's possessions were in Africa. With a few small exceptions, France dominated the African continent. Even today, many of the people of central and northwest African countries and the island of Madagascar speak a French dialect as their first or second language. In Vietnam, known then as French Indochina, much of the upper class spoke French as their primary language.

However, as you might know, much of the rest of Africa and a significant portion of the rest of the globe was ruled either directly or indirectly by Great Britain, which most people at the time recognized simply as England. The English controlled a stretch of Africa from its southern tip to Egypt. At times, as in the case of the 1898 Fashoda Incident in northeastern Africa, the English and French nearly went to war over borders, incidents, and influence. French forces did see action when they attempted to conquer or retain control of various areas, particularly in Vietnam and Algeria.

Conflicts with Great Britain were avoided with diplomacy and common sense. The wars in Vietnam and Algeria ended with a French victory. However, there was a new problem: Germany.

In 1890, two years after the death of Kaiser Wilhelm I, his grandson, Wilhelm II, who was also the grandson of British Queen Victoria and cousins with King George V of Britain and Tsar Nicholas II of Russia, fired Bismarck, who had directed German foreign and domestic policy since 1862. In place of Bismarck's calculated, insightful, and strategic foreign policy, the Kaiser acted rashly and somewhat irrationally in what he called his desire to gain for Germany "its rightful place in the sun," meaning he wanted colonial and imperial glory for his new country.

The problem was, for the most part, two-fold. Germany was a new country, and by the time Wilhelm II was ready to embark on an imperial path, France and England, among others, had already claimed much of the world or at least the desirable parts. That left Germany to seize control of what was left in Africa, namely those areas in the central and those that were very remote and relatively poor. It also seized some islands for naval coaling stations in the Pacific. However, Wilhelm wanted more, and he felt that Britain and France were intentionally keeping it out of the race for an empire, which, to a degree, they were.

In 1905 and in 1911, Wilhelm stuck his nose into problems that France was having in North Africa, specifically Morocco. In both cases, war seemed imminent, but at the last moment, diplomacy, at times led by England, kept the two European powers from all-out war.

The Path to War

As you likely know, World War One began in 1914. Why did the most costly and deadly war in human history until that time happen?

First, for years, people (mainly in the US but elsewhere as well) believed the system of alliances set in place in the beginning part of the 20th century triggered a chain reaction due to the mutual defense clauses of these alliances.

These alliances later became the Allied Powers, which consisted of Great Britain, France, Russia, and Serbia, and it was later joined by Italy and the United States, as well as a number of smaller nations. The Central Powers were Germany, Austria-Hungary, the Ottoman Empire centered in Turkey, and Bulgaria.

The alliance system did kick in, and these nations kept their promises and declared war on their mutual enemies, but they did not have to. Yes, not doing so would cost prestige and trust, but nations had gone back on agreements since the beginning of time.

So, why didn't they do so in 1914? The simple answer is the nations involved felt they had more to gain than to lose by entering the conflict.

For Great Britain, an all-powerful Germany, whose steel and coal production was already as great or slightly greater than that of the UK, with a strong navy on the Continent was too great a threat. The same was true for Russia, which shared a long border with the new power.

For France, as you can probably guess by now, the threat of Germany was three-fold. With the unity of the German states, France was no longer the most populous state in Europe. The longer war was put off (and virtually everyone knew it was coming sometime in the near future by 1898), the more the German population outgrew France. The same held true with German industrial production, which was already outpacing France. Lastly, the French saw the coalition of Great Britain, Russia, Italy, and itself as the greatest opportunity for the revenge it had been seeking since 1871.

For Germany, it believed a victorious war would, at the very least, force uneven terms from France and the likely cession of colonies from both England and France. Vast sparsely occupied lands in Russia awaited German colonization as well. This led up to what historians refer to as the Balkan powder keg. The Ottoman Empire, which had controlled much of southeast Europe for centuries, was in decline. In its place, new nations emerged or the Austro-Hungarian Empire moved in to fill the vacuum left by the Turks. The nation that concerns us most is the Kingdom of Serbia, an Eastern Orthodox nation closely aligned with Russia, which saw itself as the rightful ruler of the Southern Slavs of the Balkans, i.e., the Croats, Bosnians, Montenegrins, Slovenes, and Albanians—all of the peoples who would later make up the nation of Yugoslavia.

The problem for the Serbs was that the Austro-Hungarians, who were close allies with Germany, either directly or indirectly controlled these other Slavic lands. Though the many peoples of the area were not exactly thrilled to be under Austro-Hungarian control, they definitely did not want to be subjects of the Kingdom of Serbia. Aside from questions of religion (many South Slavs were Catholic or Muslim), the Serbs had made it no secret that as the most powerful and largest of the independent southern Slavic states, it wished to dominate the others. Under the Austro-Hungarians, the South Slavs enjoyed more autonomy than they would have under the Serbian king, Peter I.

Peter I enjoyed the life of royalty and had some say in the government, but for the most part, he was happy to let his generals and army run the country. These Serbian military men made no secret of their desire to carve out a Serbian empire in the region, and to do this, they not only built up their army but also supported underground movements within Austro-Hungarian lands where Serbs made up a sizable minority. This was especially true in Bosnia and its capital of Sarajevo.

As you may know, on June 28th, 1914, a Serbian militant movement known as the Black Hand, which was sponsored and controlled by a Serbian officer named Dragutin Dimitrijević, aka "Apis," assassinated the Austrian heir to the throne, Archduke Franz Ferdinand, and his pregnant wife. The successful assassin, Gavrilo Princip, admitted, albeit under torture, Serbia's role in the assassination, though it was denied by the Serbs.

No one believed the denial, and within two months, most of Europe was at war. At the end of the war, Germany was blamed for starting it; however, this was not the case, though the war might likely not have occurred without it playing a role.

The Serbian king and others in the government knew about plots against the Austrians. They had been going on for years, including failed assassination attempts of the Austrian emperor, but these officials had tried to discourage the militants, knowing war with Austria was doomed to fail. However, the militants enjoyed great influence in the officer corps and much of the populace, and they could not be stopped.

However, in all honesty, the Austrians had been looking for an excuse to defeat or conquer Serbia for some time. The Serbs were a serious thorn in their side, and the assassination of Franz Ferdinand, who was not a popular figure among either his own family or the conservative army officers who wanted war, was the perfect excuse to start one. In response to the assassination, the Austro-Hungarians made demands, unreasonable ones that no nation could abide by and still retain their independence. The Serbs could not accept them, and the Austrians knew that would give them the excuse they needed to go to war.

Before they presented the Serbs with their ultimatum, the Austro-Hungarians asked their powerful ally, Kaiser Wilhelm II of Germany, whether or not he would support their actions, including going to war if Serbia's own ally, Russia, should involve itself in the conflict. Wilhelm's answer is known to history as the "blank check." He told the Austrians that he would support them no matter what. Wilhelm was keen on the opportunity to both show off his army and grab what he could from the Russians.

Though the actual timeline looks different, as it took time for news and instructions to travel, this set off the mutual defense agreements that the major nations of Europe had with each other. By August 12th, 1914, much of the European continent was at war.

You may have seen pictures or old sped-up movies of the time (you can find colorized and normal speed clips on YouTube now) showing crowds of people in various countries cheering the announcement of war and the "boys" going off to war. It's hard for us to believe now, but most people were actually happy or even elated that their nation was going to war. Today, in most cases, when nations go to war, there is perhaps a grim patriotic determination to "get things done," as there was in the United States in 2001, but not actual happiness. World War One, also known as the Great War, is what changed that mindset. After all, very few people realized what kind of a war this was going to be. Their minds still pictured war as a conflict between relatively small armies of soldiers, with civilians, for the most part, being left alone. This was not to be. World War One was the first "industrialized war," and the new weapons that had been developed in the years before and during it would turn the fields of Europe and elsewhere (for instance, in Africa, where major combat took place between the Germans and English) into graveyards.

The French went into WWI believing their army was the best in Europe. They had used the years between 1871 and 1914 to modernize and retrain their men, and they could call up millions of military-aged men to serve. Their factories turned out immense numbers of shells, bullets, and guns, as did Great Britain's and Germany's.

This is not a book on military history, so the major battles will not be examined in any depth. In this chapter, we will provide you with the important facts and the results of WWI from a French perspective.

Before we get into the war, it should be said, especially for some of our American readers who might have a bias against the French military in World Wars I and II, that among the Allied Powers, the French only lost fewer men than the Russians and slightly fewer than the Germans. However, it must be remembered that the Russians were covering a greater area and had more men to begin with and that the Germans were fighting on two fronts. French deaths in WWI numbered nearly 1.4 million. Great Britain's losses, which includes Ireland, amounted to 750,000. Of course, this is still a staggering number and represents a large portion of its military-aged population. For the most part, the French poilus (the French term for their soldiers at the time, meaning "hairy ones" for their ubiquitous beards and mustaches) fought with incredible bravery and tenacity. At the Battle of Verdun in 1916 alone, the French sustained 400,000 casualties. The number of French dead at that one battle was roughly equal to the 117,000 US dead in the eight months that the Americans took part in the combat. The Battle of Verdun brought about the slogan that motivated the French to victory in the battle and the war: "On ne passe pas!" "They shall not pass!"

"On ne passe pas!" by Maurice Neumont, 1918.
https://commons.wikimedia.org/wiki/File:On_Ne_Passe_Pas_1918.jpg

Well, at least the *Boche* (the pejorative French name for the German soldier, meaning "string bean," named after the color of their uniforms) didn't make it to Paris or win at Verdun. But in 1914, and again in the spring of 1918, the Germans came close.

In 1914, the French rallied along the Marne River not far from Paris and stopped the Germans after a bloody battle. In 1918, the Germans were able to transfer hundreds of thousands of men from Russia, who had dropped out of the war after the Bolsheviks of Vladimir Lenin came to power, to the Western Front for one last push before the Americans were able to bring their full strength to bear. The Americans entered the war in late 1917. In their famous Spring Offensive of 1918, the Germans, using innovative tactics and fresh men, almost broke through French, British, and American lines to Paris, but they were stopped. After this last offensive, the Germans were no longer able to continue in any meaningful way. Like most wars, WWI was fought using the tactics and methods of the previous war, at least until its very last days. You likely have seen movies, documentaries, or pictures of troops from all nations going over the top of the trenches that covered the Western Front from the border of Switzerland to the English Channel. You probably also know that in many cases, the order to go "over the top" was a death sentence. This was because, by the outbreak of the war, weapons had changed.

Even though the French had experienced the German innovations of the rapid-firing rifle and artillery in the Franco-Prussian War of 1870–71 and then adopted them themselves, many believed the outcome was sort of a fluke, the product of bad planning and leadership. Surely, older French generals, who had grown up on stories of Napoleon I and had even known veterans of the Napoleonic Wars, said to themselves that a hard-driven attack led by able officers and driven home at the right time and place would win the day.

The vast majority of generals and politicians in the combatant nations recognized the need for the use of newer weapons, primarily the machine gun and, as the war went on, the airplane, poison gas, the flame thrower, the tank, and faster-firing, longer-ranged, and deadly artillery. However, these men did not seem to recognize how much these weapons changed warfare. Men charged over the top into fields pocked with shell holes only to be cut down like wheat at harvest.

Making things even worse was that, in the time between 1870 and 1914, industrialization had vastly improved guns, cannons, bullets, and shells, and they were being turned out and used at an unbelievable rate. To name just one country, Germany estimated it had fired over 220,000,000 artillery shells during the war. Most of these were fired in the concentrated areas of the Western Front. Artillery barrages sometimes lasted for days without end. Men went permanently insane. Many developed such incredible shell shock (the WWI-term for PTSD) that they could no longer control their bodies, in the worst cases developing Parkinson-like tremors and outright shaking. No one knows exactly how many of the casualties of the artillery bombardments during WWI were actually suicides, men taking their own lives rather than endure more shelling.

All of this led to serious problems in morale, and the French experienced it on a greater level than the other nations, though all certainly suffered from it. In 1917, mass mutinies gripped the French Army. Had the extent of these mutinies been known, some historians believe the Germans may likely have been able to win the war or at least gain Paris.

All along the line, French soldiers simply refused to fight. Some dropped their guns and walked off. Most were arrested. Many left for home. Others kept their weapons and threatened officers who ordered them "over the top." Most of the mutineers declared they would willingly defend their ground but not attack. At the time, many French politicians believed the poilus to be under the influence of a small number of socialist or communist revolutionaries, as had happened in Russia, but this really wasn't the case. Most of the mutineers—and there were thousands of them—were patriotic men who had already been asked to sacrifice a lot. They were willing to sacrifice even more but not for poor leaders who cared nothing for them. Plenty of French generals were like that, primarily the supreme commander, General Robert Nivelle, who had promised a quick victory when the French began the Second Battle of the Aisne in April 1917. Needless to say, the victory did not occur, and scores upon scores of poilus were cut down. This was when the mass mutinies began.

Though public belief is that hundreds of soldiers were arrested and brought before firing squads, the truth was that under Nivelle and then his successor, Philippe Pétain (a hero in WWI, a traitor in WWII), only about one hundred executions took place, though it's likely that not all were documented. Between the executions and reforms that took place as a result of the mutinies and changes in command, the mutinies ended. Morale was also helped by the election of the new prime minister of France, Georges Clemenceau, who promised additional reforms in the army as well as victory.

Photo of battle-hardened French soldiers on guard duty in Paris toward the end of the war. Resting on their rifles is their battle-scarred unit banner.
https://commons.wikimedia.org/wiki/File:El_114_de_infanter%C3%ADa,_en_Par%C3%ADs,_el_14_de_julio_de_1917,_Le%C3%B3n_Gimpel.jpg

By the fall of 1918, the Germans and Austrians were on their last legs. The German Spring Offensive had failed, and the Austrians were taking massive casualties in Pyrrhic victories against Italy in the Alps. In both the German and Austrian armies, soldiers began to mutiny as the French had in 1917. The leadership of the German Army knew that they could not hope to hold back the Allies on the Western Front much longer. They realized that to prevent the Allies from marching into Germany itself, terms for peace should be sought.

Let's be clear. In the fall of 1918, the German government was being run by two generals, Erich Ludendorff and Paul von Hindenburg. They, along with the vast majority of their fellow commanders, believed that continuing the war was useless. By the beginning of November, Kaiser Wilhelm II was a shell of himself (and he was not a stable person to begin with), and he was under great pressure to abdicate in favor of a civilian government headed by the popular Social Democrats. Strikes, demonstrations, and mutinies were rife in Germany and its armed forces.

Wilhelm essentially ceded power to the Social Democrats by the beginning of November 1918. They, as well as the army high command, knew the war had to end. However, in a shrewd political move, the generals declared that they would not approach the Allies for peace, for that was the government's job. And with that, one of the largest and costliest lies in the history of mankind was born, for, in November of 1918, the politicians of Germany were still behind the army, which was in power both on the front and at home. The next chapter, which touches on the lead-up to the next world war, will discuss this further.

At the beginning of November, the German government sent out peace feelers to the Americans, not the French or the British. The French would likely have rejected them out of hand, while the British were on the fence. The populations of both nations had large numbers of people pushing for the complete defeat and conquest of Germany after all the bloodshed. The US president, Woodrow Wilson, had put forward what is known as his Fourteen Points for peace. In Germany's eyes, the growing power and influence of America made it seem like the best path toward a ceasefire. After that, a permanent peace could then be negotiated. This is what occurred, and on November 11th, 1918, World War I came to an end.

Chapter 12 – Versailles and between the Wars

The Captivating History series includes an excellent book on the Treaty of Versailles, which ended WWI, as well as detailed books on both world wars. What follows here is a brief summary of the fateful Treaty of Versailles.

The Paris Peace Conference, whose members would hammer out a permanent peace to WWI, began in mid-January 1918. France was represented by its prime minister, Georges Clemenceau, a veteran politician and journalist. He was nicknamed "the Tiger" for his fierceness in defending the causes in which he believed. In January 1919, that cause was punishing Germany, the nation that had humiliated France when Clemenceau was a young man and that had inflicted over a million deaths on the battlefield and hundreds of millions of dollars in economic damages in its four-year occupation of Flanders and the western border regions, which were France's richest and most developed industrial areas.

Emotionally and psychologically, Clemenceau and the French were also keen to punish Germany for taking Alsace-Lorraine after the French defeat in 1871. Politically, Clemenceau also knew that his continued place as the head of the French government depended on taking a strong stand against the Germans, for most Frenchmen and women were eager to punish Germany for wrongs both real and imagined.

Joining Clemenceau as the main players at the Paris Conference were British Prime Minister David Lloyd George, Italian Prime Minister Vittorio Orlando, and US President Woodrow Wilson.

Wilson had established himself as a power player at the talks with his arrival in France just a few weeks before. Greeted as a savior and representative of the nation that many viewed as the guarantor of victory in WWI and the best hope for a lasting peace, Woodrow Wilson enjoyed Beatles-like popularity when he arrived in France. He was literally mobbed everywhere he went. Streets and boulevards throughout France were named after him and his country. For instance, in beautiful Mediterranean Nice, two of the main streets of the city are Avenue Woodrow Wilson and Avenue des États-Unis ("Avenue of the United States").

Wilson had formulated (actually, most of the formulation was done by aides) his now-famous Fourteen Points, which were a set of guidelines for nations to follow in the future. Wilson, who viewed these guidelines more as rules, believed that once nations adopted his principles, war could be averted forever. Of these points (found in Appendix A at the end of this book in simplified form), Points 1, 2, 3, and 14 were the foundation stones of Wilson's permanent peace plan. Point 14, which led to the foundation of the League of Nations, the forerunner of today's United Nations, was the most important to the US president; he was willing to bargain away other points if he could achieve the creation of such a league. (Ironically, because of Wilson's arrogant personality and domestic American politics, the United States Senate refused to ratify the Treaty of Versailles and join the League of Nations.)

Vittorio Orlando of Italy was essentially sidelined. Italy was viewed as not having a right to the same voice as the other major powers and was essentially given table scraps in its post-war desires.

Lloyd George and the British were split on how the Germans should be treated. They, like the French, had expended much blood in the war. Great Britain, which was the richest nation on Earth before the war, had gone broke by 1916 and relied on US loans to keep afloat, as did the French. Many in the United Kingdom wished the same type of revenge as the French did, but many, including Lloyd George, had misgivings about treating Germany too harshly.

Aside from the return of Alsace-Lorraine to France, both Great Britain and the French demanded reparations from the Germans. Diplomatically, reparations are monetary penalties for the damages caused by war. The French demanded an exorbitant amount. The British argued among themselves and finally settled on an amount less than the French had demanded and more than the Americans had proposed.

Both the British and Americans were concerned that if exorbitant reparation payments were demanded, Germany, which was an economic powerhouse before the war, might never recover. This would affect their trade and the economies of the other European nations, which could possibly throw the world into a depression. The French did not care. They wanted payback.

In their minds, they were entitled to it, and objectively, they were. Many people criticize the Treaty of Versailles for its treatment of Germany and the part it played in the rise of Adolf Hitler, but Versailles was comparatively mild compared to the Treaty of Brest-Litovsk and what it demanded of the Soviet Union (what Russia became after 1917) when Lenin sued for peace. In that treaty, the Soviets were forced to give up nearly 20 percent of its land and millions upon millions of dollars in reparations, among other things. Thus, German complaints about Versailles fell on deaf French ears.

Perhaps what rankled the Germans the most was a clause put into the treaty that is known as the "War Guilt Clause." This meant that Germany bore responsibility for starting the war, which it clearly did not. However, since the end of the war, both the Ottoman and Austro-Hungarian Empires ceased to exist, instead consisting of small, poor rump states that had no money or influence. Germany was the only Central Power left, and it had never been invaded or even shelled. German industry was intact. The Germans had also "signed" the "Blank Check" to Austria, which allowed the war to accelerate and spread. During the war, the Germans had invaded neutral Belgium and conducted a harsh and atrocity-laden occupation. In the eyes of the French and British, as well as many Americans, Germany started the war.

The Treaty of Versailles laid down the outlines of the peace. A dozen or so ancillary treaties listed the details. In the end, the Germans had no choice. Their army was in shambles. They were facing communist revolutions in parts of the homeland. Their economy was a mess. The WWI chapter needed to be closed so Germany could move on, or so the thinking went. The Social Democrat politicians and diplomats representing Germany in Paris signed the treaty. And from that moment on, the German armed forces and new right-wing extremist parties (the Nazis were but one of many) would blame the Social Democrats for signing away Germany's "honor," its economy, its army, and more. The men that Hindenburg and Ludendorff put forward to sign the treaty were known by many in Germany as the "November Criminals," named for the month in which the hostilities ended. Among the people calling them that were Paul von Hindenburg, Erich Ludendorff, and an Austrian-born German Army veteran named Adolf Hitler.

William Orpen's *The Signing of the Treaty of Versailles in the Hall of Mirrors.* Seated at center left with the mustache is Georges Clemenceau. Dead center is David Lloyd George. To the left of Clemenceau is Wilson, then Orlando of Italy.

Chapter 13 – WWII

For France, the Second World War, at least in terms of human life, was less costly than the first. And while the First World War most certainly left a lingering psychological, emotional, and political legacy as we will soon see, it is perhaps the disaster and division of WWII that left a greater impact.

Though the German invasion of France in 1940 was absolutely an unmitigated disaster for France, it should be remembered that about half of the approximately 220,000 French military deaths that took place in WWII took place in that short period. Today, many people in Great Britain and the United States falsely believe that the French simply laid down their guns after the first few shots were fired and raised the white flag of surrender. Yes, there is a marked contrast between the performance of the French military in World War I and the beginning years of World War II, but to overlook those deaths is wrong. By comparison, the United States fought for about ten years in Vietnam. The total killed in action was just under 60,000 men. This does not diminish the sacrifice of those men but illustrates the great bloodshed that took place.

Toward the end of the German invasion, Prime Minister Winston Churchill of Great Britain, dismayed by the reports he was getting about the lack of French resistance and the beginnings of large-scale surrenders, asked, "Why don't they fight?" Of course, Churchill was, well, Churchill, and he likely would've fought until the Germans had invaded his own home. However, his view was tainted by the experience of WWI. In the First World War, Churchill had been Britain's first lord of the admiralty, and he resigned in disgrace over a battle in which he played a large part. After that, he voluntarily fought on the frontlines of the Western Front for six months, where he admired the French soldiers and officers he met and saw before he returned to England to serve as the minister of munitions for the remainder of the war.

World War I was not World War II. To put it simply, the difference lay in how Germany fought. The Germans utilized the new technologies that had been developed during and after WWI, and they had much better field commanders and a better plan than the French did. At the end of the First World War, France had a huge standing army and occupied small parts of western Germany, which it would continue to do to varying degrees until 1922 and again from 1923 to 1925 after it felt Germany had reneged on parts of the peace treaty. However, like most nations after a prolonged conflict, the French people and its soldiers wanted normalcy, and demobilization began on a large scale.

As the 1920s merged into the Great Depression of the 1930s and people all over the world became more concerned with surviving, they became less and less concerned about what was happening in other countries. Within France, political extremes grew, just as they did elsewhere. On the left, communists and socialists (from the more radical to the moderate) saw that the sacrifices of WWI seemed to have meant nothing: the rich were still rich and growing richer. The poor, and now much of the middle class, was growing poorer. Germany was a rising power again by this point, and it seemed to many on the left in all nations that the "conservative powers that be" were more interested in using Hitler to contain the Soviet Union and socialism of all kinds than they were in improving the lives of the people. In Britain, as well as France, people asked, "Is this why we fought the war?"

In France, those on the right wing both admired and feared Hitler. The French political right, like its left, was splintered into many factions and viewpoints, but as the 1930s went on and fascism spread from Italy (1922) to Germany (1932–33) and then to Spain (1936), more French conservatives became fascist in outlook themselves. Before the war, this meant that while they admired Hitler's government and many of its principles (including violent anti-Semitism), they were all in favor of a strong and assertive French military and foreign policy to both compete with and counter Germany and, to a lesser degree, Italy.

Of course, most people inside France in the 1930s were moderate in their political views, but generally speaking, politics usually finds a balance, and unless threatened directly, moderates tend to remain silent. Unfortunately, in the 1930s, things in France continued to get worse, not better, and the ranks of those on both ends of the political spectrum grew while those in the middle began to feel helpless in the face of both domestic and foreign events.

In a way, France was at war with itself before the outbreak of WWII. The 1920s saw great changes around the world and in France. Internationally, France saw its influence wane as the power of the United States grew. Economically, politically, and culturally, America was becoming a superpower, and within France, many either welcomed the change coming from across the ocean or resented it.

Economically and politically, France was still a world power, but it was clear to almost everyone (at least outside France) that she was in decline, at least in comparison to the United States. In reality, not much could be done about that.

Culturally, changes coming from the United States came in the form of music, literature, and the arts, including the new medium of film. Charlie Chaplin was as popular in France as he was in the United States (of course, Chaplin was British, but his films were made in Hollywood). American influence also began to be felt in the world of fashion, which had long been dominated by France. While many, especially among the young and urban populations, embraced these changes and trends, many older French people and those living in smaller towns and the country saw these changes as symptomatic of French decline, and they looked for someone to blame. They blamed the left, while those on the left began to view the right as backward, chauvinistic (both in terms of the role of women and nationalistically), racist, and out of touch.

Interestingly, many black American jazz musicians, like Josephine Baker and Louis Armstrong, made a second home in France. There were two reasons for this. The urban French loved jazz, and, for the most part, at least in the cities, the French were much more racially tolerant than most Americans.

However, France also had an ugly side. While many accepted black Americans, they were a sort of novelty. The French retained their colonial empire after WWI and even expanded it into the Middle East, which meant that growing numbers of immigrants from Asia, the Middle East, and especially Africa came to France for economic gain. This spurred a backlash among many in France, and even highly educated and French-speaking men, such as the future leader of North Vietnam, Ho Chi Minh, could only find menial jobs as dishwashers and the like.

On the right, many French believed that France should be for the French, not outsiders. And increasingly, those outsiders came to include French and other European Jews, many of whom had lived in France for centuries. It's an axiom that when times get bad economically or otherwise, scapegoats are looked for, and in Europe, ever since the fall of the Roman Empire, that meant blaming the Jews.

Anti-Semitism has a long and ugly history in both France and the world. There are clear historical reasons for it—not that those reasons are justified or acceptable; they are not. That story is too long for this book, but suffice it to say that while France, generally speaking, was more accepting of its Jewish countrymen than most other nations in Europe, especially those in the east, anti-Semitism still existed.

This was made clear in the famous Dreyfus affair in the late 19th century. Briefly, French military officer Alfred Dreyfus, who was Jewish, was accused of passing French military secrets to the Germans. Dreyfus was convicted on the flimsiest of evidence (he was later exonerated) and sentenced to life in prison on the notorious Devil's Island prison off the coast of South America. The trial, which took place in the late 1890s, captivated and consumed France from top to bottom, famously including the writer Émile Zola, who came to the defense of Dreyfus and had to flee the country because of it.

When Dreyfus was convicted, he was paraded publicly in Paris, where he was stripped of his insignia and disgraced. The crowd began to chant anti-Semitic slurs and almost got out of control. Though it was later shown that another officer had betrayed his country, the Dreyfus affair exposed the deep anti-Semitism within France, which many believed was not there. When the Germans occupied France, that latent anti-Semitic feeling came to the fore.

One last thing about pre-war France. In France, as in many other countries, the Great Depression showed the vast differences between the rich and poor. Additionally, France had become an industrial power, and millions of people worked in factories throughout the country, though agriculture still played a huge role in the life of the nation (as it does today). Throughout the 1920s and especially in the 1930s, strikes and other protests took place in an attempt to improve the economic lives of the workers. At times, these strikes and demonstrations were put down violently, oftentimes including fatalities.

Those not involved directly either supported the strikers in their desire for a better life or condemned them for making a bad situation worse. In the eyes of many in France, both moderates and conservatives, many of the strikers were self-proclaimed socialists or, even worse, communists following the line put out by Moscow, home of the Comintern, or Communist International. These strikes helped the workers on some occasions, but they also brought down governments and further divided France.

The Maginot Line

In the 1920s, military thinking underwent a series of revolutions. The advent of the airplane, especially the long-range bomber, the submarine, and, perhaps most significantly for France, the tank changed the way military men thought about war. However, one revolution took hold within much of the French military, that of static fortification.

Hoping to avoid a repeat of the carnage of men going over the top of trenches, French generals, especially its minister of war in the late 1920s and first two years of the 1930s, André Maginot, began to find a way to defend France. They wanted to prevent another German invasion, major French casualties in future wars, and the need for a large standing peacetime army, as going without one would allow more men to contribute to the economy. The result was the famous (or infamous) Maginot Line, which was constructed at a great cost between 1930 and 1939.

The Maginot Line was a modern wonder, running some 280 miles from the Swiss border to the Belgian border with France (though, with its twists and turns, it ran a total of 900 miles). Massive walls, cannons, machine guns, bunkers, tunnels, headquarters, canteens, and small underground factories were contained in the line. It was virtually impregnable to frontal assault.

Retractable cannons and machine gun turrets of the Maginot Line today.

The problem with the Maginot Line was three-fold. First, it gave the French a defensive mindset, so when the time for offensive action came, many French officers were ill-prepared. Second and most importantly, the line did not stretch to cover France's border with Belgium in any meaningful way, which means the Germans could simply drive around its main fortifications to the south. Third, when the Maginot Line was outflanked in 1940, French military and civilian morale plummeted, which makes sense, as they had been told that they were safe behind its fortifications for years. This was made even worse when it was realized that for all the money and resources spent on the line, over five thousand additional tanks and five battleships could have been built.

The French only began to build fortifications along the Franco-Belgian border in the last two years before the war when it received signals from the Belgians that they might once again declare neutrality in any coming war (not that it had saved them in WWI) or might choose to not fight against an overpowering Germany. By the time actual combat broke out in 1940, the Maginot Line along the Belgian border was porous, with huge gaps between installations, many of which were only partially complete.

Why didn't the French build the Maginot Line along the Belgian border to begin with? One, it was thought that building the line there might indicate to the Belgians that the French would not fight for them in the coming conflict. Two, French and British military doctrine called for Allied troops to move forward into Belgium to prevent a repeat of WWI. Three, it was costly—immensely costly—and the Great Depression was still taking place.

The War

On September 1st, 1939, Germany invaded Poland, and the British and French, having signed a mutual defense pact with the Poles, declared war on Germany on September 3rd. Everyone in France and Britain prepared for immediate conflict. It did not come. From September 1939 to May 1940, the two sides fought what many sarcastically called the Phony War. Yes, there had been combat in Norway when the Germans invaded that country in April 1940, but that was far away and relatively inconsequential, at least to most Frenchmen.

Additionally, the French had launched a minor offensive into the German Saar region, penetrating about six miles without much resistance. They went no farther for reasons that still baffle historians, but with no real German reaction, many in France believed the Nazis were afraid of attacking France again.

Of course, we know this was one of the grossest misjudgments in history. The Germans had precise plans for their invasion of France, and on May 10th, the Germans unleashed the "Blitzkrieg ("lightning war") against France, Belgium, and Holland. British and French troops rushed into Belgium as agreed. The bulk of the French Army waited for the main German invasion along the Maginot Line.

The Germans did invade Belgium, and slowly (then rapidly, after events occurred in the south), they pushed back the British Expeditionary Force (BEF) and the French. Along the Maginot Line, the Germans allowed the French to see and hear what they thought was the bulk of the German Army. The Germans shelled, bombed, and launched local attacks along the strongest part of the Maginot Line to hold the French in place and to fool them into thinking the main attack would come there.

Meanwhile, on the borders of France, Belgium, and Luxembourg, in the "impassable" (or so it was thought) Ardennes Forest, the bulk of the Germans' tanks moved forward undetected. The Maginot Line did not cover the area of the Ardennes. And why would it? The forest was too thick and the roads too bad for a large force, especially an armored one. This means the Germans attacked the French at the perfect place: between their mobile army in Belgium and the static Maginot Line. Within days, the Germans had penetrated deep behind French lines and were moving toward the English Channel to cut off the BEF and French forces in Belgium and to move behind the Maginot Line in the south.

What many people don't know is that the French had more and better tanks than the Germans. What they didn't have were better officers, better trained men, a fighting spirit, and a better plan.

In the years prior to the war, the French High Command had allowed itself to believe that the Maginot Line would be effective and that the next war would be fought as the last had. Obviously, they were wrong on both counts. They would have been better off listening to maverick officers, most notably an officer named Charles de Gaulle, as they had independently developed and studied other ideas of mobile warfare in what would prove to be the "Age of the Tank." These officers, like the vast majority of their German counterparts and a handful of British officers, believed that the use of massed armor against an enemy's weak point, in combination with strong air and artillery attacks at the point of assault, was how future wars would be fought. French, British, and American tank doctrine placed small groups of tanks within infantry units as support units and not as the main weapon of war. As you can see from the map on the previous page, the Germans cut off the bulk of the French and British forces, which resulted in the BEF's evacuation at Dunkirk and the mass surrender of much of the French Army. It should be remembered, however, that two important things happened in that evacuation. A large number of French soldiers went into exile in England and formed the core of the Free French Forces, and that, given the right motivation, the French could fight. One reason the British were able to evacuate so many men, in addition to their own tenacity, air cover, and still supreme navy, was the tenacity of the French in holding the Germans back. The French under de Gaulle had also put modern tank warfare into action in a counteroffensive at Arras, temporarily halting the Germans there.

On June 22nd, 1940, the French officially surrendered to Hitler at Compiègne in the same train car they had used to dictate the terms of the ceasefire of WWI. When the ceremonies were finished, Hitler had the train car blown up.

Prior to that, on June 14th, German troops did what had previously been thought impossible: they marched down the Champs-Élysées in Paris. The famous picture below, taken from a film clip, captures the feeling of most Frenchmen and women at the time.

Weeping Parisian from NARA Ww2

All was not completely lost for France, however. With an invasion of England already in mind and other future plans, including a war on the Soviet Union, Hitler allowed the French to govern themselves in a semi-autonomous area known as Vichy France, named for its capital at the southern city of Vichy.

France occupied zones 1940-1944

In charge of the Vichy government was the hero of WWI, Marshal Philippe Pétain. In the years since the first war, Pétain and the men loyal to him had become increasingly conservative to the point of being fascist. Many of them looked to Hitler as a role model, and when given the opportunity, they wasted no time in implementing fascist policies in Vichy.

At first, this did not include the same kind of persecution Jews were facing in other parts of the Nazi empire, despite pressure from the Germans. However, as time went on, more and more anti-Semitic policies were enacted. Still, many Jews from occupied France fled into Vichy, as it was a place of relative safety when the Germans began rounding up Jewish people in the occupied parts of France in the late summer of 1941.

The history of the Holocaust in France takes up thousands upon thousands of pages. Comparatively speaking, fewer Jews (as a percentage of the pre-war population of some 400,000) were killed than in other European countries. A great deal of this was due to the brave French people who helped to evacuate large numbers of Jews to Britain, Spain, and Portugal, as well as others who helped to hide them from their persecutors. In all, about 75,000 French Jews perished in the camps of the about 400,000 living in France before the war.

Though the French may have averted the kind of horror that took place in Poland and the USSR, the Nazi occupation of the country and its puppet state in Vichy, which ceased to exist as a "state" in late 1942 due to German fears of an invasion there, illustrated that many French, like many people in other countries, would turn a blind eye to or, worse, take part in the persecution of an entire people based on their birth.

This brings us to those who did not turn a blind eye or join the fascists: the famed French Resistance.

The Resistance began almost as soon as the combat ended. At first, resistance meant slowing down work, not being pleasant to the Germans, and providing safe shelter to French soldiers, who were required to report to the Germans before returning home or heading to prisoner of war camps, among other "smaller" actions.

Most Frenchmen, however, preferred to see which way the wind blew, and in 1940/41, it was blowing from Germany. At the time, Germany seemed invincible, and many people came to terms with that. Some welcomed the Germans, while others tolerated them. Most did not resist. Even to the end of the war, those active in the Resistance was a small percentage of the population, though it grew to sizable numbers by 1944. Estimates range from 100,000 to close to 500,000 men and women, the latter playing an exceedingly important role as agents, saboteurs, and in leadership.

The face of the Resistance ultimately became that of Charles de Gaulle, who left France and immediately began organizing a government in exile, an army, and a resistance movement. De Gaulle is both loved and hated within France and without to this day, but no matter how one feels about him, it cannot be denied that Charles de Gaulle (who was seriously wounded multiple times, captured, and organized escape attempts in WWI) was brave, cunning, supremely confident, and above all, patriotic. On June 18th, 1940, he made what is known to history as the Appeal of 18 June from England:

The leaders who, for many years, were at the head of French armies, have formed a government. This government, alleging our armies to be undone, agreed with the enemy to stop fighting. Of course, we were subdued by the mechanical, ground and air forces of the enemy. Infinitely more than their number, it was the tanks, the airplanes, the tactics of the Germans which made us retreat. It was the tanks, the airplanes, the tactics of the Germans that surprised our leaders to the point to bring them there where they are today. But has the last word been said? Must hope disappear?

Is defeat final? No! Believe me, I speak to you with full knowledge of the facts and tell you that nothing is lost for France. The same means that overcame us can bring us to a day of victory. For France is not alone! She is not alone! She is not alone! She has a vast Empire behind her. She can align with the British Empire that holds the sea and continues the fight. She can, like England, use without limit the immense industry of United States. This war is not limited to the unfortunate territory of our country. This war is not finished by the battle of France. This war is a world wide war. All the faults, all the delays, all the suffering, do not prevent there to be, in the world, all the necessary means to one day crush our enemies. Vanquished today by mechanical force, we will be able to overcome in the future by a superior mechanical force. The destiny of the world is here. I, General de Gaulle, currently in London, invite the officers and the French soldiers who are located in British territory or who would come there, with their weapons or without their weapons, I invite the engineers and the special workers of armament industries who are located in British territory or who would come there, to put themselves in contact with me.

Whatever happens, the flame of the French resistance must not be extinguished and will not be extinguished.

Most people did not hear the speech, especially in France, but his words, along with another more widely heard speech on June 22nd, spread by print throughout the country and helped keep alive and spark the spirit of resistance in France.

The Resistance was not one movement. Not all Resistance fighters listened to de Gaulle. Some were led by other officers. Some of the most active Resistance cells were run and manned by communists taking orders from Moscow. Others were just individuals acting according to their conscience, but as the war went on and as the British and Americans began to recognize de Gaulle as the leader of France in exile, more and more people and groups gelled around de Gaulle, at least loosely.

Resistance acts took many shapes. Much of it was reconnaissance, reporting on German activities of all kinds, whether it be economic, military, or political. Some were acts of sabotage, and there were some assassinations. Much of the Resistance was in the form of disseminating information, such as underground newspapers, leaflets, and graffiti. By doing this, Resistance fighters let the French know there was a resistance movement all around them, that they were not alone, and not to collaborate with the Germans. Since much of the Resistance's activity was against its fellow Frenchmen cooperating with the Germans, things became extremely violent, and in essence, there was a French civil war within WWII.

The Appeal of 18 June above a memorial to a Resistance fighter: "In this house lived Alexandre ROCHAIS born on 3 August 1886 a fighter of the 6th section of ARAC, arrested 9 June 1943, assassinated 18 September 1943 at Buchenwald." These signs are ubiquitous in France.

Though there were many heroes of the Resistance (and one can see signs on buildings throughout France honoring their sacrifice, like the one above), one man, besides de Gaulle, has become the face of the Resistance: Jean Moulin, a man of extraordinary bravery.

Jean Moulin was a civil servant, a regional governor or "prefect," before the war. When the Nazis took over, he was almost immediately arrested and tortured for defending French African colonial troops against false charges of rape. He was released when he refused to bend and used a shard of broken glass to cut his own throat, almost taking his life in the process.

Upon his release, he sought out other like-minded people and joined the Resistance. He soon came to the attention of de Gaulle as someone who knew many within France and who was an organizer and a patriot. Over the course of the next two and half years, Moulin, aka "Rex," served as de Gaulle's eyes and ears in France, many times just escaping capture. Sadly, though, he was betrayed from within by a collaborator, and he was taken by the Germans, tortured, and sent to Germany on a train, where he arrived dead. Today, his remains are honored in the Pantheon in Paris, a monument and memorial to the great Frenchmen and women of history.

Modern French stamp honoring Jean Moulin.
https://it.wikipedia.org/wiki/File:Jean_Moulin_timbre.jpg

For almost every major act of resistance, the Germans punished the population as a way to turn the rest of France against those who were resisting, which was a tactic they used everywhere. For every German soldier killed or attacked, hostages were taken and, many times, executed. In 1944, as the Germans were attempting to send troops from southern France to attack the Allied landing in Normandy, one of their most notorious units, the 2nd SS Armored Division "Das Reich" was bombed incessantly by Allied planes and harassed by Resistance units. In response to a report that a German officer had been killed in the area, one company of Das Reich went berserk, wiping out the nearby village of Oradour-sur-Glane in central France. This included the deaths of civilians locked in a burning church. Six hundred people, including 247 children, were killed. Today, Oradour stands exactly as it was on the day following the massacre, a silent memorial to those who fell during yet another tragic moment of the war.

Oradour-sur-Glane, France.
Two Wings, slight edit by Calibas, CC BY-SA 3.0
<https://creativecommons.org/licenses/by-sa/3.0>, via Wikimedia Commons
https://commons.wikimedia.org/wiki/File:Car_in_Oradour-sur-Glane4.jpg

Outside of France, de Gaulle's Free French grew slowly with Allied help and a regular infusion of escapees from the Continent. In 1942, they proved their worth in a brave battle at Bir Hakeim in Libya. Though it was a military defeat, the outnumbered French at Bir Hakeim held off a much larger German force for a month. The German officer in command said after the war that he had not fought a superior opponent throughout the entire war.

In 1944, Free French commandos and air and naval forces took part in the D-Day landings, and later that summer, they aided in the invasion of southern France, which was named Operation Dragoon. As part of both of these landings, Resistance fighters, many times joined by Allied agents and Special Air Service troops from Great Britain, helped by reporting on German troop movements, attacking reinforcements and communications centers, and destroying trains and bridges. US President Dwight D. Eisenhower later said that the Resistance was like having an extra division behind enemy lines.

On August 25th, 1944, Free French troops led the way into Paris, where they were soon joined by Charles de Gaulle. There was still fighting in the streets, and as the six-foot-six de Gaulle marched through the streets to Notre-Dame, German snipers shot in his direction. De Gaulle did not flinch.

De Gaulle and Resistance leaders marching down the Champs-Élysées with the Arc de Triomphe in the background, 8/25/1944.
https://commons.wikimedia.org/wiki/File:The_Liberation_of_Paris,_25_-26_August_1944_HU66477.jpg

French troops fought through the winter and advanced into Germany, occupying the southwestern quarter of the country as their zone of control as part of the post-war peace.

Conclusion

Charles de Gaulle presided over the French Fourth Republic from 1944 until his resignation in 1946. He left the office as he was disgusted over the infighting taking place within the political parties of France. In the vacuum left by the general, a variety of mainstream political parties, including the right, the left, and moderates, enjoyed periods of time in power. Left out of power was the extreme right, which had virtually ceased to exist after the defeat of Hitler and the betrayal of Marshal Pétain, and the radical left, which was represented by the French Communist Party, perhaps the most powerful political entity in the year or two immediately after the war.

When WWII ended, many in France wanted to see a return to the French influence and power that had existed before 1940. This was both delusional and not to be. France had been eclipsed in power by both the United States and the Soviet Union from the moment Paris fell in 1940, and the nation was never to be the same player on the international stage again.

Still, this did not stop France, with the support of the United States and Great Britain, from attempting to regain control of its former colonies. In North Africa, Algeria fell back under French control. The French zones of control in the Middle East (Lebanon and Syria) became independent nations. French colonies in Central Africa were regained only to be lost by the early 1960s, mostly bloodlessly.

Vietnam was a different story. The story is long and complicated, but suffice it to say that beginning in 1946, the French attempted to reestablish their control of the country, which began a war that increased in ferocity until 1954 with the stunning French defeat at the hands of the Vietnamese in the north at Dien Bien Phu.

In 1962, a simmering eight-year guerrilla war ended France's ownership of Algeria. The war was marked with atrocities on both sides, but the role of French troops was especially criticized at home in the light of post-war anti-imperialism and the documentation of many incidents on the new visual medium of television. The end of the war in Algeria, which was encouraged by Charles de Gaulle, who had returned to power in a bloodless sort of coup in 1958, establishing the Fifth Republic in the process, provoked ultra-nationalists in the army, specifically the elite Foreign Legion, to attempt a military coup to overthrow the government, which was put down harshly.

The 1960s were a tumultuous time for France, as they were for much of the Western world, especially the United States. In 1968, riots broke out throughout France, especially in Paris. The demonstrations and violence of 1968 in France were multi-faceted. Part of these disturbances had to do with many being opposed to America's war with Vietnam. When WWII ended, many French, having experienced German occupation, felt the reoccupation of Vietnam and Algeria was wrong. Times had changed, and the time for imperialism was over. This view was widely held, but it was primarily held by younger generations who were born just before, during, or just after WWII. Many of these people felt a kinship with the Vietnamese or somehow felt a need to atone for French involvement in the region—hence their anti-American stance.

These riots also occurred because many in France felt that the WWII generation, which ruled the country, was out of touch and that it was time to move on from outdated policies and outdated thinking. Similar to the United States, the more liberal areas were urban, while the rural areas were more conservative. Also, like the USA, a culture war developed between liberals and conservatives, not only about politics but morals as well.

Internationally, the policy of de Gaulle and France after de Gaulle retired in 1969 tried to carve out an independent foreign policy. Though France was anti-communist, it also had a strong streak of anti-Americanism. This might seem odd and ungrateful to Americans, but this anti-Americanism generally did not come from a place of ingratitude, as they recognized America's part in its liberation in WWII. It came from French resentment at being replaced as a great power, American heavy-handedness and imperialism, and a desire to control its own destiny. Though most people recognized that France would support the West should a conflict develop between NATO (North Atlantic Treaty Organization) and the Soviet Union, France did not join NATO fully until 2009. It did, however, construct its own nuclear deterrent, which, though smaller than that of the US, Russia, and China, is nonetheless capable of laying waste to the entire globe.

Today, France is seen as a relatively steadfast yet sometimes critical ally of the United States, and it plays an important peace-keeping role in the world, both diplomatically and militarily. France has often sent peace-keeping forces to its former colonies in Africa and supported the US War on Terror with troops and other forces.

At home, it took many years for France to recover from WWII. Immediately after the war, it seemed to many, both in France and elsewhere, that most Frenchmen had been part of the heroic resistance movements against the Nazis, even in the parts of France controlled by French collaborationists. Between the end of the war and the late 1970s, this view changed. As you can see in the movie listed in the bibliography at the end of this book, *The Sorrow and the Pity*, many French people simply tried to get by as best they could during the war, supporting neither the Nazis nor the Resistance. It is thought that many people collaborated to one degree or another and that a smaller number actually actively resisted.

Some did both, like French President François Mitterrand (1916-1996), a power player on the international scene in the 1980s. Mitterrand's role in WWII came under intense scrutiny in his later years. It turned out that he, like many Frenchmen and women, had played both roles, collaborationist and resistor, at various times. The questions and issues (resistance versus collaboration, etc.) brought up during this time in France are still felt in the country today.

Today, France is one of the most developed nations in the world. Its current president, Emmanuel Macron, has become a world figure in his own right, claiming French leadership in the war on climate change and attempting to wrestle with serious problems in the country, especially in the areas of terrorism, immigration, minority rights, and employment issues, all of which promise to continue into the foreseeable future.

Part 2: Charlemagne

A Captivating Guide to the Greatest Monarch of the Carolingian Empire and How He Ruled over the Franks, Lombards, and Romans

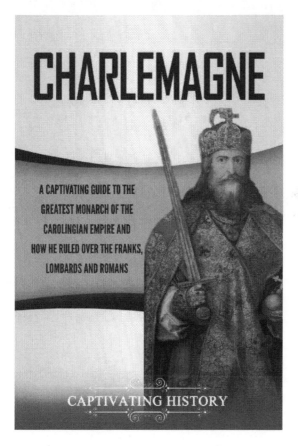

Right action is better than knowledge; but in order to do what is right, we must know what is right.

- Charlemagne

Introduction

Warrior. Ruler. Patron of the arts and language. Terrorist. Brutal oppressor. Protector of the good. Guardian of Christendom. Father of Europe. There are so many different ways in which Charlemagne can be described, and yet the man himself is often seen as an enigma. Depending on the viewpoint of history, he could have been either a monster or a guardian angel. Yet, as with most men, the truth lies somewhere in between. The truth is that he was human.

Charlemagne, crowned emperor of Rome and king of the Franks and Lombards, was the third ruler of the Carolingian Dynasty. He is also known as Charles the Great, and greatness certainly is a fitting word to describe his illustrious rule of 47 years. He added huge tracts of land to the Frankish kingdom, reformed everything from administration to currency to language, and changed the dynamics between the church and state forever—a defining influence on the entirety of Europe during the Middle Ages.

But Charlemagne also lived as a human being, a man who loved, lost, made mistakes, and endured the full spectrum of emotions. A man who was never truly satisfied with his achievements, whose constant thirst for more was never satiated.

Although he longed for more, it is safe to say that he will forever remain as one of the most influential figures throughout all of history. And this is his story.

Chapter 1 – Before the Great King

The name of Charlemagne is one that will ring familiar to many, a name that has been invoked by many powers in the centuries since he reigned, from the Holy Roman Empire to Nazi Germany. We all know that Charlemagne was some great king of France. What many don't realize is that Charlemagne was the king of France before the name of France even existed.

In truth, Charlemagne was the king of a far greater territory than modern-day France, one which encompassed six modern countries of Western Europe. This territory was known as Gaul. And the people that Charlemagne ruled would eventually give their names to the land we know as France today. They were called the Franks, and their history stretches back centuries before their first great king was born.

An Early History of the Franks

No one really knows how long ago the Frankish tribe began. Our first records of them come from the time of the ancient Romans, who sought to conquer these people; by that time, the Franks were already a large, efficient, and warlike tribe. They probably originated somewhere in northwest Germany along the banks of the Rhine when a group of smaller tribes came together—perhaps uniting against a common enemy—and formed a confederation. Thus, ruled by two powerful families named the Ripuarians and the Salians, the Franks were born.

They didn't call themselves the Franks, though. This name was given to them by the Romans, and it meant "ferocious," a title that they earned in blood. When Rome expanded into Gaul throughout the first few centuries CE, they became the first people to make lasting records of the Franks, and they clashed with a tribe of "barbarians" that proved to be far more organized than the Romans had expected. Even at the height of its imperial power, Rome may have striven hard against the Franks and even conquered Gaul, but they couldn't seem to stamp out the Franks' fighting spirit. In 287 CE, the Romans had no choice but to sign a treaty with the Franks, which ended in the recruitment of many Frankish soldiers into the Roman army.

The Romans soon discovered that the Franks made far better friends than enemies. In fact, the Franks, fighting on the side of Rome, proved to be such strong soldiers that their Roman colleagues began to make up legends about them. The most enduring of these legends is that the Franks were descended from Trojan warriors. Troy, in its time, had been legendary for its prowess. Romantic as this idea may be, sadly, it's highly unlikely to be true.

Nonetheless, the Franks became an integral part of ancient Rome's mighty army. Within the next 200 years, the number of Franks in the Roman army grew so much that they outnumbered all other soldiers who were not Roman citizens. This turned out to be a good thing. The Franks would become an invaluable asset in Rome's fight against one of history's most intimidating characters: Attila the Hun.

The Huns were a nomadic tribe from Asia and Eastern Europe that had been growing quietly in the shadows for decades by the time that Attila became their king in 445 CE. Attila loved hunting, drinking, and women. He also loved conquest, and unlike the Hunnic kings that had gone before him, Attila had a greater ambition than simply ruling a handful of tribes. In the next six years, he managed to unite the wild and warlike Huns into a single unstoppable force that would bring devastation to the very doorstep of the Roman Empire.

It all started with a beautiful girl named Honoria. As the sister of Roman Emperor Valentinian III, Honoria was a princess of Rome. She was one of the most important women in the world, but her opinion was of no importance whatsoever, especially when it came to whom she would marry. Valentinian wanted to marry her off to a boring old Roman officer for the sake of strengthening family ties. Hating the idea, Honoria decided that she would find herself another husband, one that could make even Valentinian quake in his boots. She wrote a letter to Attila the Hun, enclosing a ring and proposing marriage.

Honoria's bid to control her own fate was short-lived. As soon as Valentinian found out, he promptly married her off to the Roman officer anyway, but it was too late to stop Attila. He'd been promised a Roman princess for his bride, and he would have her, no matter what. Invading Gaul, he began to sack city after city, burning them down in a bid for Honoria.

Much of Gaul itself was a part of Roman territory at the time, but the Franks and their neighbors, the Goths and the Visigoths, were free people, and the Romans faced harsh defeats against Attila before they realized that their only hope of beating him was to fight fire with fire (or barbarians with barbarians, in this case). Roman General Flavius Aetius, a gifted, if prejudiced strategist, formed an alliance with numerous Gallic tribes. The Franks were among them. They came to the aid of the besieged city of Orléans, forcing Attila to abandon the siege and begin a slow flight back toward his homeland. It was a flight he could not sustain. His army ran out of food and water, and having no choice, Attila turned to face the oncoming Romans and their barbarian allies.

Bolstered by their Frankish allies, the Romans came face to face with their Hunnic adversary on the Catalaunian Plains in 451 CE. The battle that resulted was an utterly brutal one for the Franks. Aetius favored his Roman soldiers and viewed barbarians as expendable, so he sent the Franks into horrific danger, resulting in high Frankish casualties while the Romans stayed in comparative safety. Nonetheless, the Franks were fearless, earning their name of "ferocious" as they fell upon the flanks of the Huns. Attila was put to flight again that day, and it was the only time he would ever be defeated.

Attila did not return to Gaul. He was likely planning to do so, but in 453 CE, the Hunnic king met with an unlikely end for such a warlike man. Being polygamous, Attila decided that if he couldn't have Honoria at the moment, he'd simply take a consolation prize to tide him over before he could claim his Roman princess. This proved to be a girl named Ildico, and she would be the death of him—literally. On their wedding night, Attila drank himself into a coma. As he lay in his drunken stupor, his nose began to bleed. The bleeding was not catastrophic, but his drunken state was, for he'd slipped so deeply into an alcoholic coma that he couldn't even sense the fact that his own blood was steadily trickling into his windpipe. Attila drowned in his own blood that night.

The Rise of Clovis

At the time of the Battle of the Catalaunian Plains, the Franks were led by their king, Merovech. His name would become legendary not because of his role in the defeat of Attila the Hun, but because of the grandson he'd leave behind after his death: Clovis.

Merovech's son, Childeric I, died thirty years after the defeat of Attila, leaving the Frankish people in the hands of his son, Clovis, who was only fifteen years old at the time. It was an era in which child rulers often caused terrible grief and trouble for their subjects. A fifteen-year-old, in the modern day, would hardly be considered a suitable ruler for an entire tribe of people. The Franks had much to fear, such as their king growing up into a tyrant or, perhaps worse, a squabbling regency that could erupt into a civil war. But, unlike many others in history, this teenage king would grow into a mighty ruler.

Clovis proved to be a fearless warrior and an adept strategist. He came to power with an ambitious vision: to see all of Gaul united underneath his rule. The only trouble was that Gaul wasn't even under Frankish rule at the time. Instead, it belonged to the Romans.

As evidenced by Flavius Aetius's treatment of the Franks during the Battle of the Catalaunian Plains, Romans may have lived alongside the Franks, but they still believed that they were deeply inferior to the Romans. This prejudice was evident all over the Roman Empire, and Clovis had had enough of it. He must have heard his father's stories of how his men had been butchered like pigs on the plains while the Roman soldiers watched. Clovis was done with Roman rule.

In 486, when he was just twenty years old, Clovis turned on his erstwhile ally, Syagrius, the Roman governor of Gaul. Syagrius met Clovis in an open battle and was soundly defeated by the young Frankish king. The governor fled to another "barbarian" ally, Alaric II, the king of the Visigoths (not to be confused with his great-grandfather, Alaric I, the man who sacked Rome). It proved to be an unwise move. The Visigoths had been killed on the Catalaunian Plains just as the Franks had; besides, Alaric had no intentions of angering Clovis. When Clovis sent messengers to him demanding that he hand over the Roman governor, Alaric was quick to comply. Syagrius was sent to Clovis, who promptly beheaded him. And so, the Roman control of Gaul came to a resounding end. In fact, the entire Roman Empire was in its death throes by this point, and Clovis's killing of Syagrius was one of the final blows that would be struck to the dying empire.

Now that the Romans were out of the way, Clovis set about uniting the whole of Gaul under his rule, conquering those Frankish leaders who dared to stand against him. He killed many of them, forcing their tribes to join him and forming Gaul into a single powerful territory under one Frankish king. By the beginning of the 6th century, Clovis controlled everything from the British Channel to the Alps. His territory included modern-day France, Luxembourg, Germany, and the Netherlands, as well as parts of Switzerland and northern Italy.

Clovis, like generations of Franks before him, was a pagan; he served numerous traditional gods, just as his ancestors had. But for the past 500 years, a new name had been spreading throughout the world from its birthplace in the Middle East. Even Rome had abandoned its gods and astronomers to follow this religion. It was Christianity, and it was spreading slowly over the known world.

Clovis had come into contact with some forms of Christianity during his rule. Not only had he known Romans, who were Catholic, but he'd also met with the Goths, who followed Arian Christianity. Clovis had no quarrel with the Christians, but he had no intention to convert either. But according to his biographer, all that changed during a battle with the Alemanni tribe around 503 CE.

Clovis Converts

The Alemanni were winning.

Clovis's troops were engaged in full battle with the Germanic tribe, which Clovis was trying to beat into submission, a tribe whose lands he'd hoped to add to his growing territory. Now, though, it seemed as if the Alemanni were not simply going to resist him: they were going to destroy him. Wherever Clovis looked, he could see his men were dying.

Clovis was by no means inexperienced in battle. He'd been king for more than twenty years, and he'd spent every one of those years fighting against some enemy, usually an enemy of his own making. But he'd never seen things this dire before. He knew that he was about to be routed, perhaps even killed, and the earth had been stained blood red as his men died right and left. His own blade ran scarlet with blood, and yet more and more enemies came wherever he looked.

He knew that he might not make it home this time, not from this campaign, and his heart fled back to the woman he loved: the Burgundian princess he'd married. Clotilde, like most of her people, was a Catholic. They were happily married, but there was one thing they'd never agreed on: religion. For years, she'd been imploring him to turn from his traditional faith and serve her God. Clovis had always refused. But now, it seemed that his gods had abandoned him. They seemed powerless in the face of the raging Alemanni.

Clovis was desperate. He wanted to get home, by any means necessary, and he prayed aloud to the God his wife served. Incredibly, before his very eyes, a miracle happened. The tide of the battle began to turn. The Alemanni threw down their weapons, turned their backs, and fled as though the Franks had fallen upon them with chariots of fire.

Or so goes the story of Clovis's conversion as told by Gregory of Tours, a historian from the late 6th century. According to Gregory, Clovis returned to Clotilde, utterly humbled. Once he'd told her everything that had taken place during the battle, Clotilde convinced the Catholic bishop of Reims to preach to Clovis. Many conversations took place between the two men, and in the end, Clovis converted. He was baptized inside a small abbey in Reims, and so the Franks became a Catholic people, or at least their king did.

Regardless of how accurate Gregory's account is, Clovis most certainly did convert to Christianity, namely to Roman Catholicism. He had defeated the Romans nearly twenty years before, but now he adopted the religion of his enemies. And so began the long and complicated history of the Roman papacy and the Frankish kings.

The Merovingian Dynasty

Clovis was more than just a king and a conqueror. He was the founder of a dynasty known as the Merovingian dynasty, named after Clovis's grandfather.

By the end of Clovis's reign, Gaul—and the Frankish people—had become one of the most important powers of Western Europe. The Western Roman Empire had fallen, with its last emperor deposed in 476; by the end of the 5th century, even the last twitches of its corpse had faded. The resulting vacuum was quickly filled by the Eastern Roman Empire and, increasingly, by the rising might of Gaul. This power would be a long-lived one.

Clovis, however, would not share the same happy fate. He died in 511 at his capital, Paris, apparently of natural causes. The empire he'd forged would stand for centuries, and the dynasty he'd founded would rule Gaul for over 200 years.

The Merovingian dynasty governed Gaul from the time of Clovis in the late 5th century to the rise of the Carolingian dynasty—whose most famous king we'll be studying in this book—in the 8th century. Known as the "long-haired kings" for their unique appearance, the Merovingians soon made a name for themselves as being adept and powerful rulers who unfortunately often resorted to simple tyranny.

The spread of Christianity over Western Europe did not come as easily as the snap conversion of Clovis I. Once the Merovingians had closely allied themselves to the Roman papacy, they realized that the papacy was emerging as a greater power than the empire in which it had been born. The title of Western Roman Emperor had faded into oblivion, but the title of Roman Catholic Pope was one that began to command respect throughout Europe. The Merovingians saw him as a useful ally, and they were determined to bring their realm under Catholic control, often for purely political reasons.

Thus, the Merovingians forced evangelism with the edge of the sword, persecuting the pagans that still observed ancient Frankish traditions. As their control over the realm grew, and as other nations began to show the mighty Franks more and more respect over the next 200 years, the Merovingians' appetite for power became insatiable. Their actions were motivated solely by politics, and this would eventually prove to be their downfall.

After years of closely allying with the papacy, the Merovingian kings began to appoint secular leaders in church positions. Laymen performed religious duties, something that the Roman Catholic Church did not tolerate. Clashes with the papacy ensued, and by the beginning of the 8th century, the Merovingians' long-standing alliance with the pope had all but ended.

A number of other factors contributed to the decline of Merovingian power, and the once-great long-haired kings had become so lackadaisical and feeble that they were now known as the "do-nothing kings." Rome's power was gone, and the papacy itself was threatened. The time was ripe for a new ruler to rise in Western Europe and bring unity back to the scattered people. And that ruler would be a Frankish king.

Chapter 2 – Rise to Power

An equestrian statue of Charlemagne in Paris near Notre-Dame Cathedral.
Arnaud 25 Attribution-ShareAlike 3.0 Unported (CC BY-SA 3.0)
<*https://creativecommons.org/licenses/by-sa/3.0/deed.en*> *via Wikimedia Commons*
https://commons.wikimedia.org/wiki/File:Charlemagne_Notre_Dame.jpg#file

With the Merovingians' hands tied, Francia—the country that had risen as the home of the Franks when Clovis's Gaul gradually shattered into numerous small kingdoms—nonetheless needed to be governed. Power did not simply disappear when the

Merovingian rulers gave it up. Instead, it dissipated into the hands of others, namely, the Frankish mayors of the palace.

In Francia during the 8th century, the mayors of the palace played a similar role as the modern-day British prime minister. Kings and queens still ostensibly ruled, but in matters of state and government, they were little more than figureheads. The real power belonged to the mayors, and the greatest mayor of them all was Charles Martel.

Battle of Tours, 732

Charles knew that the odds were stacked overwhelmingly against him.

The Frankish commander had arrayed his troops in a square formation around the wooded plain, across which a mountain wind swept with icy cold. He waited now, ready for an attack at any moment, and he was facing an enemy that had grown as quick as cancer—and twice as deadly.

Abd al-Rahman, also known as Abd er Rahman, the commander of the Muslim army that was rapidly bearing down upon Francia, was a formidable enemy. His cavalry was unlike anything that Western Europe had ever seen before. Swarthy men armed with bows and scimitars rode light-footed horses that never seemed to tire and moved with a speed and agility that the lumbering European cavalry could never hope to match. This combination was one that Europe found almost unbeatable, as that cavalry could mow down any army, and Charles knew that infantry units pitted against cavalry forces almost always ended in disaster. Yet here he was, ready to face Abd al-Rahman with a group of Frankish infantrymen. Greater armies than his had fallen and been destroyed at the blades of those Muslim horsemen.

The Umayyad Caliphate's roots went back almost exactly one hundred years. After the death of the Prophet Muhammad in 632, the Umayyad Caliphate emerged as the leading Muslim power, and its religious fervor drove its campaigns from continent to continent. North Africa and the Middle East didn't stand a chance. Now, the Umayyads had set their sights on Europe, and their conquest swept north and west like an uncontrollable flame. Already, the Duchy of Aquitaine, itself a part of Francia, had fallen to their trampling hordes.

Charles was the last line of defense to prevent the whole of Francia from falling to Abd al-Rahman. His group of infantrymen was the only thing that stood between Francia and the Umayyad Caliphate, and he knew that defeat would mean more than just the loss of land and life. It would mean the loss of Frankish culture. The Franks were still profoundly Catholic, while the Umayyads were profoundly Muslim. Not a soul in Francia would be left unaffected by the occupation of the Umayyads. Charles knew that he was standing at a crossroads in history itself. The stand he had taken near the city of Tours would send aftershocks through the centuries to come.

On October 10th, 732, Abd al-Rahman finally attacked. The vicious cavalry composed of Arabs and Berbers fell upon the Frankish infantry without mercy, and Charles's lines began to buckle. If the Battle of Tours had ended there, the same way that most of Abd al-Rahman's battles ended, then history itself would have quaked to its very foundations. The Umayyad soldiers would have crushed the Franks, the plain slick with mud and blood, and Abd al-Rahman would have pushed on unhindered to Paris itself.

It had happened over and over again in the past, but it did not happen on that day, for Charles struck at the Muslims again and again with a ferocity they had not grown to expect from the Europeans, a ferocity that earned the Frankish leader the name of Charles Martel: "Charles the Hammer." That hammer forged Europe on the anvil of the Umayyads that day, and incredibly, his infantry stood against Abd al-Rahman.

Meanwhile, behind enemy lines, Charles's scouts were heading fast to the Umayyad camp, which had been practically abandoned during the fighting. Frankish prisoners from Aquitaine were waiting there to be rescued, and the scouts made quick work of what guards were left, then set to freeing the prisoners. The camp was piled high with the bountiful spoils of the Muslims' conquests so far. Soon, word reached the battlefield that the camp was being robbed.

The Umayyad soldiers were hard pressed by Charles, and they were tired of fighting, as they were facing the very real possibility of defeat. When they heard that their booty was being carried off, they began to break ranks in a panic, rushing back to defend their camp. Chaos erupted throughout Abd al-Rahman's lines. Charles and his men pushed them harder, pressing home their newfound advantage, and somehow, incredibly, the Frankish infantry put all the Umayyads to flight. Those swift horses were sent bolting for home, many with empty saddles. Abd al-Rahman was pulled down and killed, and his army fell into chaos and fled.

Somehow, Charles Martel had turned the Battle of Tours into a victory, and it was a victory that would change global history forever. The man who fought it had already had plenty of experience in battle; in fact, he had paid for his title in blood.

Charles Martel

Charles was supposed to have inherited his title from his father, Pepin the Middle, who was the mayor of the palace before him. Charles considered the title to be rightfully his; he was, after all, Pepin's oldest son. Unfortunately, Charles Martel turned out to have the same enemy as Cinderella: a wicked stepmother. Plectrude, Pepin's second wife, sought to gain power for herself. She persuaded Pepin to disinherit Charles and make his grandson, Theudoald, his successor instead. Theudoald was a little boy at the time, while Charles was already well into his twenties and proving himself as a capable young man. Fearing that Charles and his supporters would overthrow her, Plectrude had the young man imprisoned after Pepin's death in 714.

Charles refused to languish in prison while Plectrude ruled as regent for his young nephew. Escaping from prison, Charles fled to another Frankish kingdom, Austrasia. Here, he found considerable support. The Austrasians considered him the rightful heir and were reluctant to be governed by a regency, so they provided him with the men and troops that he needed. Charles trained them personally, and after four long years of civil war and campaigning against Plectrude (as well as conquering Bavaria and Alemannia), he was finally able to claim his title of mayor of the palace.

His battle for the title provided him with invaluable experience, which would stand him in good stead when Abd al-Rahman arrived nearly twenty years later. His resounding victory against the Umayyads halted their progression into Europe, sending them back to the Middle East, a move that would change history forever. Yet that victory came at a high price.

One of the things that Charles had learned during his campaigns against his stepmother's forces was that conscripts were simply not good enough. Traditionally, during this feudal period, rulers would go to war primarily with fyrdmen—serfs that had received little training and possessed some rudimentary armor and weapons. These men were not career soldiers; they were farmers, and they spent more time tilling the land than training with their weapons. Charles had formed a standing army in Austrasia, a body of men dedicated to nothing but warfare, and it had proven to be the difference between victory and defeat. His was one of the few standing armies that the Umayyads would ever face in Europe, which may be why the Battle of Tours was a Frankish victory.

Standing armies, however, were rare for a reason. Serfs earned their own keep and went to battle for little or no pay, but soldiers needed to be fed, housed, and paid wages. In order to afford the army that had defeated the Umayyads, Charles had to resort to desperate measures. He began to seize large tracts of land that belonged to the Catholic Church, using them to generate income in the form of taxes, money that would have otherwise gone to the papacy. Even though Charles's conquest of the Umayyads may very well have saved the widespread occurrence of Catholic Christianity in that part of the world, the papacy was nonetheless deeply disgusted with him for taking their land. His actions caused a terrible rift between the rulers of Francia and the popes of Rome.

Nonetheless, Charles left behind a powerful legacy, and that legacy would only be expanded by his son and grandson who succeeded him.

Pepin the Short

As victorious as Charles was in warfare, he was unlucky in love. That's not to say that he had trouble finding a wife. After his sensational escape and flight to Austrasia, Charles married a girl there, Rotrude of Hesbaye. However, they enjoyed only six years of marriage together before Rotrude died. She left Charles with five children, including two sons. He named one Pepin after his father, while the other was called Carloman.

After Rotrude's death in 724, Charles headed off to campaign once again in Bavaria, where he came across another woman that could soothe his grieving heart. Her name was Swanahild, and she was nobly born, a fitting second wife for the most powerful man in Francia. She would bear him another son before his death, whose name was Grifo.

After the Battle of Tours, Charles would govern Francia for another nine years until his death in 741. He was around the age of 55 (his date of birth can only be guessed at). Instead of choosing a single heir from among his sons, Charles decided to divide the power between the two sons he had with Rotrude. He gave the larger lands of Neustria to Pepin, while Austrasia went to Carloman. Grifo was entirely left out, a fact that would soon lead to trouble for his two older half-brothers.

When he became mayor of the palace alongside Carloman, Pepin had already chosen a wife. Her name was Bertrada of Laon. Bertrada was a distant relation of Pepin's, and for that reason, their marriage was not sanctioned by the Church for several years. The Catholic Church was still against Charles Martel and his family thanks to the Hammer's treatment of Church lands, and the religious establishment sought any opportunity to bring disrepute to Charles's name, including their rejection of Pepin and Bertrada's marriage.

So, it came to be that, one year after Pepin became the mayor of the palace, Bertrada gave birth to a baby who would technically be born out of wedlock. The child was a strong and healthy son, and his parents named him after his grandfather. Perhaps they hoped that some of Charles Martel's greatness would rub off on little Charles. Little did they know that their son would grow up to become the greatest king that Francia had ever known.

* * * *

The boy would eventually be called Charlemagne, but as a child, he was known simply as Charles. Likely born in Aachen, Charles moved with his parents to the capital city of Paris soon after, where Pepin reigned and little Charles grew up. Not much is known of the boy's childhood. He was educated in the abbey of Saint-Denis by its abbot, who appears to have enjoyed teaching a student who was both enthusiastic and intelligent. As well as his native tongue, Charles learned both Latin and some Greek, and he could read and write as well. Literacy, at the time, was a privilege given only to the highborn and the rich—there had even been kings who could neither read nor write. Being literate in multiple languages was a noteworthy achievement in those days.

Being an only child at the time, Charles enjoyed having his mother's full attention lavished upon him. His father, however, was continually distracted. Pepin was fighting hard to defend his power.

Ever since Charles's father, Pepin the Short, and uncle, Carloman, had gained control over Francia, they had constantly been fighting to defend their power against their slighted half-brother. Backed by his mother's people, the Bavarians, Grifo was determined to grab what he believed to be his rightful share of Francian power.

For the first several years of Charles's life, his father was off campaigning against Grifo. Despite the fact that Pepin and Carloman had always had a tenuous relationship at best, they had no choice but to work together if they wanted to hold on to their own power. They finally succeeded in besieging Grifo's army and eventually pushed through his defenses to arrest him. Grifo was lucky that his half-brothers didn't kill him. Instead, he was forced to live out his days in a monastery, cut off from the outside world and incapable of holding any type of earthly power again.

Carloman would eventually share Grifo's fate. Slowly, Pepin began to pressure his brother, fighting for his vision of a unified Francia under a single ruler. It's unclear exactly why Carloman gave up his title and prestigious life. He may have done so voluntarily; it is also possible, however, that Pepin pressured Carloman into abandoning his title and becoming a monk himself in 747 when little Charles was only six years old. Carloman's power was left to Pepin, and thus, Charles's father became the sole ruler over all of Francia and one of the most powerful men in Europe.

However, before Carloman could join a monastery, he did make one very important political move. Mayors of the palace had the right to choose and appoint the kings of Francia from among the Merovingian family. Before his abdication, Carloman had chosen Childeric III, making him the figurehead king of the Frankish people. This move greatly chafed Pepin. He couldn't stand having any rivals to his power, not even one that had no real capacity to influence the government, and it seemed to him to be senseless to have a king who did nothing.

Pepin wanted Childeric gone. But many of the Franks were used to the idea of kings, and they'd never known a time when they were not governed by Merovingians. In order to get rid of Childeric, Pepin would need the backing of a strong ally. He could think of only one ally who had both the strength to bend the will of the Frankish people and the motivation to support a new Frankish king, and that was Roman Pope Zachary.

The papacy's soured relationship with the Merovingians—and, most recently, with Charles Martel—had cost it an important ally, one of the few powers in Western Europe that would have taken up arms to protect the pope. Large tracts of land belonged to the papacy in Italy, and the greedy surrounding kings were eyeing that land, hungering to add to their domains. Prominent among those were the kings of the Lombards, a Germanic tribe that had settled in Italy and established itself there as a powerful kingdom.

Pepin knew that Zachary was desperate—perhaps even desperate enough to form an alliance with the son of a man that the papacy fervently hated. He decided to reach out to Zachary in the form of a letter, which he dictated; Pepin, unlike Charles, was likely illiterate. He told Zachary that he considered it to be a grave injustice that a man with no real power should hold the title of king of the Franks, while the person who was doing all the heavy lifting would only be called the mayor of the palace. Pepin's intention was clear. He wanted to oust Childeric and make himself the king.

Zachary was delighted to receive Pepin's letter. He saw a wonderful opportunity to procure an ally who had proven himself in his war against Grifo and who commanded the army that had stopped even the Umayyads in their tracks. He swiftly responded, and soon, he found himself on his way to Paris.

In 751, Childeric III, the last of the Merovingians, was formally deposed. Zachary anointed Pepin as the king of the Franks—the first of a dynasty that would later be named the Carolingian dynasty, although it was not named after Pepin but after the ten-year-old boy who watched from the sidelines as his father's coronation took place. It must have been heady stuff for little Charles to watch the sparkling crown being placed upon his father's head, knowing that he was Pepin's eldest son. Someday, that crown would be his own. Perhaps at that moment, Charles knew, for the first time, the thrill of power.

Shortly after Pepin's coronation, Zachary returned to Rome and died there that same year. He was succeeded by Pope Stephen II. Stephen, who had once been a Roman aristocrat, found himself in charge of a deeply threatened papacy. The Lombard king had captured the Exarchate of Ravenna shortly before Stephen became the pope, and it was obvious that the king was now setting his sights on Rome. Stephen turned tail and fled. He ran to the safest place he could think of: Paris. Pepin welcomed him with open arms, giving him sanctuary, and Stephen gratefully anointed him a second time in 753. The Lombard threat continued to grow, and Stephen begged Pepin to do something. As his power was firmly cemented in Francia itself, Pepin resolved to campaign against the Lombards.

Twelve-year-old Charles watched his father depart at the head of the great professional army that had beaten the Umayyads. This time, Charles was old enough to understand the risk that Pepin was taking. One can imagine that the sound of a marching army was one that the boy would never forget. And when Pepin returned soon afterward, with the Lombards soundly defeated and with Stephen installed once again in Rome, Charles's mind was made up. He, too, would be a glorious warrior one day. He wanted to win great battles, just like his father.

In gratitude for Pepin's actions, Stephen held another anointing ceremony for the Frankish king. This time, Charles and his brother Carloman (a toddler at the time) were anointed as well, as Pepin was eager for the boys to be established as the heirs to the Francian throne. Being anointed as the future king at the age of twelve must have been heady stuff for young Charles.

As for Pepin, he had not only defended Stephen's lands, but he had also expanded them into what would eventually become the Papal States. Stephen was eternally grateful, and Pepin's actions formed his most lasting legacy: the alliance between the Carolingian kings and Rome. Charles didn't know it yet, but Pepin's actions would someday change his life.

* * * *

By the time that Charles was a teenager, he had been joined by two more siblings. The first was a brother named Carloman, nine years Charles's junior. The second was a little sister called Gisela.

Charles and Carloman were trained in all the noble arts of young princes, considering that they were now heirs to a throne instead of just to a title. In fact, Charles may have had his first taste of battle around this time, as older teenage sons occasionally went to war with their fathers in this era. Pepin had been dealing with scattered rebellions all over his kingdom, especially from the particularly troublesome Duchy of Aquitaine, ever since he ascended to the throne, and in the latter part of his reign, these rebellions became more and more common.

Pepin was thoroughly engaged in keeping his own kingdom together when disaster struck once again for Rome. Stephen had died in 757, leaving his title to Pope Paul I. A new Lombard king, Desiderius, ascended to his throne at about the same time. Desiderius was an ambitious king and was determined to achieve what his predecessor had been unable to: rule over Rome. He began to march on the Papal States, and Pope Paul begged Pepin for help. But Charles's father was too busy fighting to keep his kingdom intact. He couldn't give aid to the papacy, no matter how much he wanted to.

This sorry state of affairs would continue for a full decade. As Pope Paul I watched in fear for the marching legions of Desiderius's army, Pepin struggled to contain the revolting Aquitanians, a battle that would eventually take him to his grave. In 768, the 54-year-old Pepin was on his way back to Paris after yet another campaign in Aquitaine when he died. It's unclear what exactly caused his death, but the most likely explanation is that he was mortally wounded in battle. He died at Saint-Denis, in Neustria, on September 24th, 768.

Charles was 26 years old when his father died, and Carloman was 17. Like his father before him, Pepin was reluctant to leave his kingdom to a single heir. Instead, he made Charles and Carloman the co-rulers of Francia. And it would soon become evident that—like their father and uncle—they had little desire to share the throne.

Chapter 3 – Sibling Rivalry

Without reliable sources to tell about Charles's and Carloman's childhood, we can only speculate on what their relationship was like as they grew up. In truth, they may not have had much of a relationship at all. The nine-year age gap between the two boys meant that they couldn't play together like most siblings do, which could have placed Carloman in the role of annoying tag-along little brother. However, it is more likely that they never really spent time with one another.

To make matters worse, it would appear that their personalities could not have been more different. Charles was vivacious, unstoppable, fiercely fearless, and impulsive. He dreamed of battles and kingdoms, of wars and splendor. On the other hand, Carloman was a quieter, more bookish type, a scholar and philosopher rather than a warrior prince. He was slow to act and quick to err on the side of peace, perhaps even verging on cowardice, especially in Charles's eyes.

Many may have considered Charles to be the kinglier of the two. He was, after all, the older brother; he had even been in a battle with Pepin on the campaign that claimed the old king's life. Yet perhaps Pepin viewed Charles as impulsive rather than decisive. Strangely, when Pepin divided his kingdom between his sons—who would reign as co-kings but hold their own lands and territories—he gave the majority of the land to Carloman. Charles had to make do with a far smaller share.

This chafed appallingly at Charles, and perhaps with good reason. He was 26 when his father died, making him far older, more experienced, and certainly much more able at defending the kingdom than Carloman. Charles had ridden out to war against Aquitaine. He had witnessed firsthand the gruesomeness of the battlefield, the cries of the dying, the blood running thick upon the Frankish earth. He must have felt that it was grossly unfair of Pepin—the father with whom Charles had stood shoulder to shoulder against their foes—to leave the majority of his lands and power to Carloman, who'd probably been safely sheltered in some fortress while this was happening.

Their relationship declined quickly and dramatically. In fact, hotheaded Charles may not have been far from marching his men on his own brother, thus plunging Francia into a harsh civil war, when something else drew his attention: the very same duchy whose rebellion had led to the death of his father.

The Rebellion of Aquitaine

Ever since the days of Charles Martel, Aquitaine had been a particularly troublesome duchy of Francia, as evidenced by Pepin's long and bloody struggle against them—a struggle that had eventually claimed his life. For eight long years, Pepin constantly fought against the duke of Aquitaine, Waiofar. Their bitter feud was horrifically destructive and not only on the battlefield. Surrounding peasants, farms, and peaceful little towns were all affected by the blight of war. It's possible that Charles had been by his father's side for every blow struck in the battle for supremacy. He was certainly a part of that last fateful campaign. It was in far-flung countries that Charles would someday claim his title of Charles the Great, but it was on the hills of Aquitaine that he was forged from an academic prince into a fine and furious warrior.

His tall figure grew hard and lean, his hands dexterous with weapons, and his body flowed in unity with that of a powerful cavalry horse.

In the eighth year, with Charles still fighting alongside his father, the drawn-out struggle finally seemed to be drawing to a close. The people of Gascony, a nearby area and ally of Aquitaine, had fallen to Pepin in battle. Pepin's scorched-earth method of warfare destroyed countless towns, fortresses, and farms, leaving Waiofar without the resources to battle Pepin, who could draw on resources from the rest of his lands to fuel his armies. Waiofar himself remained ever elusive, never tasting the sharp edge of Charles's blade no matter how hard the warrior prince fought to bring him to bay. Eventually, it was his own men who turned against him. Some say that Pepin's messengers had turned Waiofar's own soldiers into assassins, perhaps promising them money in exchange for Waiofar's head. It's possible, though, that there were more insidious enemies—like fear, doubt, and hunger—responsible for the treachery of the Aquitanians. Either way, the war was practically over when they turned on Waiofar and killed him. Aquitaine and its allies surrendered, and Pepin rode home wounded but triumphant. He wouldn't live to enjoy his victory, dying on his way back to Paris.

As Charles arose to take the throne of the Franks, the Aquitanians realized that Pepin's death was an opportunity. Charles had not yet made himself so famous in battle as to frighten the Aquitanian lords; he was still a fledgling king, after all, youthful and inexperienced. Hastily, a kinsman of Waiofar—possibly his son—rose up to take the title of duke of Aquitaine. His name was Hunald II, and so, the conflict of two fathers became the conflict of two sons.

As soon as unrest began to rise again in Aquitaine in 769, just a year after Pepin had died, Charles was ready to leap into action. The blade of his sword was thirsty for vengeance. He was eager to put down the Aquitanians and avenge the death of Pepin, and he believed there was only one way to achieve his goal: war. After mustering the armies he had at his disposal, though, Charles realized that he didn't command the same fighting force that Pepin had. Most of Francia's armies were under Carloman's command. Much as Charles hated his brother, he needed him if he wanted to win this war, and so he was forced to humble himself and go to Carloman for assistance.

To his credit, Carloman did agree to meet with Charles. He left his home in Burgundy and brought some men down to an unspecified meeting place—possibly Paris—in order to discuss the matter of Aquitaine with his brother. Charles didn't want a discussion, though. He'd already made his decision: he was marching on Aquitaine, and Carloman was coming with him. But the eighteen-year-old king refused to be forced. He wanted nothing to do with the war that had taken their father, and, taking his armies with him, Carloman turned around and rode back to Burgundy.

Meanwhile, Hunald's strength was growing, and Charles's blood was up. Even though he had nowhere near the fighting force that he wanted, Charles refused to stand by and watch Hunald reclaim the lands that Pepin had fought so hard to protect. Perhaps it was because Carloman had not been in those battles that he did not understand the sacrifices that Pepin had made in order to gain some control over Aquitaine. But Charles had been there. And even if his brother refused to ride with him, he was going to war.

Advancing to Bordeaux, Charles established his men there, building a new fort at Fronsac. His army wasn't as large as he'd hoped it would be, but he was determined to beat the Aquitanians nonetheless.

Meanwhile, Hunald was not faring as well as he'd hoped either. Waiofar had not been defeated in one fell swoop. Instead, his numerous small allies—the Gascons, the people of Bourges, and others—had slowly crumbled away as Pepin beat away relentlessly at them. If Hunald was to hope to fight Charles, he would need allies. Sending his men out on guerrilla raids in a hopeless bid to hold off Charles's army, Hunald rode to Gascony looking for help. The Gascons had assisted the Aquitanians in the past, and Hunald hoped they would fight together once more.

Unfortunately for Hunald, Duke Lupus II of Gascony was not so eager to make war with the Frankish king. When Hunald arrived at Lupus's court, help was not what he found. Instead, Lupus had him arrested, bound, and then dragged before King Charles.

Charles's campaign was over before it had truly begun. Pepin may have been the one who truly subdued Aquitaine and Gascony, but it was Charles who accepted their final surrender after years of fighting. Hunald was delivered at his very feet just as Syagrius had been delivered to Clovis: a helpless prisoner. Yet, strangely enough, Charles failed to execute Hunald as he might have done. Executions of enemy kings were commonplace at the time, but Charlemagne would use a different tactic. The age of chivalry was close at hand, and while few real men of the Middle Ages would live up to its legendary code, Charles, in this one instance, had mercy. He sent Hunald to live out his days in a monastery in peace, albeit robbed of all his ambitions.

Lupus, too, surrendered to Francia, and so, Charles won his first campaign without hardly striking a single blow. Aquitaine had fallen at last at the feet of Francia.

With the rebellion crushed, it was time for Charles to start looking to an area of kingship that perhaps did not appeal to his hot young blood the same way that war did: diplomacy. And in the Middle Ages, marriage was one of diplomacy's most important forms.

Charles's First Love – Or Was She?

The first romantic relationship recorded in Charles's life may not have been very romantic. In fact, it's likely that there was little real romance at all in the lives of the nobility at the time. Charles was never given the opportunity to choose his own wife or to marry for love. Instead, Pepin chose wives for both Carloman and Charles before his death.

Little is known about the women that Pepin had chosen to wed his sons, except that they were both Frankish and noble. He likely chose them from families that would strengthen the crown's political alliances. Either way, Charles and Carloman may have had little or no say in the matter, although it was likely none judging by how short-lived Charles's marriage was.

In fact, Charles's relationship with Himiltrude may not have even been a marriage at all. We're not sure that the Church ever truly sanctioned their union, but it's unclear why not. She might have been a concubine rather than a wife to Charles, or she could have been bound only by *Friedelehe*, a poorly understood Germanic relationship that seemed to have been some kind of betrothal or even a stand-in for a Church-approved marriage.

Either way, their relationship began in 768, the year that Pepin died, and she certainly looked fitting when she stood beside the tall and powerful Charles. War had hardened and tanned him, and despite his somewhat ungainly proportions, he was a sight to behold with his rich golden hair and powerful size. And according to his contemporaries, Himiltrude was splendid beside him. In fact, one writer described her as possessing "surpassing majesty" as she stood adorned with gold beside her royal lover.

Their relationship might have been loveless, but it was definitely not childless. While Charles was off fighting in Aquitaine, Himiltrude brought their first and only child into the world. The kings of the time customarily named their sons after their fathers, signifying that their sons were their heirs and would carry on their legacy. Just as Charles had been named after his grandfather, Charles Martel, he named his baby Pepin after his own father. Sadly, it would soon become apparent that the boy was badly deformed. He would later be known as Pepin the Hunchback.

While Charles may never have wed Himiltrude at all, Carloman wasted no time in marrying the bride Pepin had chosen for him, another Frankish noblewoman named Gerberga. Carloman likely married her in 768 as well when he was only seventeen. In the span of three years, they became parents to two sons, the eldest of whom was also named Pepin. Carloman may have been the quieter of the two brothers, but his choice of name for his son signified that he was by no means ready to surrender his crown. Instead, Carloman was convinced that young Pepin would someday be co-king alongside Charles's son of the same name.

Once again, after the Aquitanians were defeated and the two young princes were born, the kings may have come to blows if it hadn't been for a new diplomatic mission. And this one would change Charles's home life dramatically.

Desiderata, the Lombard Princess

In 756, the death of King Aistulf of the Lombards had precipitated chaos in the Lombard Kingdom. Aistulf's rule had been ambitious, as evidenced by his repeated bids to claim the papal lands, but when he died, he left his kingdom without a strong heir. The first claim to the throne would have lain with his brother, Ratchis. Ratchis, however, had moved to Monte Carlo and taken up a monk's habit. Accordingly, the dukes of the Lombard Kingdom all had their eyes on the throne.

It was the duke of modern-day Tuscany who moved most decisively. His name was Desiderius, and he amassed an army, setting his sights on the throne of the Lombards. With King Pepin the Short of the Franks still occupied with fighting the Aquitanians, there was nowhere for Pope Stephen II to run, and he could only watch in horror as civil war loomed among the Lombards.

But Desiderius had other foes to deal with. In the face of Aistulf's death, Ratchis did the unthinkable: he revoked his vows and announced his own claim to the throne. His leap from monk to king was viewed as a terrible sin by the Catholic Church, in whose eyes the monastic vows were meant to be lifelong.

As Italy teetered on the brink of civil war, Desiderius realized that he and Pope Paul I (Stephen's successor in 757) had a common enemy: Ratchis. Ratchis wanted the same throne that Desiderius did, and he had spurned the Church that Paul now stood for. Setting aside his ambitions for the Papal States for now, Desiderius turned to the pope and offered him a truce—and a deal. He would surrender some Lombard towns to the pope's control if Paul would offer Desiderius his support and acknowledge him as the king of the Lombards. Ready to get his revenge on Ratchis, Paul was quick to accept Desiderius's offer. An uneasy peace was forged between the papacy and the Lombards, and Ratchis wisely decided to flee, leaving the throne open for Desiderius, who quickly seized power and became the king.

The relationship between the papacy and the Lombards, unfortunately, would not remain so stable. Desiderius never lost his thirst for the Papal States, and with no other major enemies to occupy him, Pope Paul I was well aware that the Lombard king could invade at any moment. Unfortunately for Paul, his only real ally, Pepin, would spend the rest of his reign embroiled in the conflict with Aquitaine. After Paul's death in 767, Desiderius went as far as to interfere with the papal succession, crowning a pope of his own choosing, who reigned only briefly before he was rejected by the Romans.

It was only when Charles took the throne, and Aquitaine had finally been subdued, that the new pope, also named Stephen, began to see a glimmer of hope against Rome's old foe. This time, however, help from Francia did not come in the form of armored knights riding in to rescue Stephen III. It came instead in the form of diplomacy, and it was not Charles who brought the diplomatic mission to Italy but his mother, Bertrada.

It's unclear who exactly initiated the negotiations of peace between the Franks and the Lombards, Desiderius or Bertrada. Both had valid reasons for seeking something more solid than the unhappy truce between the Lombards and the papacy. Desiderius had no desire to make an enemy of Francia, as that had been Aistulf's fatal mistake. And Bertrada, impressed though she must have been by Charles's conquest in Aquitaine, was well aware that her son was no match for Desiderius just yet. He had only been king for two years, after all, and the rebellion in Aquitaine had already been all but crushed when he took the throne.

So it was that the queen mother of the Franks and the king of the Lombards came together in peace, and they solidified that peace in the most medieval way possible: by marriage. Desiderius had fathered at least four lovely daughters, and he chose one of them to be sent to Francia to marry a man who had been the enemy of her people. Her name is somewhat disputed. History knows her well as Desiderata, which may not be accurate; some sources suggest that "Desiderata" was recorded in error and actually referred to Desiderius himself and that her real name was Gerperga. This name, however, may have arisen through confusion between Charles's wife and Carloman's wife, who was named Gerberga.

Either way, the Lombard princess was likely little more than a teenager when she found herself being sent across the mountains with the Frankish queen mother to be united in marriage to an unknown king. One can only speculate how frightened the girl must have been as she traveled to Francia. She must have heard the stories of how Pepin had put the Lombards to flight and butchered her own people, and now, she had no choice but to marry his son.

The pope was no more pleased with the marriage than Desiderata was. He had hoped that Charles would come charging gloriously over the mountains and defeat the Lombards in battle, not marry one of their princesses. However, there was little that he could do to stop the wedding from happening, and so, King Charles of Francia married Princess Desiderata of the Lombards in 770. To do so, he had to put Himiltrude aside.

It's difficult to ascertain what Charles's marriage to Desiderata was really like. There are no real records of the personal nature of their relationship, yet it's no leap of the imagination to think that there couldn't have been much love between them. Desiderata could have done worse than Charles—at least he was young and handsome—but both of them had still been forced into marriage likely against their will. It's possible that neither had seen the other before their wedding day, and Charles would probably have been much happier to ride into Italy and subdue the Lombards with the edge of the sword rather than marry into their family.

Either way, there appears to have been little intimacy between them. In their one year of marriage, Desiderata would bear no children.

The Brink of War

It's easy to speculate that Charles's loss of Himiltrude and his marriage to Desiderata did little other than to fuel his hatred for Carloman. Carloman was married with two healthy sons and was still in control of most of Francia, despite the fact that it was Charles who had had to fight the Aquitanians alone, Charles whose child was born with a deformity, and Charles who'd been forced to put aside his wife and marry a Lombard princess.

By 770, Charles and Carloman's relationship had soured dramatically. Once again, civil war loomed. With the rebellion crushed and the Lombards dealt with, Charles had no one to fight except his brother. It's possible that Francia might have descended into civil war or that Carloman would have suffered the same destiny as his ill-fated uncle of the same name: being quietly forced into life as a monk.

But before any of this could come to pass, tragedy struck Carloman and his small family in 771. Despite being only twenty years old, Carloman died out of the blue. By all accounts, his death came about as the result of natural causes, perhaps a catastrophic hemorrhage. He left Gerberga and their two sons behind, as well as an empty throne.

The vacuum left by Carloman's death was one that Charles was only too eager to fill, even though it was not rightfully his. In the years that followed, the fight for Carloman's throne would swallow up several nations into its sour belly—and it would begin to pave the way for Charles's rise from co-king of Francia to Holy Roman emperor.

Chapter 4 – To the Pope's Rescue

A 15th-century depiction of Charlemagne and Pope Adrian I.
https://commons.wikimedia.org/wiki/File:Charlemagne_and_Pope_Adrian_I.jpg

The tragic early death of Carloman would shake the foundations of several countries, France and Italy among them. Yet no one was as unexpectedly and harshly affected as Gerberga and her two little boys.

Like everyone else, Gerberga hadn't expected Carloman to die so soon, and his death shattered her world. Whatever her feelings had been for her husband, he had provided her with protection and stability in a world where noblewomen and their children could easily become targets. She knew that Charles hated Carloman, but the latter had held enough power that Charles hesitated to attack him outright. Now, Carloman was dead, and Gerberga's protection against Charles was gone.

If it hadn't been for Charles, Gerberga's life might not have changed much after Carloman's death. She would have become a regent for her son Pepin, who would have taken his rightful place as king in due time when he was old enough. In the meantime, Gerberga would have been one of the most powerful women in the known world. But she knew that Charles would have no respect for the rightful succession of his brother's throne. She wasn't sure what he would do to her or to her two toddlers (the eldest of whom was only three years old), but she knew that it wouldn't be good. She had to get away from Francia if she wanted her son to be king—or even to survive at all.

As Charles was hugely popular in Francia itself, Gerberga knew that it would be no use at all to attempt to find sanctuary in her home country. Instead, she could think of only one ally strong enough to protect her and her boys from Charles: Desiderius, the king of the Lombards. His truce with Charles, despite Bertrada's best efforts, had been short-lived. A few months before Carloman died, Charles had rejected Desiderius and his people on every conceivable level, as he had divorced the Lombard princess.

Divorcing Desiderata

Divorce, as we know it today, did not exist in the Middle Ages. The concept of simply ending a marriage was utterly unthinkable at the time; marriage vows were truly binding for life. And while lower-born people, such as serfs and peasants, could escape the notice of the Church and simply abandon their spouses, the nobility did not have that choice.

There was no legal way to actually end a marriage in Charles's time, no matter how intolerable it may have felt. However, a marriage could be terminated if it could be proven that it had never been valid in the first place. This process, called annulment, was the only way that noble-born people could escape from a union that they could no longer bear. There were a variety of reasons why marriages could be annulled, including infidelity, marriage under false pretenses, or consanguinity—being too closely related. This was a particular favorite of nobility at the time since most nobles were related to each other somehow, and the Church officially disallowed marriages between people who shared any ancestors in seven generations.

Another reason for annulment, however, was infertility. This may sound strange, but in an era where producing a viable heir could mean the difference between decades of peace and years of turmoil for an entire country, fertility was vitally important in noble marriages. Birthing an heir was a massive part of every queen's responsibility. And here is where Desiderius's daughter appears to have failed Charles.

After a year of marriage, Desiderata had still failed to give birth to an heir for Charles, and he turned to Pope Stephen III, asking for the marriage to be annulled. Stephen was very ill at the time, but he was more than happy to destroy the alliance between the Franks and the Lombards, as it was an alliance he had never approved of, one that could have meant disaster if the Lombards ever decided to invade Rome as Desiderius often threatened to do. He briskly annulled the marriage, and Desiderata was sent back to Italy, a rejected queen, forced out of the title she'd never asked for.

It's hard to say exactly why Charles really wanted to end his marriage to Desiderata. He did have a valid reason to be concerned about his lack of an heir; with Carloman's two boys as healthy as ever, Charles was feeling pressured to have a son of his own who would be a more capable king than Pepin the Hunchback. However, poor Desiderata had hardly been given a chance to prove herself as a fertile queen, having been married to Charles for only a year.

Another possibility was that Charles had found a different woman and realized that marrying her would be a much smarter move politically than staying with Desiderata. This seems likely, as he had hardly sent Desiderata way from him before he was standing in a wedding ceremony. Her name was Hildegard of the Vinzgau, and she was only about thirteen years old at the time. However, marrying her would win Charles an ally he desperately wanted. Hildegard's father was a powerful count who owned a vast amount of land within Carloman's part of Francia. He would have been a dangerous enemy if he had allied with Carloman, but when Charles married Hildegard, he turned the count into a useful friend. Perhaps divorcing Desiderata was done explicitly in order to marry Hildegard and build an alliance that could help Charles if he decided to make war on Carloman after all.

One can easily speculate that Charles truly could not tolerate living with Desiderata. Marrying her had hardly been his own idea after all. Perhaps their relationship had simply devolved to such a disgusting point that Charles could no longer stand it and would do anything to escape from their relationship, even to the point of damaging his truce with Desiderius.

On the other hand, it's entirely possible that breaking the peace with the Lombard Kingdom was exactly what Charles had wanted. Charles was hungry to expand his power. He had already conquered Pepin's old enemies, the Aquitanians; he may have been spoiling to do the same to the Lombards.

Either way, divorcing Desiderata was a disgusting insult to Desiderius, destroying what little friendliness there had been between the Franks and the Lombards. The atmosphere was as ripe for war as dry undergrowth for a wildfire. All that it needed to ignite was one small spark—and that spark came with the death of Carloman on December 4th, 771.

War Begins with the Lombards

Gerberga's flight to the Lombard capital of Pavia could not have been an easy one. There were only two ways for her to reach Italy in safety: either by sea or by land. The sea routes were treacherous at best, made almost impassable in winter; the mountain passes would have been similarly perilous in midwinter. She could not have hoped to cross the mountains by carriage. Instead, she would have had to ride, with her one- and three-year-old sons too young to control their own ponies.

It's difficult to imagine how hard this journey must have been for Gerberga. For starters, she was little more than a child herself; if she had wed at thirteen, the traditional age for princesses, she would have been only seventeen or eighteen at this point. Winter was cruel, and the road was long. It would have been a grueling trek across a frigid, friendless landscape for this young mother and her little boys.

Yet somehow, Gerberga managed to reach the court of Desiderius, where she was welcomed with caution. Desiderius knew her as the sister-in-law of his chief enemy now that Charlemagne had rejected Desiderata, but he could also see an opportunity in her desperation. When Gerberga begged him for protection, Desiderius realized that he could provide much more. In fact, if he could, he would try to make her two sons the kings of Francia. He recognized the fact that Charles was a dangerous enemy. He also realized that having a client king of his on the throne of Francia would give him an important ally on the very doorstep of his enemy. If he could get little Pepin onto the throne of Francia, he could be Pepin's regent, controlling a large part of Charles's country. Or, even better, Charles would be engaged in a civil war in his own land and leave the Lombard Kingdom alone.

For Pepin to be made king, however, the papacy would have to be on board with Desiderius's plans. And Desiderius's relationship with the papacy had done nothing but decline since he meddled with their affairs after Paul's death in 767. Stephen III viewed Desiderius as a grave enemy. Yet the Lombard king was as wily as he was powerful, and even though he hadn't been able to determine the next pope, he still had friends in Rome. Stephen III was sickly and uninvolved, and Desiderius hoped that perhaps one of his Roman sympathizers would be able to overrule the pope and show the Lombards some support. His ultimate goal was for Carloman's sons to be anointed as kings, just as Carloman himself, as well as Charles, had been back when Pepin had first put the Lombards to flight in the 750s.

His plan might just have worked if not for another ill-timed death that would ultimately doom Desiderius and all of his schemes. In 772, shortly after Gerberga arrived at Pavia with her children, Pope Stephen III died. Desiderius scrambled to try to intervene in the papal succession once more; however, he was unsuccessful, and to his horror, Stephen was replaced by Pope Adrian I. Adrian was as anti-Lombard as it was possible to be, and he had no love for Desiderius.

Desiderius quickly had to abandon any hope of getting Pepin and his little brother anointed. Instead, he left his schemes of seizing Frankish land behind and focused on protecting his own. Back in 757, when Desiderius had first become the king of the Lombards, he had done so by bargaining with the pope of the time, offering to surrender certain cities to him in exchange for papal support against Ratchis. Conniving as he was, Desiderius had never actually surrendered those cities to Rome, a fact that Stephen had conveniently ignored. Adrian, on the other hand, did not plan on turning a blind eye. He confronted Desiderius, demanding that the Lombard king keep his word and give up several cities in

Ravenna to papal control.

Desiderius would not be so easily cowed. He had never given in to the popes' demands before. Surely, he could conquer Adrian just as he'd conquered the popes before him. Desiderius immediately refused to surrender the cities; instead, he decided that it was high time to launch the invasion he'd been threatening to begin for decades. He attacked the Papal States themselves, and Adrian found himself cornered just as Stephen II had been in the time of Aistulf.

At first, Adrian was determined to handle Desiderius on his own. He was the pope, after all—one of the most powerful men in Europe—and he was sure he could protect his lands and people against some petty Lombard king. But it quickly became evident that Adrian's armies were no match for Desiderius. As he faced the very real threat of losing Rome entirely to the invading king, Adrian realized that he had no choice. After holding out against Desiderius for several months, he began to look for an ally to turn to. And like the popes before him, Adrian would see that his only hope was the king of the Franks.

In 773, word reached King Charles from Rome, and he met with Roman ambassadors at Thionville. At the time, he had just returned from his first hard war with the Saxons (which will be explored in a later chapter). The war had shown that he was not only a battle-hardened warrior, who was capable of suppressing revolts in his own realm, but that he also was a king who could subdue entire nations. What was more, he had just repudiated Desiderata, so his relationship with Desiderius was clearly no longer a friendly one.

Even though Adrian hadn't had much communication with Charles yet, he suspected that the young king might prove to be a strong ally for the Church. Charles had not only conquered the Saxons, but he had also Christianized them, sometimes brutally. Whether or not he actually followed the values of the Church was one thing, but it was clear that his political alliance lay with the Catholic Church.

For those reasons, it was little surprise, although it must have been of great relief to Adrian, that Charles responded swiftly, ready to fulfill his role as the protector of Rome, despite the fact that Desiderius's own ambassadors had also traveled to Thionville to meet with him. Charles was no friend of Desiderius. Still, his appetite for war had been tempered by experience, and he hoped he would be able to cool Desiderius's temper without violence. There was little hope of solving their problems with diplomacy, so Charles decided to try bribery instead. He offered Desiderius a bribe of an unknown amount of gold in exchange for the cities that Adrian demanded.

Desiderius, however, would not be cowed by a young Frankish king. He had a trump card up his sleeve: Gerberga and her sons. If he could beat Charles in battle and force Adrian to anoint Carloman's son Pepin as king, he could put a client king on the throne of Francia. Desiderius was ready for war, and Charles's earlier reluctance vanished. There was nothing else to do besides to march an army over the Alps and meet Desiderius in battle.

The Siege of Pavia

As the winter of 773 approached, Charles gathered his powerful standing army and approached the Alps. He was aided by a strong and experienced commander: his uncle Bernard, a son of Charles Martel himself. It wasn't long before their invasion was met with strenuous resistance. At the very feet of the Italian Alps, Desiderius had set his army in array, ready to do battle with the Franks.

Charles had grown wiser during his battles with the Saxons. Instead of marching directly on Desiderius as he had done with the Aquitanians, the young king started to look for a weakness. He would find the same weakness as one of the first Frankish kings did hundreds of years before when meeting with the intimidating Attila the Hun: Desiderius had failed to protect his flanks. A sneak attack on the flanks of the army could prove devastating, and so, Charles and Bernard split up and sneaked down through the frosted mountainside, then pinched Desiderius's army between the two of them and fell upon the Lombard flanks with unexpected savagery.

The battle was brief. The Lombard army was devastated, scattered across the snow by Charles's powerful army, and Desiderius had no choice but to flee. His border shattered, he realized that his only hope was to protect his capital, Pavia.

Founded in 220 BCE as a Roman settlement, then named Ticinum, Pavia was already more than five centuries old by the time Desiderius rode back to it with his tail between his legs. It had already had a long history haunted by ignominy. Always a powerful city in Italy, it had even been the seat of Romulus Augustus, the last emperor of the old Western Roman Empire. He had been defeated there in 476 CE, and now, Desiderius had to face the grim reality that his fate could be very much the same. The last emperor of Rome had sought safety at Pavia, and the last king of the Lombards now did the same.

Withdrawing his army and people into Pavia, Desiderius locked its great gates and dug in, preparing for the siege that was now inevitable. Charles and Bernard marched up to the city and took their time in laying a siege. There was no need for them to catapult great rocks into the walls or mount ladders and grappling hooks up to its towering battlements; they had a far greater weapon than that: starvation. Simply by preventing anyone from leaving the city, the Franks could secure their victory.

Well, almost anyone. One Lombard did escape the beleaguered capital, and it was Adelchis, the single son of King Desiderius and the one-time brother-in-law of Charles. He fled Pavia as fast as he could ride, not simply for cowardly reasons. Instead, he had an important mission: he had to protect the one great asset that could be Desiderius's last hope, Carloman's family. Gerberga and her two sons were holed up in Verona, a hundred miles away from the siege.

Upon reaching Verona, Adelchis realized that the Lombards' situation was utterly dire. They were surrounded by powerful Franks, and Charles had proven to be more than a match for Desiderius. If Adelchis was going to find a way to beat his ex-brother-in-law, he was going to need more than just the late Carloman's son and apparent rightful heir to the throne of Francia. He'd need a powerful ally, one that could face both the Franks and the Romans.

The most obvious choice was an old enemy of Rome, the Byzantine, or Eastern Roman, Empire. While its split from the ancient Western Roman Empire in 285 CE was peaceful, a decision made by Emperor Diocletian when he realized that the Roman Empire as a whole was too large for one emperor to administrate, the split had proven to open a great rift between the two halves. Everything about the Byzantine Empire was different from their Roman counterparts, not least their religion, as they were Eastern Orthodox Christians instead of Roman Catholics. The Byzantine emperor would have no qualms about facing the Roman pope.

But Adelchis's efforts proved to be too little, too late. Even as he begged the Byzantines for help and struggled to scrape together an army of his own, Adelchis's enemy was hot on his trail. Leaving the capable Bernard in charge of the siege at Pavia, Charles rode after the young prince, determined to stamp out every last hope that Desiderius had. Verona fell quickly before Charles's onslaught. Adelchis once more abandoned the conquered city, fleeing to Constantinople, and Carloman's little family was left without any protection from their vengeful uncle.

It would appear, however, that Charles stripped them of their titles yet spared their lives. It's uncertain exactly what happened to Gerberga and her two little boys, but there is no record of their deaths. As was Charles's habit, they were likely forced to join an abbey and live out their lives in quiet anonymity, even though the blood of princes and kings flowed in their veins.

With the sons of both Carloman and Desiderius dealt with, Charles returned to Pavia, which was still under siege. It would remain that way for around ten months. There was no need for dramatic battles this time. Charles and Bernard waited calmly for starvation to do its work. In fact, Charles himself didn't spend all his time at Pavia either. He journeyed three hundred miles to celebrate Easter in Rome in the spring of 774, where he was gratefully received by Adrian.

As summer came in green abundance to the foothills of the Alps, the citizens of Pavia failed to experience nature's beauty and bounty. Instead, they were starving. Desiderius could watch them die no longer. He had no choice but to surrender, and Charles triumphantly plucked the crown from the emaciated Lombard king. Desiderius may have expected that he would be forced to pay tribute to Charles or rule underneath him, but Charles was not content with simply forcing Desiderius into submission. Instead, he wanted Desiderius's titles for his own. The last king of the Lombards was cloistered and stripped of his titles, and Charles had himself crowned as the king of the Franks and Lombards. It was around this time that people first began to call him Charles the Great or Carolus Magnus, a name that would eventually be shortened into its modern-day version of Charlemagne.

The remaining Lombards were divided on what they could do now that Charlemagne was ruling over them. Some dukes wisely allied themselves with Charlemagne and lived peacefully under his reign; others couldn't face life under the Franks and fled over the mountains to modern-day Genoa. Still others, however, waited in the hopes that Adelchis would return from Constantinople. The young man was treated well there and eventually did get the military support he'd wanted. Years later, in 787, Byzantine

Empress Irene would attempt to cultivate an alliance between the Byzantines and Charlemagne by soliciting his daughter's hand in marriage to her son. When her offer was rejected, she gave Adelchis an army and sent him off to attack Italy.

Adelchis returned at last to be the new hope for his people, but their hope would turn out to be false. The Lombard duke of Benevento, Grimoald III, had been more or less forced to fight on Charlemagne's side, and together with the Frankish forces, he soundly defeated Adelchis. The Lombard prince's campaign was over before it had even started, as he fought only one battle that was such a resounding defeat that it brought about an official end to the Lombard Kingdom forever. It rallied briefly a few years later when Grimoald himself attempted to throw off the Frankish shackles that bound him, but Charlemagne's sons quickly defeated him.

As for Adelchis, no one knows his ultimate fate. He may have died on the battlefield or fled once again to live out his days in Constantinople, a failed hero without any titles.

Chapter 5 – The One Defeat

Conquering the Lombard Kingdom placed Charlemagne in charge of one of the largest kingdoms in Europe. He had established himself already as a force to be reckoned with, but his appetite for expansion was never satiated. In fact, it only grew, and with everything peaceful on the Italian front, Charlemagne was seeking a new direction in which to expand. He was already involved in the Saxon Wars in the east; now, he turned his eyes to the south. And this tumultuous part of Europe was ripe for conquest.

The State of the South

Ever since his first conquest in 769, the thoroughly subdued people of Aquitaine had been meek and biddable. This was helped by the fact that Charlemagne appointed several of his most powerful allies as dukes over the surrounding areas, such as Toulouse and Bordeaux. But while Aquitaine was behaving itself nicely, Gascony was quite another affair.

Lupus II, the duke who had so willingly betrayed Hunald, which had led to the conquest of Aquitaine in 769, had quickly submitted to Charlemagne. Now, however, he had grown tired of submitting to marauding Franks. He would not go belly up again so easily.

While Gascony officially belonged to Francia, the reality was very different. Its people—largely members of the Basques—saw themselves as independent warriors who would not be so easily shunted around by some Frankish king. The Basques were an ancient people. They endure to this day as a unique ethnic group, with mysterious origins and a culture that grew in almost complete isolation, leading to enormous distinctions from their surrounding peoples. Everything from their language to their DNA is unrelated to the surrounding tribes.

The Basques were a proud, independent, pagan race in the late 8th century, and Charlemagne, with his orderly empire and Christianization policies, was determined to change that. He was eager to suppress them, trampling them down into an easy highway all the way to the Pyrenees, which formed the southern border of France with Spain. If he could cross the Pyrenees, he stood to invade the lands that lay even farther south. And these were particularly appealing to Charlemagne as they were ruled by some of the greatest enemies of the Roman Catholic Church: the Muslims.

Ever since Charles Martel had faced the Umayyad Caliphate on the battlefield of Tours nearly fifty years before, Muslims and Christians had been locked in a continuing battle. Charles Martel had succeeded in driving them back out of France, but they were still in control of almost the entire Iberian Peninsula. However, these Muslims were not all members of the Umayyad Caliphate. Instead, many of them were Abbasids, and they were no friends of the Umayyads.

The governor of Hispania—modern-day Spain, including some other territories on the Iberian Peninsula—was Sulayman al-Arabi, an Abbasid. He was feeling increasingly threatened by the emir of Cordoba, an Umayyad, and he knew that he needed to find a way to keep his lands under his possession before the sweeping Umayyad hordes took over. Forming an alliance with two other powerful Abbasids—Abu Taur of Huesca and Husayn of Zaragoza—he agreed with them that they needed to seek an alliance with another power. Any power, so long as it would stand against the Umayyads.

As surprised as Charles must have been to receive Muslim ambassadors, he was eager to find out more when he realized that they were seeking a military alliance. Fighting alongside the Abbasids could provide the perfect opportunity to crush Gascony. What was more, Charles was seeking to expand into Hispania itself, driving back the Muslims, starting with the Umayyads, and growing an ever-greater Roman Catholic empire.

In 778, Charles decided to accept al-Arabi's offer of alliance. He knew that he would be facing his most formidable enemy to date if he marched on the Muslims, and so, he mustered the biggest army he could. Pulling every spare man into the massive ranks of his power, he marched at last over the Pyrenees. Sending one half of his army over the eastern part of the mountains and leading the rest over the western part, he crossed through the passes without mishap, soon arriving in Hispania to a warm welcome from al-Arabi.

Al-Arabi was ready to do battle at once. Their first target was Zaragoza. While its leader, Husayn, ostensibly was an ally of al-Arabi's, Charlemagne's enemy had beaten him to the city. The Umayyad Caliphate had sent one of its most important generals to secure Zaragoza: Thalaba Ibn Obeid. But it would seem that Ibn Obeid had underestimated Husayn's power. For whatever reason, he was unable to subdue Zaragoza, and Husayn clapped him in irons and imprisoned him.

Charlemagne and al-Arabi likely didn't know this, though. They marched on Zaragoza to liberate it from the Umayyads only to find it firmly under the control of Husayn, whose ego had become rather inflated by his recent capture of Ibn Obeid. Having conquered the Umayyads all by himself, Husayn decided that he didn't need help, especially not from some Christian Frankish king with an ulterior motive. He refused to allow Charlemagne and al-Arabi entrance into the city.

Charlemagne was enraged. Al-Arabi had promised him that controlling Zaragoza would be a walk in the park thanks to Husayn's involvement, and now, he'd been betrayed by his new allies. Deciding he'd been wrong to ally himself with the Abbasids after all, Charlemagne arrested al-Arabi and laid siege to Zaragoza.

The siege, however, was short-lived. Husayn was stubborn, and Charlemagne had begun to realize that capturing Hispania with its messy politics wasn't going to be as easy as he had first assumed. After a month's siege, he reached a truce with Husayn, agreeing to leave the city alone in exchange for certain prisoners and a rather substantial amount of gold and treasure. Husayn gratefully accepted, and Charlemagne turned around, setting his sights on his real target: Gascony.

With al-Arabi still in chains with his army, Charlemagne set about subduing the Basques who lived on both sides of the Pyrenees. His goal was not so much to capture the territories—officially, they belonged to him already—as it was to simply break the spirits of the Basque people. His soldiers were permitted to do as they pleased, and they pleased to destroy everything. They crashed into towns full of innocent people, setting houses and farms alight, driving women and children through the streets, razing entire villages to the ground. Homes, lives, and businesses were taken, destroyed, and left as scattered ashes and black scars of charred earth.

The remaining Basques were relentlessly oppressed, abused in every way by Charlemagne and his soldiers. They were hopelessly mistreated, and to add insult to injury, Charlemagne did not spare their capital, Pamplona. He did not destroy this city; after all, it was important to an economy that now had to pay him tribute. Instead, he simply stripped away its defenses, laying it bare and vulnerable to any form of invasion. He had its walls—the pride and protection of any medieval city—pulled down. Pamplona was left as naked and beaten as a peasant in the stocks.

This would prove to be a fatal mistake. Pulling down Pamplona's walls had been easy, but breaking the spirit of its people would turn out to be all but impossible. Instead of growing submissive, the Basques became bitter and angry. Their duke was determined not to give in the way he'd done nearly a decade before. And while the Basques could not hope to meet Charlemagne in a pitched battle, there was another way that they could get back at him for all he had done to their people.

Their plans were enabled at last when they received help from a fellow enemy of Charlemagne, the family of Sulayman al-Arabi. He was still being dragged around with Charlemagne's army, a prize prisoner, like some captive wild animal for the masses to gawk at. They were determined to get him back, and the Basques were more than ready to help.

So, even as Charlemagne plundered and pillaged wherever he would, his one and only downfall was being plotted in the mountainsides of the Pyrenees.

The Battle of Roncevaux Pass

By the warm summer of August 778, Charlemagne decided that his southern campaign was over. He may not have won Zaragoza as he'd hoped, but the Basques had been thoroughly defeated, and the governor of Hispania was with him in chains. Saxony was calling him west for further warfare, and he would later return to conquer Hispania. It was time for him to go home.

Charlemagne began to lead his vast, bloated army back over the Pyrenees, this time keeping them all together in one trampling, destructive mass of men and horses. The baggage train, in particular, was grossly swollen with prisoners and plunder. Huge amounts of treasure had been laden into carts drawn by beasts of burden. Charlemagne's army was a mighty one, but it was also massive and slow, and it crawled across the mountains under the heaviness of its power.

The Basques, on the other hand, were as quick as mountain goats on the rocky passes. Armed with spears and going on foot, they knew the landscape better than anyone, melting in and out of the mountains like wild animals. They knew that the perfect place for an ambush was the narrow Roncevaux Pass. Arraying themselves among the rocks and foliage, armed to the teeth and ready for vengeance, aided by Al-Arabi's family, the Basques waited.

Oblivious of the little army hidden in the rocks mere yards from them, Charlemagne's soldiers marched merrily through the pass, grown perhaps a little careless from the easy and wanton destruction they'd wrought on the Basques. The bloated baggage train trailed along behind, weighed down with treasure, prisoners, and provisions for the soldiers. Surrounding and following the baggage train was the rearguard, a considerable force of some of Charlemagne's best men who brought up the rear of the army and protected the baggage train. Charlemagne's rearguard was commanded by several of his most high-ranking officers, including Roland, the military governor of the Breton March. Charlemagne was confident that they would be able to protect his army against some unforeseen rear attack.

His confidence was misplaced, not so much because of the competence of the commanders but because of the unexpected savagery with which the Basques and their allies would fall upon him.

Hidden in the surroundings of Roncevaux Pass, the Basques and Abbasids waited, biding their time until the great mass of Charlemagne's army had passed by. When only the baggage train and the rearguard were in sight, they launched their attack in their unseen hundreds.

The first that the Frankish commanders knew of the ambush was the sound of javelins and arrows hissing through the air, then the deadly slap as sharp projectiles met human flesh. As screams rang out, the Frankish commanders frantically searched for an invisible enemy. They never had the time to organize any real defense. By the time the Franks realized that Basque and Abbasid soldiers were attacking them, their enemies were already pouring down from the mountainside, armed with spears, knives, and short swords. Charlemagne's men were surrounded in moments; the fighting was quick, brutal, and significantly one-sided. All of the training Charlemagne's commanders received, many of whom would have been raised with warfare in mind, proved to be no match for the surprise attack that now faced them. They began to die quickly.

The Battle of Roncevaux Pass was not so much a fight as it was a slaughter. The Frankish soldiers never really stood a chance, not against such a well-planned ambush driven by such a burning desire for revenge against all the evils Charlemagne and his men had committed against the Basque people. Every single member of the Frankish rearguard was killed. The rest of Charlemagne's army escaped relatively unscathed; the rearguard sacrificed itself in slowing down the Basques and Abbasids long enough for Charlemagne to get the rest of his men out of the pass and onto open ground, where no one would dare to face him in a pitched battle.

It was still a crushing defeat for the Franks. Even though the rearguard was a comparatively small part of Charlemagne's army, it had included some of his very best commanders, and there was some turmoil in Francia due to the death of so many high-ranking men. To add insult to injury, all of the treasure that Charlemagne had accumulated in that campaign—including the gold that Husayn had paid him to leave Zaragoza alone—had been carried off by the Basques. Perhaps worst of all, Sulayman al-Arabi had gone free.

His children had rescued him, and so, Charlemagne ended up not conquering the Abbasid rulers of Hispania, instead making a great enemy out of them. Sulayman al-Arabi himself, however, would not live long enough to be an enemy of Charlemagne. He was killed just two years later by the ever-treacherous Husayn of Zaragoza.

The Battle of Roncevaux Pass would go down in history as the only major defeat that Charlemagne would ever suffer. It was a tragedy in its time for the Franks, especially for Charlemagne, but throughout the rest of his long and warlike rule, Roncevaux Pass would be the only time he drank of the bitter draft of defeat. While not all of his battles would end in decisive victories, never again would he taste of it.

Unfortunately, while Charlemagne may have learned something from Roncevaux, he certainly did not learn how to treat his subjects better, especially those who were pagans or practiced any of the other traditional religions. His Christianization would always remain legendary in its brutality, and few people suffered more than the Basques. The Saxons would also be horrifically oppressed throughout the three decades of war that Charlemagne would wage against them.

The Battle of Roncevaux Pass would become the stuff of legend centuries after the end of Charlemagne's illustrious rule. In the 11th century, 300 years after the battle itself, it became the inspiration for *The Song of Roland,* an epic poem penned by some long-forgotten medieval poet, possibly Turold. The poem, a breathtaking 4,000 lines in length, was hugely popular throughout the late Middle Ages, and it remains the oldest surviving piece of Frankish literature. While its version of events is not fully historical—it glamorizes the Franks as tragic heroes, carefully omitting the brutalities committed against the Basques, and it also includes magical swords and some fictional characters—it remains an impressive and enduring piece of writing.

As for Charlemagne himself, he did not return swiftly to the site of his only defeat, but it remained a thorn in his side for decades. At the turn of the century, however, Charlemagne decided to finally deal with his unfinished business in the Pyrenees. He returned in a series of campaigns and won a belt of territory stretching across the northernmost part of modern-day Spain. This belt would serve as a buffer between Muslim Hispania and Christian Francia, and it became known as the Spanish Marches. It was composed of a series of tiny countries, little more than provinces. Most of these were absorbed by Spain or France at some point in history, now forming modern-day Catalonia, but one of these puny territories still endures as an independent country to this day.

The Principality of Andorra, located right on the border of France and Spain, considers its roots to lie in the edge of Charlemagne's sword. Andorra is a beautiful little place, filled with mountain valleys, and it serves as a hub of tourism and trade, thanks to its low taxes. It has only about half the square mileage of New York City, and its population numbers about the same as the town of Hammond, Indiana (around 77,000 people).

The Children of Hildegard

When Charlemagne returned to win the Spanish Marches around the year 800, he was not alone. In fact, Charlemagne himself did very little of the legwork in that campaign; most of the actual fighting was done by his son, Louis the Pious. Born in 778—the same year that his father suffered the defeat at Roncevaux—Louis was only one of many children that would be born to Charlemagne and his teenage bride, Hildegard.

Hildegard turned out to be a suitably fertile bride, which was highly satisfying to Charlemagne after the disappointment of Desiderata. Hildegard was only fourteen years old when she produced a legitimate heir in 772: a son named Charles the Younger. From there, she would have a child every year for four years running. In 773, she had another son, who was originally named Carloman.

In 774, Charlemagne and Hildegard had their first daughter, Adalheid; she was born during the Siege of Pavia and tragically died on the journey back to Francia. In 775, another daughter would follow, who was named Rotrude. Poor Hildegard would have a short break of a few years then, only giving birth again in 778. As if to make up for it, she had twins this time, both boys. They were named Louis and Lothair, but Lothair tragically died as a baby. The surviving boy, Louis, would become one of Charlemagne's most famous and important sons.

Before Hildegard's death in 784, she would give birth to three more children, all girls, named Bertha, Gisela, and Hildegarde. By the time she died, Hildegard had become the queen of one of the greatest territories in the whole of Europe. She was a mother to princes, princesses, and even kings. As Charlemagne's kingdom began to grow into an empire, he sought to further consolidate his power by crowning his sons as kings underneath him. In 781, the pope crowned two of Charlemagne's sons. Louis was crowned the king of Aquitaine at the tender age of three years old, while Carloman, aged eight, was crowned the king of Italy. At this point, Carloman was renamed Pepin. This was a clear message from Charlemagne that he considered Pepin to be the rightful heir to his throne. It also perhaps could have been a message saying that he now considered Himiltrude's son, Pepin the Hunchback, to be unworthy of his crown.

Charlemagne's beloved Hildegard turned out to be as perfect a queen as any medieval king could hope for. She accompanied him on most of his campaigns, pregnant and often with small children, enduring the unhappy circumstances of warfare as well as thousands of miles of uncomfortable travel. Having given Charlemagne nine children, she never birthed a stillborn or suffered a miscarriage, at least according to contemporary chroniclers.

Motherhood was not Hildegard's only calling. She was very much involved with the Church and distributed large amounts of her wealth to churches, abbeys, and monasteries. There is also evidence pointing to the fact that Hildegard was more than just a pretty face. Although contemporaries praised her beauty, which they may not have had a choice in doing, considering she was married to the most powerful man in their part of the world, she appears to have been intimately involved in Charlemagne's administration, helping with some of his governmental decisions. Today, some churches consider her a saint.

A horrific blow came to Charlemagne in 783. Hildegard had recently given birth to her last child, a little girl named after her mother. The child was born sometime in 782, and this time, Hildegard's fertility would prove to be her downfall. The queen's youthful body, which had birthed nine babies and was only 25 years old, could take no more. The birth was a traumatic one, and while Hildegard held on bravely, she ultimately did not survive it. She died on the last day of April and was buried on May Day at an abbey in Metz, where candles were burned on her grave every day for years afterward at Charlemagne's bidding.

Chapter 6 – The Burning of the Sacred Places

Ary Scheffer's 19th-century depiction of Charlemagne accepting the submission of Widukind at Paderborn.
https://commons.wikimedia.org/wiki/File:Charlemagne_742_814_receiving_the_submissi on_of_Witikind_at_Paderborn_in_785_Ary_Schefferr_1795_1858.jpg

September 778 must have been one of the hardest times of Charlemagne's life. A frigid French winter descended upon his army, which was still a long way from home, and they had already traveled the 500 miles from Roncevaux to Auxerre. If Charlemagne was heading to his usual seat at Aachen, he still had 300 miles to go; even if he was going to Paris, he still had 100 miles left to travel. It must have seemed like a very long way to the disheartened Frankish king who'd just buried many of his best commanders and closest friends. He had also just suffered his first and only major defeat.

At Auxerre, Charlemagne began to demobilize his giant army, and we can only imagine that his thoughts were set on the comforts of home. He'd been ruling for ten years and spent most of them in active warfare. But his warring days were far from over. In fact, they were just beginning, and when Charlemagne was at Auxerre, he learned that his fighting for the year was not yet done. Word came to him from the northeast. The Saxons were revolting—again.

The Saxons

This wild, warlike Germanic tribe had been a prolific and intimidating people for centuries. Originating along the North Sea coasts of Germany, the Netherlands, and Denmark, they had threatened all kinds of European powers, from the ancient Romans to the Vikings, and now, they were becoming a thorn in the side of the Carolingian Empire.

Sadly, little is really known about the Saxons and their culture, and their side of history's story has seldom been told. We know that they were named *Saxons* after their choice of weapon: the *seax*, a brutal, short, nimble sword that often spilled the guts of those who considered themselves more civilized, and at close quarters to boot. They spoke a Teutonic language that would become the precursor to the English you're reading right now. Unfortunately for us, the Saxons did not write. They were an illiterate people, and so, their only surviving contemporary histories are those of their enemies.

The earliest records of the Saxons, as with many of these tribes that had no use for the written word, belong to the ancient Romans. As the Roman Empire expanded into Gaul, the Saxons resisted strenuously, and they would be a thorn in the Romans' side until the very end of the empire. Britannica (modern-day Great Britain) was a hotbed for Roman-Saxon conflict, as the Saxons were expansionists as well. Childeric I, the Merovingian king who fought Attila the Hun alongside the Romans, would be one of many Frankish kings to fight the Saxons. He was a part of one of the last Roman armies to wage war on this fierce tribe.

The Saxons also practiced paganism, worshiping a variety of deities related to the earth and other parts of their surroundings. There are also some parallels with the Norse gods. Trees were particularly important in their religion, as well as Irminsul pillars, sacred monuments to their gods. Sacrifices were important as well, including some instances of human sacrifice. This ancient religion was largely separate from the Christianity that was creeping steadily throughout the world, and it touched every aspect of Saxon culture.

To the growing Roman Catholic Church, the presence of such a large pagan society was practically inexcusable. Widespread efforts were made to convert the Saxons, some of them in the form of peaceful missions, others in oppressive bouts of warfare.

The mission of Boniface was one of the first steps toward the Christianization of Saxony. In the early 8th century, a nobleman from the Christian Saxon Kingdom of Wessex named Wynfrith approached the Roman pope, determined to make a dangerous foray into the heart of the Saxons' country. The pope gave Wynfrith his blessing, changing his name to Boniface.

Boniface was well into his middle age by the time he reached Saxony, but his older age could not suppress his religious zeal. He was described as a blunt man, tactless at times and grumpy, and eager with his ax; he felled numerous sacred Saxon trees. However, Boniface and his followers did not carry weapons.

Building churches wherever he went, Boniface baptized many Saxons, but Christianity didn't quite stick. A group of pagan Saxons fell upon him and his companions deep into Saxony in 754. It is unclear whether they were simply bandits or seeking to destroy this change to their way of life. Either way, the result was the same. The unarmed clergymen were all killed.

As a result, by the time Charlemagne's rule began, the Saxons were still largely pagan. They remained the carbon opposites of the Rome-loving Franks with their literate kings and orderly ways. To make matters worse, the border of Francia and Saxony was poorly defined, often running through open country with no real way for the local people to know which land belonged to the Saxons and which to the Franks. This caused crime and turmoil in the area, as the enemy tribes murdered one another and sabotaged property.

It was clear that the Saxons were a problem that Charlemagne would have to deal with sooner or later. And he did so at the very first opportunity.

The Saxon Wars Begin

In the first few years of his rule, Charlemagne was very much occupied with internal Frankish troubles. The suppression of the Aquitanian rebellion was his first order of business, and it was rapidly followed by his sneaky attempts to get rid of Carloman.

Four years into his reign, though, in 772, things had settled for the young king. Carloman had died, the Aquitanians were thoroughly suppressed, and yet Charlemagne's appetite for warfare and violence was barely getting warmed up. The logical next step was to turn to his most troublesome border, that with Saxony.

Gathering a powerful army, Charlemagne lost no time in marching northeast to Saxony. The Saxons were warlike in their own right, but they stood little chance against Charlemagne's organized army. Few could ever stand against him in a pitched battle; the Saxons, it would appear, had no hope at all. Charlemagne mowed them down, burned their towns, cut down their villages, and finally reached one of their most treasured sites of all: an Irminsul pillar. These great wooden pillars were utterly central to the Saxon faith. Its name meant "world-pillar," and it was related to Yggdrasil, the "world-tree" that anchored and connected all the worlds of the Saxons' belief. To remove that Irminsul pillar was to cut down a great cornerstone of Saxon culture. And that was exactly what Charlemagne did when he came upon one such pillar near Paderborn, the home of the Engrians, whom he beat into submission with the edge of the sword. They were already a defeated people when Charlemagne cut down their pillar. And while many were baptized into Christianity, one must consider that very few of them did this willingly. Perhaps some, having seen their Irminsul fall, clutched at the new hope that was offered them, but many had seen their fellow Saxons die at the edge of Frankish blades and knew that they had no real choice.

Charlemagne's campaign was going well, and he probably could have pushed even farther into Saxony if it was not for the fact that Rome needed him. In 774, he received word from beleaguered Pope Adrian and headed off to fight Desiderius of the Lombards, leaving Saxony to its own devices.

With the great king thus out of the way, the Saxons were finally free to take their revenge, and they did so with desperate violence. Saxon raids were launched on all kinds of Frankish settlements and garrisons. Even the church at Fritzlar, which had been built decades before under the supervision of Boniface himself, was threatened; according to the chroniclers, however, it was miraculously spared from fires. Many other buildings were not so lucky. Franks were killed, their property plundered, and the Saxons felt they were finally taking back what Charlemagne had stolen.

A particularly brutal fight took place when a group of Saxons disguised themselves as Frankish soldiers. They smuggled themselves into the Frankish ranks while their enemies were out on patrol and marched right into the Frankish camp. As soon as the men had let down their guard, the Saxons turned against them and took their revenge. The Franks were taken completely unawares. Many of them were killed before the Saxons made their escape.

Charlemagne, freshly back from subduing the Lombards in 774, was as quick as ever to retaliate against the rebellious Saxons. He rode to the rescue of the Franks, and now that he himself was at the head of his army, it proved to be far more successful against the Saxons. The rebels were beaten back out of the territory that the Franks had claimed. It was clear, though, that the war of 772/73 had not been enough to subdue the rebellious Saxons. Charlemagne would have to formalize his power.

Little did he know that the fight to absorb Saxony into his territory was twenty years away from being over.

A War of Faiths

In 777, a few miles away from the remnants where an Irminsul pillar had once stood, Charlemagne called a great assembly at Paderborn. This was deep within the Saxon territory that the king had claimed, and he demanded the presence of Saxon leaders, ostensibly for diplomatic reasons, but truly, it was clear that Charlemagne was eager to show his power. He wanted the people to know that even their greatest leaders had to be at his beck and call.

And the vast majority of them were. They had already endured five years of violence, and they were ready for peace in their land, even at the cost of freedom. Most of the Saxon rulers were quick to submit to Charlemagne at Paderborn. One, however, was totally absent, a powerful leader named Widukind. Little is really known about this Saxon's life, but he was an adept military commander and a force to be reckoned with in Saxon society, and as such, his rebellion was no small cause for concern. However, he could not be found in the length and breadth of Saxony. He had fled to the Vikings, sheltering with King Sigfred of Denmark, who appears to have been his father-in-law.

At this point in time, Charlemagne was not much bothered with Widukind—an attitude that would prove to be a mistake. But to Charlemagne, what was one rebellious tribal leader now that the entire country was on its knees before him? Content that the assembly of Paderborn had firmly established him as the supreme ruler over the Saxons, he left once more, this time for the disastrous campaign in Hispania.

So it was that the brokenhearted Charlemagne, grieving the friends and companions that had died at Roncevaux Pass and disassembling his army as winter approached, was disgusted to hear that the Saxons had organized a rebellion once again. And this time, they had fallen upon the Franks with a special depth of hatred that more than matched the brutality with which the Saxons had been treated. This time, their hatred was directed not only to the people who had invaded their country but also to the religion they touted. The Saxons were on a rampage up and down the banks of the Rhine, butchering all in their path, burning churches, and even sexually abusing nuns—an utterly unthinkable act to the Christian mind.

Charlemagne was immediately incensed. Despite the fact that winter was approaching and his army was exhausted from its hard defeat and long march home, he could not allow the Saxons to keep wreaking havoc on his people and their culture. The main body of the army had already scattered back home, but Charlemagne's own bodyguard was still with him. This powerful regiment likely consisted of strong cavalry that could travel swiftly and also pack an enormous punch, the precursors of the knights that would emerge later in the Middle Ages. They were known as the *scara*, and they stood ever ready to do the king's bidding.

Although Charlemagne himself would remain in Francia, the *scara* rode as fast as their horses would take them to the border of Saxony. After arriving in the "barbarian" land, the *scara* fell upon the Saxons with swift brutality. Despite their relatively small numbers, the Franks succeeded in putting an end to the Saxon rampage. It would be Charlemagne's only real victory for the year of 778.

It must have been a good one, though, because 779 brought about the beginning of the end for the Saxons. The *scara* alone had wrought so much havoc on the Saxons in battle that they were beginning to realize that fighting Charlemagne would be a foolish endeavor. When Charlemagne returned to Saxony that year, tribes from all over the country came to see him, seeking to give him their submission and asking to be baptized and allowed to live in peace. Again, some of them may truly have decided to convert to Christianity, but it's not difficult to assume that most of them were simply motivated by fear. If they submitted to Charlemagne and gave up their religion, at least they would be allowed to live in something resembling peace. Some of these tribes had never even met with Charlemagne before; they had only heard of what he'd done to their fellow countrymen and decided to choose surrender over war.

After that, Charlemagne appears again to have decided that the trouble in Saxony was finally at an end. In 780 and 781, he was occupied with Frankish affairs and traveled to Rome in order to have Pepin and Louis the Pious crowned as the kings of Italy and Aquitaine. (Charles the Younger would be made king of the Franks in 800.) He would only turn his attention back to Saxony in 782. This time, it would be done more peacefully. After all, the Saxons had been largely peaceful for several years by this point, not daring to show any resistance to the Franks after the violence they'd experienced at the hands of the *scara* in 778.

Charlemagne decided that it was time to hold another assembly and check on his relations with the Saxon leaders. Perhaps this time, even Widukind would be brought to heel. These hopes, however, were unfounded. Many Saxon leaders came in submission, but Widukind was a no-show, and riding through the Saxon countryside, Charlemagne could see that the people at large were not quite as subdued as their leaders. Little knots of Saxon rebels were everywhere, no doubt hoping for Widukind to return from Denmark with an impressive Viking army and overthrow this arrogant Frank once and for all. In fact, there were rumors in Saxony that Widukind had already returned and was summoning an army to stand against Charlemagne.

Still, there was little cause yet for Charlemagne to actually fight battles against them. That was until the year 782, a year in which Charlemagne would show his darkest side.

Beyond Saxony, there were more Germanic tribes that continued to live in freedom, and these were constantly rebelling along Charlemagne's new Saxon border. These rebellions, however, were small and easily crushed by Charlemagne's noblemen without his personal involvement. One such nobleman was Count Theodoric, the head of a small portion of Charlemagne's army that included numerous noblemen who were not only high-ranking officials but also close companions to Charlemagne himself. Still, they were men of war, and both they and Charlemagne thought nothing of it when he asked them to ride out against one such rebelling tribe and suppress them.

En route to the border, Count Theodoric came across a different enemy than he'd bargained for. Widukind really was back in Saxony again, and he was causing trouble wherever he went. Most recently, he'd stirred up a group of Saxons who had formerly submitted to Charlemagne. They found Theodoric as he rode merrily off to war. Accounts differ on what exactly happened next. Some write that the Saxons fell upon Theodoric in a surprise attack reminiscent of the ambush at Roncevaux Pass. Others say that Theodoric came across the rebels, perhaps during a minor skirmish, and began to make plans to go out against them. Before he could do so, however, some of the minor lords in his employ decided that they'd do it themselves. They were loath to lose all of the glory of battle to Theodoric himself and decided that they'd win themselves some honor. Instead, they found nothing but death and defeat at the hands of the Saxons.

Charging out against the Saxons in disarray and without their most capable commander, Theodoric's men found themselves briskly surrounded, outnumbered, and then killed by the thousands. It was a bloody battlefield that day; even Count Theodoric himself, perhaps as part of the onslaught or perhaps in an attempt to rescue his endangered men, was killed. It was a horrible defeat for the Franks at the hands of Widukind, and once again, it was a crushing blow for Charlemagne.

Only four years after the stinging tragedy that had been Roncevaux, Charlemagne was once more confronted with grief, loss, and humiliation by the deaths of so many of his noblemen and friends. He was enraged at the fact that this barbarian rabble had been able to take so much from him. This was, after all, the Middle Ages; inequality was part and parcel of life there, and the idea that some lives were infinitely more valuable than others governed every aspect of society. To Charlemagne, the death of Count Theodoric was worse than the loss of a thousand ordinary soldiers. And it was abundantly clear that the Franks already viewed the Saxons as inferior.

Before Charlemagne could summon his men and ride out against the Saxons, their own people stepped forward to solve the problem. Petrified that Charlemagne's wrath against Widukind would have devastating repercussions for their own peaceful people, many of the Saxons that had allied themselves with Charlemagne took it upon themselves to identify and capture the rebels. They brought thousands of rebels to Verden, where they would await Charlemagne's judgment.

The king's next action is one that is almost inconceivable in the sheer scope of its violence and wanton destruction of human life. Perhaps one can attempt to delve into the psychology of this decision. Emotion was not something that medieval kings were taught how to deal with; grief was an everyday part of their experience, and as men, they were expected to keep a stiff upper lip and never allow this pain to show. But Roncevaux had struck Charlemagne deeply, much more deeply than simply causing him humiliation. He had never been allowed to process the deep personal losses he had suffered that day. Instead, they had festered like an abscess on his soul, and that abscess had burst with the death of Theodoric. Overwhelmed by helpless rage and unspeakable bereavement, Charlemagne turned to violence.

Perhaps this move could be thought of as political. The Saxons had been a thorn in Charlemagne's side for ten years. Making an example out of these rebels might put an end to years of war and ultimately allow him to seek greater territories to conquer.

Still, it's impossible to justify what Charlemagne did next, much less understand it. The king reacted in a movement of unspeakable violence that can hardly be comprehended, one that rivals many of the bloodiest moments in history and which speaks powerfully to the dangers of absolute power. Faced with thousands of Saxon rebels, unarmed and bound, Charlemagne decided that there was only one way to deal with them. They would all be killed—and not only killed but gorily beheaded. All of them, in a single day.

Four thousand five hundred men died that day, creating a scene of carnage that is almost impossible to imagine, let alone describe. The swish and chop of axes or swords slicing human heads from their shoulders must have filled the air. The amount of blood must have been nearly unthinkable, spurting, running, pooling, soaking into the earth, a stain on the memory of that place forever.

Thousands of Frankish soldiers were employed to carry out the dark deed. One is almost afraid to imagine the screams, the pleas for mercy, the horror in the hearts of those waiting to die as they watched their compatriots being butchered like sheep in a gruesome manner that was robbed of any semblance of dignity.

The scope of Charlemagne's awful massacre is so vast and the logistics so complicated (how do you kill 4,500 people, one by one, in a single day?), that many historians dispute whether it ever actually happened. Thanks to Saxon illiteracy, the only contemporary account is found in the royal Frankish annals, which may have employed a degree of hyperbole in order to make Charlemagne seem more terrible and glorious. However, there is little reason to doubt that Charlemagne's treatment of the Saxons was intensely brutal. By 782, they were a broken and defeated people.

Widukind himself, however, was not part of the army killed at Verden. He had escaped once more, fleeing again to his Viking allies.

Decades of Warfare

If it had been Charlemagne's hope to end the Saxon Wars with the Massacre of Verden, then he had spilled the blood of 4,500 people in vain. The Saxon Wars were a long way from over, thanks in part to the survival of Widukind.

Having committed this unspeakable atrocity—one bordering on genocide—against the Saxon people, Charlemagne's next step was to consolidate his power in a more orderly manner. He had struck terror into the hearts of the Saxons; now, he had to show them what it meant to live under a Frankish king. He sat down to compose a set of laws that would dictate the Saxons' new way of life, including restrictions on the religion they were allowed to practice. In short, any form of paganism was punishable by death, although a suitably repentant transgressor could be pardoned by a priest. The Saxons had no choice at all. Or rather, they had an impossible one: they could uphold Christian traditions or die.

In secular areas, however, the Saxons were allowed to keep their traditional laws. The Franks characteristically did not interfere much with the everyday secular trespasses of their subjected peoples, allowing them to maintain their old laws as long as they converted to Christianity.

Still, in that time, law and religion were almost inextricably linked. Robbing the Saxons of their own belief system was a fundamental change to their entire culture and way of life, one that most of them had not willingly chosen. Bursts of sporadic rebellions continued across Saxony.

However, during 783, Charlemagne was much too occupied to launch another campaign against them. This turned out to be a year of yet more loss and personal tragedy for him. It was the year in which he lost the woman who had been a pillar of his present life and guarantee of his dynasty's future: Hildegard. To make matters worse, that same year, his mother also died. Bertrada had been more than Charlemagne's mother; she had been an important, albeit unofficial, adviser to him. The two most important women in his life were lost to him within a year. And since he'd lost so many of his closest allies at Roncevaux and in Saxony, Charlemagne found himself feeling lost.

He moved fast, however, to remarry, even though Hildegard had given him numerous viable heirs. Charlemagne's quick remarriage was unlikely to have been a move to secure the future of his family's rule. Instead, he was struggling to cement his power in the present. The woman he married is little known to history, but we do know that her name was Fastrada and that she came from East Francia. This wedding was undoubtedly a political move. Although the chroniclers attest that he and Fastrada had an emotional bond, an alliance with a powerful East Francian family would strengthen Charlemagne's war with Saxony. Fastrada would give him two daughters during their marriage, Theodrada and Hiltrude, both of whom became abbesses.

Charlemagne couldn't waste much time in picking himself up from the latest losses in his life, for he had to return to Saxony in order to put an end to the continuous rebellions there. He rode out against the Saxons in 784, and for the first time, he was accompanied by one of his sons in this campaign. Charles the Younger was only twelve years old, but medieval society already considered him a man. Maturity had to come quickly for medieval princes, and it was time for him to prove himself as a worthy successor to the warrior king who had fathered him.

The campaign Charles joined turned out to be a long and difficult one. Widukind was back in Saxony, fighting tooth and nail alongside his renewed band of rebels. The Franks truly had their work cut out for them in suppressing the many small flames of revolt that flickered all across the country. Widukind was likely outnumbered and under-resourced, but he was an excellent strategist, and he kept the Carolingian commanders on their toes. Widukind's rebellion was so powerful that Charlemagne would not see his home all year. Instead, he took a risky decision and remained in Saxony throughout the winter, sending his men out to fight in the bitter cold and blowing snow. It was a baptism through fire for young Charles. His armor already hung heavy on his youthful shoulders, and now, he had to deal with it in the freezing cold as well.

Charlemagne's hard decision paid off. Slowly, the Franks ground away at the Saxon resistance until even its leader could no longer keep fighting. In 785, Widukind finally gave up. He surrendered and pleaded with Charlemagne for a promise that he wouldn't be harmed if he turned himself in. Charlemagne gave his solemn word, and Widukind courageously, considering what Charlemagne had done with his last set of prisoners, went before him.

Perhaps the screams of Verden were still ringing in Charlemagne's ears, and maybe there was some kind of regret in his heart for what he had done. Instead of harming Widukind, Charlemagne kept his promise. The rebel leader was baptized into Christianity, and from there, he disappears from history. It's possible to speculate that he, too, may have ended up cloistered in some forgotten monastery, living out his life in peace but not freedom.

Such would eventually be the fate of Saxony itself. Even though Widukind was conquered in 785, it would be almost twenty years before the Saxon Wars would be declared over, although the scale of violence was much diminished compared to the first decade of warfare. Some hope came to the Saxons in 793 when Denmark decided to get involved and the Vikings began to raid the Franks; however, these forces were defeated so soundly that Saxon refugees were no longer able to enter Denmark in 798. It was the beginning of the end for the Saxons, and the last rebellion took place in 804. After that, Saxony officially belonged to Charlemagne. It had become yet another piece of his kingdom, a kingdom that had now grown into something even bigger. Something that would, by the time the Saxon Wars were over, grow into an empire.

Chapter 7 – More Conquests

A golden bust of Charlemagne.

The conquest of Saxony was still not enough for the growing appetite of this expansionist ruler. In fact, even while he was still waging the Saxon Wars, Charlemagne was already seeking other territories to conquer.

As his sons grew into what counted for manhood in the Middle Ages, Charlemagne was supported by them as he sought to expand his lands. Louis, king of Aquitaine, was sent to campaign in the south, where he eventually won most of Spain. Pepin was campaigning on the borders of Italy, while Charles the Younger fought with his father in Saxony. Charlemagne's empire began to expand in all directions, wreaking devastation on the surrounding peoples. But first, there was some conquering to be done within Francia itself.

The Bloodless Bavarian Conquest

Duke Tassilo III of Bavaria had been Charlemagne's rival ever since he was a little boy.

His father, Duke Odilo of Bavaria, had long been a friend of Charles's father, Pepin the Short. More than that, Odilo was family. He had married Pepin's sister (Charles Martel's daughter), forming a powerful alliance between the dukes of Bavaria and the mayors of the Frankish palace. When Pepin became a king, the alliance still held firm.

Yet power and alliances in the Middle Ages were always tenuous at best, as they were always just one dead nobleman away from crumbling, and things fell apart in 748, the same year that Charlemagne was born. Tassilo, Odilo's son, was only seven years old at the time. He was left orphaned and alone, and Pepin was quick to take the boy into his own household and raise him as a ward of the Frankish royalty. While family compassion may have played some role in Pepin's decision, he undoubtedly also saw an opportunity. By raising Bavaria's rightful duke, Pepin had a trump card up his sleeve if Bavaria itself should ever slip through his fingers.

This was exactly what happened nine years later when Grifo, Pepin's illegitimate brother, attempted to seize Bavaria. Sixteen-year-old Tassilo was abruptly thrust into his role as the duke of Bavaria, and Pepin ousted Grifo, placing Tassilo on the throne instead. The boy had been raised as if he was a son of Pepin's, so it was no difficult task to make him a vassal to Pepin, thus effectively securing Bavaria as Pepin's territory.

Tassilo appears to have been quite content with this arrangement, which was fairly usual for the time. He married one of Desiderius's daughters, forming a strong alliance with the Lombards, and also had a fairly good relationship with the pope.

Things grew sour for Tassilo in 763 when he was a grown man and Pepin was at war with Aquitaine. The Frankish king called on Tassilo to help him, but the latter had alliances with some Aquitanian nobles who were in revolt. He was unwilling to go to war against them and declined to come to Pepin's aid, even though, as he was Pepin's vassal, he had already sworn fealty to the king many years ago. Abandoning Pepin to his fate, Tassilo may have indirectly helped cause the king's death five years later.

This obviously complicated Tassilo's relationship with Charlemagne. The two rulers had grown up in the palace together, and just as Carloman must have always felt a few steps behind his older brother, Charlemagne would have grown up resenting Tassilo. The young man was always much further ahead in his education as a ruler and a warrior than Charlemagne was simply because he was seven years older. One can imagine that this chafed Charlemagne's budding ego. He was, after all, the crown prince of Francia; why should he be made to feel so inferior to some simple duke?

Thus, there was likely some rivalry brewing between Charlemagne and Tassilo, one that Charlemagne would not forget even after he had proven himself to be the greatest king that Francia had ever seen. Added to this, Charlemagne had lost Pepin the Short when he was still a young man, and the memory of his father's tragic early death still stung. In grief, he may have been looking for someone to blame, and Tassilo was a handy scapegoat. Perhaps if the Bavarian duke had ridden to Pepin's aid—the man who had raised Tassilo and given him power and a title—when the former king had asked, then Charlemagne's father would have lived to fight another day.

Either way, Charlemagne clearly wanted Tassilo out, and he wanted Bavaria for himself as well. To take over the duchy legally, he would have to get help—and that help would have to come from Pope Adrian. Only Adrian could declare Tassilo as unfit to rule, thus allowing Charlemagne to take over Bavaria without force and without damaging the territory he wanted to claim for himself.

Luckily for Charlemagne, the pope was no friend of Tassilo. His relationship with Tassilo had been fairly good, but Tassilo had not been as quick as Charlemagne to repudiate his Lombard wife. Accordingly, when Adrian needed help against the marauding Lombards, Tassilo had not responded.

In 788, with things quietening down on the Saxon front, Charlemagne decided that it was time to deal with his old rival. He approached the pope for help, and Adrian quickly declared Tassilo an oath-breaker thanks to his failure to support Pepin in the Aquitanian campaign. Tassilo was thus unfit to rule. His titles were stripped from him, and he was packed off to a monastery, Charlemagne's favorite solution for troublesome nobility. All of Tassilo's rights to Bavaria were formally handed over to Charlemagne in 794, and the duchy was divided up into small counties and became a part of Francia.

The Fall of the Great Ring

As Saxony was assimilated into Charlemagne's growing empire, the Franks found themselves coming into contact with more and more "barbarian" tribes as their borders pushed out farther. One such tribe, and perhaps one of the most formidable, was the Avars.

This nomadic Asian tribe, which consisted of quite diverse peoples, had been ruling over the steppes of Asia and Eastern Europe for centuries. After the fall of Attila and the end of the Hunnic Empire, the Avars had been quick to flow into the power vacuum that Attila left behind, and they rapidly proved themselves worthy of being his successor. Like the Huns, they were adept horsemen who consistently used stirrups long before their neighbors, a considerable advantage as having stirrups on the saddles of their swift warhorses allowed them greater stability and speed. Thus, they could fire arrows from the backs of galloping horses with immense accuracy. They were also one of the first people to use the trebuchet, which would become an important part of siege warfare in medieval Europe.

By 626, the Avars were powerful enough that they laid siege to Constantinople. They built a truly impressive fortress known as the Great Ring of the Avars, possibly located in modern-day Austria, east of Bavaria. The Ring was made of several concentric circles of wooden fortifications, with archers and other warriors in between the circles. It was a formidable fortress indeed, and the Avars ruled powerfully from within it, building a great empire.

The Avar Empire, like many others of its kind, was short-lived. Internal squabbles chipped away at its power, and by the late 8th century, it was crumbling badly. Nonetheless, the Avars did not give up on expanding their collapsing lands. They turned on Bavaria and Friuli in 788 and launched a destructive invasion.

Charlemagne had just claimed Bavaria that same year, but trouble in Saxony called him away, forcing him to allow his new lands to languish in the hands of the Avars for two long years. It was only in 790 that he could finally strike back against these fierce nomads. Along with his son, Pepin Carloman, and a powerful commander known as Duke Eric of Friuli, Charlemagne attacked the Avars.

Pepin and Eric worked together to attack the Great Ring itself, and despite its impressive fortifications, it fell before the might of the Frankish army. Cutting through all the way into the heart of the Ring, Pepin and Eric discovered a rich reward for their efforts. The Avars had been collecting booty for centuries, including some from the Frankish territories they'd so recently lost, and the central ring of the Great Ring was absolutely stuffed with gold. Charlemagne had returned to his favored seat at Aachen by this time, but Pepin proudly sent him a staggering amount of gold and treasure stolen from the Avars.

The Great Ring would not remain long in Frankish possession. It eventually fell back into the hands of the Avars, but the days of the Avar Empire were numbered. By 795, the tuduns, or governors, had realized that they were fighting a losing battle that would only cost their people in money and blood. They journeyed to meet with Charlemagne and turned themselves over as his vassals, offering him their surrender and allowing themselves to be baptized into the Roman Catholic Church.

In the process of baptizing the tuduns, Charlemagne selected one of them to become a new ruler, bestowing upon him the title of khagan, an ancient name for an Avar ruler. Khagan Abraham, who had received his new name from Charlemagne, was sent back to rule the Avars as vassals of the Frankish king. Thus, the Avar Empire officially ended in 796.

Trust between the Avars and the Franks, however, remained very tenuous. Charlemagne soon lost confidence in Khagan Abraham and led a personal assault on the Great Ring of the Avars. The fortress fell before him for the last time, signaling the end of the Avars as a whole.

There was a small rebellion sometime later, around 799, as some Avars mustered against the Franks and sallied out for their freedom. It must have felt like a noble idea to the Avars, who longed for their old way of life, but it was an ill-conceived one. Charlemagne sent a Bavarian army out against them. The Avars were defeated, the confederation of Avar tribes came to an end, and even the Avar race itself eventually intermingled with the Franks and died out.

The Defeat of the Slavs

Charlemagne's treatment of the tribes surrounding his empire was deplorable, as it often led to the end of entire races. The Slavs, however, was one tribe that he never managed to stamp out. Even though the Slavs were illiterate and their origins wreathed in mystery, their language is the root of many influential languages still widely spoken today, including Russian and Polish.

But in the 8th century, the Slavs were no one in particular, especially not to the "civilized" world. Even the ancient Romans had barely documented them, dismissing them as just another tribe of barbarians that had to be subjugated. For this reason, we know very little about the early Slavs. They may have been nomadic, and they may have originated in modern-day Poland or the Czech Republic. Either way, they were definitely pagans in the eyes of Charlemagne. They were polytheists who worshiped many gods that had similarities to the faith of the Vikings, including a ruling god of thunder and important gods of love and fertility. Although, where the Norse gods typically were more or less human in shape, the Slavic gods had many heads—as many as four in the case of their god of war.

By the time of Charlemagne's empire, the Slavs had replaced the Huns in the Balkans. They had some alliances with—and similarities to—the Avars, but they operated as an independent people, often fractured in their approach to the Franks. Still, they controlled vast tracts of territory, and there was nothing that Charlemagne hungered after more than new lands.

By 789, even though he was still busy conquering the Saxons, Charlemagne had already drafted vast numbers of them into his army. The warlike race that he had to spend thirty years conquering proved to be as valuable in his army as they had been destructive fighting against it. Eager to test out his new soldiers on some unsuspecting tribe, Charlemagne decided that the Slavs were a logical next step.

Marching the Saxons into Slavic territory, Charlemagne crossed the Rhine and moved into foreign lands that he was determined to own. The Slavs were met with the glittering ranks of Charlemagne's breathtaking army, and they wisely offered little to no resistance, capitulating quickly in the face of Charlemagne's power. He traveled across Slavic territory all the way to the shores of the Baltic. And everywhere he trod, he decided that he owned the land.

Interestingly, although the Slavs were pagans, Charlemagne was far gentler with them than he had been with the Saxons. His violent Christianization of Saxony was not repeated here in the Slavic territories. Perhaps the bloodshed at Verden had left him with regrets, or perhaps he had simply seen that that level of violence had caused more trouble in Saxony in the end than it was worth. Either way, there is little to attest to any particularly brutal treatment of the Slavs from Charlemagne's side. Instead, when they submitted to him, he simply demanded the right to send missionaries into their lands and ordered that those missionaries, who were usually peaceful and unarmed people, should be left unharmed.

There was more to conquering the Slavs than simply gaining more land and power, however. The Slavs themselves would prove to be strong allies who stood by Charlemagne with fidelity and courage as he continued his expansion.

Of course, not all of the Slavs surrendered to Charlemagne without a fight. He divided the new territory into duchies as he had done with most of his lands, and one of these, Littoral, was filled with rebels who refused to bend the knee to this foreign king. Their rebellion turned out to be a failure, however, as their own people turned against them and fought on Charlemagne's side. Pannonian and Dalmatian Slavs joined forces with Charlemagne to fight those from Littoral, located in modern-day Croatia.

Still, the Littoral Slavs were able to cause plenty of grief and trouble for the Franks, even though their rebellion was ultimately doomed. During the long and gruesome Siege of Trsat in 799, Eric of Friuli, the duke who had proven to be one of Charlemagne's most adept commanders, was killed. It was a terrible loss for Charlemagne, both personally and in terms of his empire; the experienced Eric had been an invaluable strategist, as well as a useful adviser to the young Pepin Carloman.

The Span of the Carolingian Empire

By the early 800s, Charlemagne was ruling over a truly vast territory that stretched all the way from Spain to Scandinavia, from the British Channel to the Baltic Sea. He had conquered a huge variety of peoples, from the Slavs to the Saxons, the Avars to the Aquitanians, and the Basques to the Umayyads.

His rule extended over thirteen modern-day countries: Austria, Croatia, Belgium, Slovenia, Liechtenstein, France, Spain, Switzerland, Andorra, the Netherlands, Italy, Luxembourg, and the Czech Republic. The unity of this vast realm had been unheard-of since the days of the Western Roman Empire. In fact, it's considered that Charlemagne's empire was the hammer and forge that forced the glowing metal of a scattered and uneducated part of the world into the cold, sharp steel that Europe would become in the centuries to follow.

The forging of this mighty dominion would later earn Charlemagne another title: Father of Europe. What was more, he was the first to tout the idea of Christendom, of a vast array of Christian lands united in their religion. It can be argued that his vision never truly came to pass. However, Charlemagne was filled with high ideals, and these would endure into the Middle Ages that followed. The dynamics of power and spirituality that Charlemagne introduced through his strong bonds with the pope, even as he unified vast tracts of land, would give birth to much of medieval culture—including, arguably, the Crusades.

Charlemagne was no longer just a king. The "King of the Franks and Lombards" had grown into something bigger, as the lands he controlled became something far more than a mere kingdom. With kings bowing down at his feet to do him homage, Charlemagne had grown into something that Western Europe hadn't seen since the fall of the Western Roman Empire in the 5th century.

Charlemagne had become an emperor. And it would only be a matter of time before that title was officially bestowed upon him by the only man who had that kind of power: the Roman Catholic pope himself.

Chapter 8 – An Empire Rises

Jean-Victor Schnetz's painting of Charlemagne and Alcuin of York, completed in 1830. It hangs in the Louvre today.

https://commons.wikimedia.org/wiki/File:Charlemagne_et_Alcuin.jpg

As the 8th century drew to a close, Charlemagne had become one of the most powerful people in Europe. He had unified a truly vast territory and ruled over a vast population of many diverse peoples. Even though he had shown great brutality in his conquests, he had also proven himself to be a capable administrator, as well as an adept warrior.

In fact, Charlemagne's territory was no longer a mere kingdom. It stretched over many kingdoms, and it could easily be called an empire. But for that to happen, Charlemagne would have to become an emperor.

The Roman Need for an Emperor

Charlemagne's assistance of Pope Adrian I against the Lombards in 774 had been the start of more than two decades of peace and prosperity in Rome. With the greatest king in Europe as the bodyguard of his reign, Adrian had very little to fear. No one would dare to invade his lands, not with Charlemagne backing him. Added to that, the constant stream of revenue into Charlemagne's hands was often diverted into the coffers of the Roman Catholic Church. It was a very good time to be the pope.

It would be a mistake, however, to view Adrian as Charlemagne's lap dog. Even though the pope needed Charlemagne's protection militarily, he still maintained a fiercely independent mindset, and he proved himself to be an outstanding politician. Employing peaceful diplomacy and making careful alliances, Adrian was able to greatly expand the Papal States. And where Charlemagne protected Rome, Adrian played no small role in protecting Charlemagne's budding empire. He worked hard to maintain peaceful relations with the Byzantine Empire by supporting its position on iconoclasm when he personally attended the Council of Nicaea in 787.

Adrian's relationship with Charlemagne was often tinged with rivalry. He was not always happy about Charlemagne's extensive influence over Italian lands, and tensions could arise between them when it came to Roman matters. Despite this, however, his personal relationship with Charlemagne was a close one. He might not have had Charlemagne's military strength, but he had more wisdom and experience than the king, and for twenty years, Charlemagne cherished their friendship.

That golden age for Rome came to an end in 795. Adrian, whose birthdate is unknown but who would have been quite elderly by this time, passed away due to natural causes in the winter of that year. When the news reached Charlemagne, who was leading a campaign against the Avars at the time, he was deeply saddened. In fact, he composed—by dictation—a long and poetic epitaph to Adrian, which can be seen today in the Vatican. The epitaph is a testimony to Charlemagne's close relationship with the pope; in it, he even refers to him as "father." It might not be too much to say that Adrian really did act as a father figure in Charlemagne's life, considering that the two men became friends six years after Charlemagne's loss of Pepin the Short.

Not all of the Romans, however, shared quite the same love for Charlemagne that Adrian had. Fearing that the king would attempt to interfere with the papal succession as Desiderius had done, the Romans were quick to elect a new pope. In fact, on the very day that Adrian died, the cardinal-priest of St. Susanna was consecrated as Pope Leo III.

Leo was not quite as independently-minded as Adrian had been. Aware of Adrian and Charlemagne's relationship, and eager not to make an enemy out of the powerful warrior king, he sent an envoy to Aachen with the standard of the city and the keys of the confession of St. Peter. In a roundabout symbolic way, Leo was sending Charlemagne a message that said he saw the king as the protector of Rome. Charlemagne, while deeply grieving Adrian, was ready to make friends with Leo. He sent Leo a letter that congratulated him on his recent ascension to pope, along with a large amount of treasure that had just recently been seized from the Great Ring of the Avars.

With Charlemagne backing him, Leo felt he had little to fear, and for four years, this proved to be true. But trouble brewed in Rome nonetheless. Leo's election had ostensibly been unanimous, but he was not the only papal candidate. A member of Adrian's family had also been considered, and he had many supporters. These grew more and more restless with Leo in charge of Rome. And with Charlemagne occupied with squashing an Avar rebellion in 799, they decided that there was little the Frankish ruler could do to stop them.

In the spring of 799, Leo was part of a ritual procession as he celebrated the Greater Litanies. He headed for Rome's Flaminian Gate in all his pomp and splendor as cheering crowds of Romans surrounded him. He'd been the pope for several years and was settling happily into his role, invincible under Charlemagne's protection. Or so he thought.

Without warning, a group of armed men burst from the crowd, rushing down upon the weaponless pope. Leo didn't stand a chance. He was seized and thrown to the ground, and they fell upon him with brutal violence, their hands scratching and clawing at his face. Their aim was not to kill him; it was simply to mutilate him, to make him unfit to be pope. They scrabbled at his eyes and mouth, hoping to put out his eyes and rip out his tongue. Leo's supporters were woefully inadequate. They did little to save him, and while his attackers were ultimately unsuccessful in their attempts, Leo was left alone and bleeding in the street for some time.

When nightfall came, the unconscious, wounded pope was still lying in the street. His supporters came to pick him up then and carried him off to a nearby monastery, where he recovered.

After having regained his strength, Leo realized that his protectors within Rome itself could do nothing to keep him safe from his opposition. It was an automatic reflex to turn to the man who'd been Rome's guardian angel for decades: Charlemagne. Along with a group of Roman sympathizers, Leo hurried over the Alps that summer, joining Charlemagne at Paderborn.

Of course, Charlemagne was quick to help Leo, although he could not personally journey to Rome at that time. He sent an envoy with Leo to put him back into his rightful place in the Vatican, and they returned him to Rome unmolested, then went on to search for those who had attacked him in order to imprison them. They were thrown into a dungeon to await a trial the following year when Charlemagne himself could attend to the matter.

A Christmas Coronation

When the next year came, Charlemagne had arranged his affairs so that he could journey to Rome again, visiting it perhaps for the first time since the death of Adrian. He presided over the trial of the accused who had attacked Leo. In turn, they brought charges of adultery and perjury against Leo. They could provide no evidence of Leo's guilt, but the pope was still desperate to prove himself worthy in the eyes of the people, and so, he swore a lengthy oath of innocence to Charlemagne. This was a humiliating thing to do, but it worked. The accused were condemned to death, and Leo won Roman hearts when he petitioned for them to be exiled instead of killed. Charlemagne agreed, and Leo was able to take his place as pope once more without opposition.

Still, Leo had been shaken by these events, both emotionally and politically. His enemies had been dealt with, but he wasn't sure that the Romans had much faith in him. He lacked the personal friendship that Adrian had enjoyed with Charlemagne, and he needed to do something to cement Frankish-Roman relations. So, he hatched a plan, one that likely did not have much of

Charlemagne's involvement, but one that would change his life and the course of history forever.

Charlemagne had decided to remain in Rome for the winter, celebrating Christmas in the splendor of St. Peter's. Christmas Mass at Rome in the Middle Ages was always a wonderful spectacle, filled with ceremony and celebration. St. Peter's was packed with people, many of them Europe's most important dignitaries, but none were more important than Charlemagne.

Charlemagne's biographer, Einhard, who wrote extensively on the subject of the ruler's life from 817 to 830, claimed that despite Charlemagne's tremendous power, he seldom indulged in dressing up. Usually, he wore a linen shirt, silk tunic, and otter-skin cloak as any ordinary Frankish nobleman would wear; only rarely did he don the more elaborate ceremonial garb. Still, he was a majestic sight when he did. His towering height of six feet, three inches would be tall today; in the 9th century, when the average adult male stood only five feet, eight inches, it was tremendous. On Christmas Day, Charlemagne was decked out in a flowing blue cloak that poured over his still-powerful frame, fastened by a giant golden buckle. Rich embroidery covered his clothes, jewels glittered on his fingers and at his throat, and the hilt of his sword was made of expensive metal, shimmering with precious stones.

He was a breathtaking sight as he strode up to the altar. Decades of war had given him a slight limp, and the hair that curled richly around his head was turning white, but he still exuded power and charisma. Kneeling down in prayer at the richly decorated altar, the king bowed his head.

There is a debate among historians today if he was aware of what was about to happen. Einhard says that Leo's next action was a complete surprise to Charlemagne, although others argue that he must have at least suspected that Leo had some scheme in the works. Either way, it was a splendid, unorthodox, and history-making moment. Leo strode up behind the kneeling and bareheaded king. Seizing a brilliantly decorated crown, the pope cried out, "To Charles, the most pious Augustus, crowned by God, the great and peace-giving Emperor, life and victory!" He repeated these words twice, and they rang throughout St. Peter's as he lowered the great crown on Charlemagne's white head.

Before Charlemagne could rise, Leo fell to his knees and began to anoint Charlemagne's feet with oil. Cheers broke out, and the clergymen who were present began to recite the coronation litany. With that, Charlemagne had become the emperor of Rome.

In practice, becoming emperor didn't add any lands to Charlemagne's dominion. He was effectively ruling over most of the old Western Roman Empire already thanks to his many conquests. Still, it had been more than 300 years since the last time an emperor ruled over Italy, and this new title ushered Charlemagne's lands into a new era: the era of a great empire. He was no longer simply the king of the Franks and Lombards but an emperor of a territory now known as the Carolingian Empire.

Leo's act of crowning Charlemagne had many motivations, which are still the subject of debate amongst historians, and also many repercussions, which would resound throughout thousands of years of history. One of the most immediate consequences was the conflict with the Byzantines. The Eastern Roman Empire was being ruled by Empress Irene, whose claim to the throne was shaky already and invalid—at least in the eyes of Charlemagne and Leo— because she was a woman. Under the traditional Salic law that was a simple fact of life for these men, women were simply unfit to rule. In Leo's eyes, he had crowned Charlemagne not as emperor over the western half of the Roman Empire but over the Roman Empire as a whole. Empress Irene was not amused, and considering she held territory as close to Charlemagne's borders as Venice, this was a considerable threat—one that would cost Charlemagne dearly in the years to come.

But for the first decade of Charlemagne's rule as Roman emperor, he turned much of his warfare over to his sons, and he was able to settle down and concentrate on administration. And here, he would prove to be so much more than just a military genius. Age had tempered the great man's rage somewhat, and he turned to making his empire a hotbed of culture, arts, and learning, resulting in a powerful resurgence of these gentler areas of life that would be known as the Carolingian Renaissance.

The Carolingian Renaissance

Now that he bore the same title as the rulers of ancient Rome, Charlemagne seemed to feel that he owed them a debt, and he felt obliged to revive and preserve their ideas, writings, and culture. The Carolingian Empire quickly began to grow into something reminiscent of ancient Rome, and this dive into culture and learning would not be seen again until after the Middle Ages.

One of Charlemagne's first steps was to standardize the currency used in his realm, basing this new currency on that of ancient Rome. His *livre carolinienne*, *sous*, and *deniers* were modeled on ancient Rome's *libra*, *solidus*, and *denarius*, and they would eventually become the modern-day pound, shilling, and penny. These coins were used throughout his empire, facilitating much easier trade. Measurements were also standardized, making communication easier. Perhaps for the first time, the subjugated peoples of the Germanic tribes he'd conquered were able to enjoy some benefits of being part of Charlemagne's domain.

Charlemagne also seemed to be trying to turn Aachen into a second Rome, as the architecture of the buildings he commissioned there—and elsewhere in his empire—was strongly reminiscent of Roman antiquity. The breathtaking Palatine Chapel, built in 792 and Charlemagne's personal place of worship in Aachen, is only one example.

However, it was not in architecture or currency that Charlemagne's greatest influence lay. Although he was also a patron of the arts and music, his deepest passion was for education and literature.

Alcuin of York, a British scholar, was one of Charlemagne's most beloved and trusted advisers and also one of the most influential educators of his time. Charlemagne gave Alcuin everything he needed to turn Aachen into a blossoming center of learning. In a time when even the most highborn people seldom learned to read or write, Charlemagne made waves by having Alcuin compose a standardized curriculum, bringing literacy and education all over the length and breadth of the Carolingian Empire.

Alcuin also curated an extensive palace library, a priceless treasure in the time before the printing press. The library did more than simply house dusty old books that never saw the light of day. The new wave of literacy rocking Aachen was such that the library's books were in huge demand; scholars couldn't copy them fast enough.

Books themselves were also changed at Charlemagne's patronage. Writing was evolving, growing more and more accessible. Although it was once a skill reserved only for the most highly educated of people, reading was something that increasing numbers of noble-born people were able to do. This was in part thanks to education and in part thanks to the fact that Alcuin was revolutionizing the ease of reading by standardizing the use of capital letters and even spaces between words, inventing a new form of writing known as Carolingian minuscule.

Always the Christian king—even if he behaved more brutally than the so-called barbarians at times—Charlemagne encouraged Alcuin to work on the Bible, and the scholar quickly obliged. Many full editions of the Bible were copied and distributed all over the realm, and with Charlemagne's encouragement, the diverse peoples he ruled started to translate the Scriptures into their own vernacular. Saxons, Hispanics, Avars, and Slavs were all able to study the Bible in their own languages for the very first time.

The Bible was not the only ancient text that Charlemagne would preserve, however. In fact, the Carolingian Renaissance is responsible for the preservation of almost all the classical Latin texts we have today.

Without the printing press, producing books was an incredibly long and painstaking process. Every single line had to be copied by hand, word for word, often by quiet monks laboring away in their abbeys. The ancient Latin manuscripts were no exception, and in the dark years following the end of the Roman Empire, the war-torn world had seldom had the same time and money to copy them. But Charlemagne was determined to preserve every single one. He had hundreds of copies made of each of these important books, and in fact, almost all of the classical works we still have today were copied down by the Carolingians.

Without Charlemagne's influence, we wouldn't have Marcus Aurelius's *Meditations* or the *Aeneid*. We wouldn't know Tacitus's history of the Roman Empire or Julius Caesar's own account of his conquests in Gaul. Cicero's works would have been lost forever, and Pliny's *Natural History* would have disintegrated under the brutal weight of time.

This love of learning that was instilled across the Carolingian Empire was something that Charlemagne felt keenly in his own heart. He had summoned great masters from all over his realm to teach him various subjects harking back to ancient times, such as rhetoric, grammar, astronomy, logic, and even arithmetic. He became a learned man, far more so than most medieval kings, but there was one simple skill that many of us in the modern world take for granted, yet he could never master. Charlemagne could more than likely read, but he never did learn how to write. It hadn't been a part of his early education, and he tried to learn in later life, but the skill constantly eluded him.

The great emperor had conquered so many vast territories, yet he remained defeated by the written word. This appears to have frustrated him for decades. To the very end of his life, he kept a wax tablet under his pillow and would practice his letters in vain.

The Death of Charlemagne

As Charlemagne headed into his seventies, he began to cement the plans he'd made years before. Although many of his ideas were very progressive, Charlemagne was a traditionalist when it came to planning his succession. He considered his title as Holy Roman emperor to be something of an honorary thing, not tied to heredity, and so, he decided to split his lands among Charles, Pepin, and Louis.

Fate, however, had other ideas. In 810, the conflict with the Byzantine Empire came to a head. This empire controlled Venice, but the city had lost respect for Constantinople and switched its allegiance to Pepin, the king of Italy. The Byzantines would not give up Venice without a fight, though. Pepin rode to lay siege to the city, but his plans were doomed when disease broke out among his troops. He was forced to return to his own country with his tail between his legs and broken ranks of sick men. It is possible that Pepin himself had contracted an illness there, as he died just a few months later, leaving Italy without a king.

Just one year later, Charles the Younger, the king of Francia, suffered a similar tragedy. He was childless, and it was a horrific blow when he died in 811 after suffering from a stroke.

Bereaved of two cherished sons within a few months of one another, Charlemagne had to drag himself out of his personal grief to realize that their deaths could have terrible implications for his empire. At least he had one son left: Louis the Pious, the king of Aquitaine, who also controlled the Spanish Marches. Now that his brothers were dead, Louis would have to bear the full weight of the empire on his own young shoulders. In 813, possibly too old to travel to Rome, Charlemagne summoned Louis to meet him at Aachen. He had him anointed and crowned as co-emperor over the Carolingian Empire, although Louis would never be made Holy Roman emperor as his father had. Louis also received half of Charlemagne's lands; the emperor would leave the rest to him after his death, except for Italy, which went to Pepin's illegitimate son Bernard.

Charlemagne may have been growing too old and frail to ride all the way to Rome, but he still seemed to be fairly vigorous in the autumn of 813. He spent it hunting and riding in the beautiful, ardent countryside surrounding his peaceful home, safe in the knowledge that Louis was a man after his own heart and would care for the empire like it was his own. But disaster struck that winter. The emperor developed a cough and sudden fevers that would come and go, leaving his strong face haggard and pale.

By January, it was clear that Charlemagne was dying. He had contracted pleurisy, an inflammation of the spaces around the lungs, and in the 9th century, there was no way of treating it. On January 21st, 814, depressed beyond measure and still burning with ambition as much as he burned with fever, Charlemagne took to his bed. Seven days later, he died at the age of 71, having ruled over Francia for nearly half a century.

All of Charlemagne's personal wealth was donated to the Roman Catholic Church that he had protected so fervently during his lifetime.

Conclusion

As promised, upon the death of Charlemagne, Louis the Pious became the ruler over the Carolingian Empire, while Bernard became the king of Italy. And during the rule of Louis, the Carolingian Empire was held together, but it was a very tenuous bond. Louis would have been a much better clergyman than he was a king; he was a deeply devout person, devoted to the Church, and generally well-intentioned, but he failed miserably as an administrator. Several revolts occurred during his rule.

Things only worsened when Louis died, dividing the empire among his three sons. These men were jealous and ambitious, and they fought among one another, tearing the empire apart from the inside out. This made it vulnerable to attackers from beyond its borders. The Vikings, still clinging to their paganism and terrified of suffering the same fate as the Saxons, decided to strike first before they could be invaded. They annihilated the Carolingian Empire's borderlands and were perilously close to taking over Paris when the king of Francia—Charles the Fat, Charlemagne's great-grandson—bribed them to go away in 888. With that, the Carolingian Empire had fallen.

Yet the time of the Roman Empire itself was far from over. In fact, Charlemagne's coronation may have looked like a twitch in the death throes of Rome, but it was really the beginning of a whole new era. Nearly two centuries after the coronation of Charlemagne, a new Holy Roman emperor would be crowned when Otto I of Germany marched to the aid of Pope John XII. In gratitude, the pope gave him Charlemagne's ancient title, and the Roman Empire lived on as the Holy Roman Empire. It would remain an important force in world politics until its decline in 1806.

The Holy Roman Empire was not Charlemagne's only legacy. In fact, it is difficult to imagine a leader more influential in the course of history than this king with his conquests and his renaissance. There are many everyday aspects of our modern world that can be ascribed at least in part to his far-reaching influence. Our knowledge of ancient Rome. Our concept of modern-day Europe. The vast spread of Christianity and everything that came with it. Would more of us be celebrating Yuletide instead of Christmas if Charlemagne had never ruled?

This emperor was many things, and many of them were not positive. He was a murderer, a warrior. He was tempestuous, brutal, close-minded, and arrogant. But he was also intelligent, ambitious, driven, and determined. And like it or not, our lives today are very different because of this one man who lived more than a thousand years ago.

Part 3: Notre-Dame de Paris

A Captivating Guide to One of the Most Famous Catholic Cathedrals of Medieval Europe

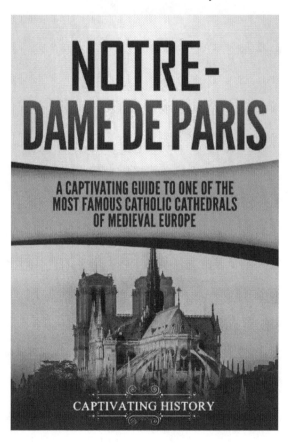

Certainly there is matter here for many large volumes, and often the universal history of humanity in the successive engrafting of many arts at many levels, upon the same monument. The man, the artist, the individual, is effaced in these great masses, which lack the name of their author; human intelligence is there summed up and totalized. Time is the architect, the nation is the builder.

- Victor Hugo, *The Hunchback of Notre-Dame*

Introduction

It was with horror and sadness that the people of the world opened their social media or switched on their televisions on April 15th, 2019, only to see terrifying pictures of smoke and flames roaring around one of the most iconic outlines in France: that of Notre-Dame de Paris. The cathedral attracts more visitors than the Eiffel Tower (an estimated 13 million annually), and it has become a favorite with tourists and Parisians alike. Mass is still conducted there regularly, and when the fire destroyed part of Notre-Dame, all of the world mourned.

There is more to Notre-Dame, however, than just a tragic fire. Almost nine centuries of history lie behind its weathered towers, and its history is closely interlinked with that of France and its people. Its story has rung out through the ages as one of hope and survival, a tale of fear and destruction turning into courage and renovation. Its characters range from novelists to saints, from daredevils to kings, from generals to emperors. Its themes stretch across the spectrum, from humanity's greatest darkness to the warmth of the human spirit; it tells stories about exceptional brutality and exceptional grace, of the greatest terror of them all and of dauntless courage. Kings were crowned here, emperors seized power, Nazis paraded the streets, and saints strove valiantly to break sieges. There were wars and revolts, there were requiems and battles, there were suicides and stunts, and there were feats of human engineering that still baffle the modern mind.

And above all, now and always, then and forever, there is hope.

The world watched Notre-Dame burn. Now, it's time for the world to hear its story.

Chapter 1 – Before Notre-Dame

The Pillar of the Boatmen, as reconstructed from pieces discovered beneath Notre-Dame de Paris

The excavation was hot, dark, and sweaty work, not made any easier by the knowledge of the mighty cathedral that towered just above. The foreman of the band of workers that were laboring away in the darkness was painfully aware that one of France's most important monuments was directly above him. He mopped his brow, looking over the row of men that were slowly and painstakingly chipping away at the soil. The work progressed at a snail's pace by hand, but the utmost care had to be taken to avoid disturbing the church above. The foreman gritted his teeth and shook his head, inwardly cursing the authorities that had decided that it was really necessary to excavate space to create additional tombs for the archbishops directly beneath the nave of Notre-Dame. Couldn't they just be buried in graveyards like normal people?

Then, a workman called out to him. The foreman raised his chin. The worker had found something—something that he didn't think should be there. A curious band of men gathered around him, and the foreman shouldered his way through, grumbling to himself about these workmen. Part of them would always be looking for diamonds when they should be moving dirt.

But when he saw it, he knew that this time the discovery was no figment of some worker's imagination. It was a strange, square piece of stone, a corner so precise that it had to have been built by human hands. The workmen murmured in awe as the foreman reached out and brushed some of the dirt away to reveal carvings— multitudes of them, etched into the stone everywhere that he was able to dig the soil away. Men and women, strange beasts, and none of them familiar to any of the men standing around. The more of the strange object that the men could reveal, the more certain the foreman became of one thing: This was no Roman Catholic relic. This was something completely different.

* * * *

The year was 1710, and a band of workmen excavating an area beneath the nave of Notre-Dame de Paris had just stumbled upon the oldest monument ever discovered in France. This work of a guild of boatmen in Roman times, called the Pillar of the Boatmen, was created in honor of Tiberius Caesar in the first century CE. It was dedicated to the Roman god Jupiter, and its skillfully carved surface featured Roman gods and fragments of the Gallic mythology of which we still currently know so little about. It had once stood in a Gallo-Roman temple located where the current Notre-Dame de Paris has stood for more than 800 years.

This temple had been a part of a very different France to the one we know today. Then named Gaul, it had not been a country in itself but was rather a part of the Roman Empire, since it was conquered by Julius Caesar sometime in the 50s BCE. Gaul was a vast territory, extending across modern-day France, Luxembourg, Belgium, and even parts of Germany, among others. Its residents were Celts, people with a complicated mythology of their own, and while they were conquered by the Romans, they did not allow their culture to die out completely. Instead, they appear to have merged the Roman gods with deities of their own, producing a new mixed culture of which we only have a few relics today. The Pillar of the Boatmen is one of the oldest, possibly the oldest, of all the Gallic sculptures that include an inscription.

It had been less than a century since the Celts' lives had been overthrown and so dramatically changed by the arrival of Julius Caesar's troops, but they would not enjoy their new Gallo-Roman culture for long. The winds of change were blowing through the ancient world, starting in Jerusalem, the capital of the ancient state of Israel. The Jewish leaders had crucified a man named Jesus Christ, a man who claimed to be the Son of God, and his followers were spreading all over the known world, preaching that their Jesus had risen again. Despite persecution, the word was spreading farther and farther. The era of Christianity had come.

Even as the guild of boatmen was building their famous pillar, Christian apostles were traveling to Gaul, spreading their message all over the Roman Empire. While at first the Roman Caesars (a Roman title that means emperor) clung to their gods, by the 4th century CE, Christianity was accepted as an official religion throughout the empire. Constantine was the first Roman emperor to convert to Christianity, even if he did so with his dying breath; successive emperors would be Christians for much of their lives.

When the Western Roman Empire began to collapse, Gaul was largely abandoned to the tribes of native people that had made it their home. In 486 CE, a Frankish king named Clovis conquered most of Gaul, carving out a new country. It was under his rule that the nation first became known as Francia (from which France derives its name), named after the Franks that now populated it. Paris, the city that had grown around the lost Pillar of the Boatmen, became the capital.

This newborn France would experience several periods of division and chaos over the next few centuries, but it was mostly united under King Charlemagne in the 8th century. France would continue to consolidate its lands and culture while England was conquered by the Normans in 1066.

Hugh Capet was crowned King of the Franks in Noyon in the late 10th century. The Capetian Dynasty would last for hundreds of years, bringing stability to France and reestablishing it as a major power in the medieval world.

Meanwhile, the Gallo-Roman temple where the Pillar of the Boatmen had stood had long since been destroyed. In its place, Childebert I—an early Frankish king of the Merovingian Dynasty reigning in the 6th century—built a basilica that he dedicated to Saint Stephen (St. Etienne in French). Descriptions from the era describe it as a large and majestic building for its time, although it was about half the size of the magnificent building that stands at the heart of Paris today.

This basilica would stand for 600 years. Bishop after bishop came and went, presiding over the most important cathedral in the capital of France, and each was content with the ancient building where generations of Parisians came to worship. Until, in 1160, a new bishop would come to power—a bishop whose ambition knew no boundaries. And for him, there would have to be a new cathedral.

Chapter 2 – The Construction of a Cathedral

The new Bishop of Paris stood in the Cathedral of St. Etienne, and he wasn't satisfied.

Maurice de Sully had seldom been satisfied. He had been born to parents so humble that his birthdate is not officially recorded, but it was probably around 1120. He should have grown up to be just another peasant boy herding cattle or tending sheep on his father's farm, but instead, Maurice had other ideas. He decided to throw himself into the study of theology, making the long journey from his hometown near Orléans to begin his studies in Paris itself. He was only about twenty years old when he made a name for himself as a professor and a preacher, and by 1159, he was the Archdeacon of Paris.

Maurice had come a long, long way from the farm boy who had once dreamed of greatness. Now the Bishop of Paris in 1160, he was one of the most important people in the entire church, despite his poor childhood. It would have been easy for him to sit back and relax now, enjoying the luxury that his position brought him. Instead, Maurice wanted to make even more changes. He gazed around the cathedral, a frown furrowing his brow. It had been big and beautiful in its day, he supposed, but right now, it was, frankly, dated. All over France, bigger and more ambitious cathedrals were being built, and the new Gothic style was all the rage. Maurice reached out to brush his fingers against the aging wall of the cathedral. Dust crumbled away at his touch, revealing the advancing decrepitude of the building. Maurice shook his head. A new Gothic cathedral—that was just what Paris needed. And just what Maurice needed to prove, once and for all, that he had left his humble beginnings a long way behind him.

* * * *

Maurice's idea came at a good time for France. While King Louis VII had had considerable trouble in his personal life— marrying Eleanor of Aquitaine a few months before he was crowned king only for her to have their marriage annulled and go off to marry the King of England in 1152—he had become king at a time of rising royal power and increasing stability. His brutal father, Louis VI, had made the royalty unpopular but far more powerful; now, Europe was occupied with the Crusades instead of fighting with itself. There was relative peace in France, and its people had responded with a building boom. Cathedrals were sprouting up all over the kingdom and the rest of the continent, and it didn't take much for Maurice to convince Louis VII that it was high time that Paris had a majestic cathedral of its own.

Plans were drawn up, although we don't know who drew them; the original architects of Notre-Dame have lost their names to history. It was decided that the new cathedral would be built upon the ruins of the old Cathedral of St. Etienne, but that plot of land alone would not be big enough. Instead, more land would have to be bought, and this was a problem since the building site was located on an island in the middle of the Seine. In order for the church to be built to the size that Maurice wanted, piles—large wooden posts—would have to be driven into the river and the island would have to be connected with another one nearby. Even that would not be enough—more land was going to have to be bought, and in the heart of a city whose population was growing by the day, it would not be cheap.

Maurice himself invested vast amounts of his personal wealth into the project. He was supported by the French Crown, which poured almost unthinkable amounts of money into building the new church. Despite being embroiled in an embarrassingly unsuccessful war against his ex-wife's new husband, Louis VII was quick to open the royal coffers for this new cathedral. He considered himself a pious king, having been a key part of the Second Crusade despite tremendous personal danger; this was possibly also as a result of the fact that he was still wracked by guilt after a massacre in Vitry during his brief and foolish conflict with the Count of Champagne. Louis' willingness to spend money on the new cathedral was a good thing though: in today's money, Notre-Dame would have cost the equivalent of about one billion U.S. dollars.

There was now money to buy the expensive land for the cathedral to be built upon, but there were still endless acres of red tape to wade through in order for the land to be officially transferred. This proved to be one of many delays; nonetheless, in 1163, the cornerstone was laid, and construction began. Stone was quarried (or pilfered from Roman ruins), hundreds of builders were employed, and the work went quickly for almost two decades.

Everything about Notre-Dame was new and experimental. For centuries, architects had been creating square, squat buildings with fat walls and few windows; this was the only way they could see large buildings bearing the weight of their roofs. Yet in the past few decades, technology had accelerated. Architects could now design taller buildings with more windows, creating a newer and more elegant style, and so, the Gothic church was born. While not the first, Notre-Dame was a fairly early example.

By 1182, the choir, its aisles, and the high altar were complete. The altar was consecrated and the first Mass held there that year, but the cathedral itself was far from finished. Its nave, facades, and intricate decorative work still had to be done, a square still had to be leveled and built in front of the cathedral, and a whole new street also had to be built in order to connect the mighty building with the rest of Paris more easily.

Louis VII had been dead for two years by this time. His son, Philip II, would add mightily to French territories and power. He allied with the son of his father's ex-wife, Richard the Lionheart, King of England. Together, Philip and Richard would launch the Third Crusade, aiming to capture Jerusalem. Their efforts, despite reclaiming some of the lands back that Sultan Saladin had taken during his war with the Crusaders, proved to be a failure. Their friendship was destroyed, and the two kings went to war with each other. It was only Richard's death that saved France at all—he was on the verge of defeating Philip completely when he was succeeded by John Lackland. John proved to be far less of a fighter than his brother, and he was quickly defeated.

The construction of Notre-Dame continued unabated. Maurice de Sully had died peacefully in 1196, having at least celebrated one Mass inside his mighty new church, even if he didn't see its completion. When Louis VIII, the son of King Philip II, was succeeded by Louis IX—now known as Saint Louis for his peace and piety—it was a boon for the building of Notre-Dame. Louis was a supporter of Gothic architecture, as well as being devotedly religious, and he continued to pour funds from the royal treasury into the building of the cathedral. This was a good thing as the architects had discovered a flaw in their plans. The original architects had underestimated the weight that the thinner walls of the cathedral would have to support. Its massive roof, constructed with planks from thousands of oak trees, was simply too heavy, and stress fractures were spreading through the stone walls. Something would have to be done, yet with the king so strongly supporting the Gothic style, simply making the walls thicker was out of the question.

The solution was innovative and elegant: flying buttresses. These beautiful arches, anchored on one end into the walls of the cathedral and built into heavy and powerful pillars on the other, kept the more open and airy look of Notre-Dame whilst preventing it from collapsing beneath its own weight. Notre-Dame became one of the first cathedrals ever to be built with flying buttresses.

The work continued on gorgeous statues of biblical characters, the intricate transepts, and the Western facade. By 1250, the characteristic two towers crowning the Western facade had been built, and work continued on adding gargoyles and the hundreds of figures in the tympanum.

Meanwhile, Louis IX and his successor Philip III both died in unsuccessful crusades. The new king of France, Philip IV, was a strong administrator and one of the most powerful kings that France would ever have. He had authority even over popes and emperors. After his death, his three sons ruled, continuing the Capetian line of succession, until Charles IV, his youngest son, died. Charles' death in 1328 would plunge both France and England into a century of darkness and conflict. He left no direct heir, and the man next in line to the throne of France was seated upon the throne of England. A distant French relative, Philip of Valois, would hurriedly be crowned, but it was too late. The Hundred Years' War between England and France would rage for more than a century.

Yet Notre-Dame was almost finished, and nothing would stop her, not even the longest conflict in European history. Paris itself was in constant peril as the balance of power swung wildly from one side to the other, but construction continued.

Finally, in 1345, the cathedral was completed. It was named the Notre-Dame de Paris: "Our Lady of Paris." It had taken almost 200 years to build, but it was finished at last.

The Hundred Years' War, however, was far from over. And its strange and crazy turns would soon see Notre-Dame honored with its first-ever coronation.

Chapter 3 – A Curse and a Coronation

Henry VI was only ten years old, but he was the king of two nations who was already being forced to defend one against the advances of a jealous rival.

The Hundred Years' War had been raging for more than ninety years. Little Henry barely understood what was really going on; his coronation in England two years earlier had been a long and tedious ceremony for a mere seven-year-old boy, and he wasn't sure that his French one was going to be much more interesting. For the adults surrounding this hapless child, however, the French coronation was a vital part of the war that they feared they might be losing. Only a decade earlier, the English had been so resoundingly winning the war that the French king of the time had little choice except to sign the Treaty of Troyes. Its terms granted the French princess' hand in marriage to the English king, then Henry V; it also disinherited the French king's son and heir, so that the resulting offspring of the union between Henry V and Catherine of France would be the new king of both England and France. Henry VI, the now ten-year-old boy who found himself being carried into Paris on the back of a pure white horse on a wintry day in 1431, was that new king. But the disinherited French prince, the Dauphin Charles, was not inclined to give up his throne so easily. Aided by the mysterious Joan of Arc, he had been seizing power back, and now the English knew that their position in France was in grave jeopardy. Crowning little Henry in Paris would be an effort to reassert his—and, thus, England's—authority.

Paris was the second choice of where to hold Henry's coronation. Traditionally, French kings had been crowned in Reims, but that was now under the Dauphin's control: even though Joan of Arc had been executed by the English in May of 1431, the Dauphin had only continued to grow in power since her death. Paris was the second-best option, and there was only one church in the capital of France whose grandeur befitted such a pompous occasion. And so, decades after its construction, Notre-Dame became the site of a king's coronation.

Henry had little regard for any of this. He just walked along the street, covered by a gorgeous and gaudy canopy of gold and blue, which was borne on either side of him by his guards and servants. Crowds lined the street, shouting; Henry, who didn't speak much French, wasn't exactly sure whether they were cheering him on or trying to intimidate him. He was surrounded by people, but there was no trusted guardian nearby to give him courage as he approached the mighty church that towered before him.

The sight of the cathedral itself was enough to give him a moment's pause. He had been crowned in Westminster Abbey in England, a beautiful and impressive place in itself, but its grandeur had been worn away in his mind by sheer familiarity. This place was something else entirely. The facade of it was covered in statues and gargoyles; they gazed down at him, by turns stern and sneering, as he moved in short steps toward the enormous building. Two huge towers crowned its top, so high above that Henry had to tip back his head and squint in order to see all the way to the top. Its three giant arched doorways gaped wide, like three mouths about to swallow him into a future that he didn't understand.

But one thing he did know: He didn't have a choice. Fate had decreed that he would be born to royal parents, and so, he embraced his fate. Henry squared his narrow shoulders, fixed his eyes on the central doorway, and walked forward into his destiny.

* * * *

Henry's coronation at Notre-Dame was evidence for what it had become over the 86 years since its official completion: the home cathedral of Paris. It was, by this point, one of the most impressive buildings throughout the length and breadth of France. Its inspiring architecture, varied as it was through the mingling styles of the many architects that had worked on it during its long construction, had already become a national landmark.

Yet Notre-Dame was not only the setting for hundreds of Masses, requiems, beautiful services, and glorious ceremonies. Indeed, even before its completion, the mighty church would bear witness to one of the bloodiest and most controversial executions to take place in medieval France.

* * * *

The year was 1314. For seven long years, the Knights Templar had been suffering at the hands of an angry king. Philip IV was on the throne of France; the last crusade had just ended in dismal failure, and thousands of knights had made the tiring trek back to Europe. Spurred on by a continent ruled by popes who were more powerful than kings, knights had once streamed to the Holy Land in a bid to claim it for Christendom. And none of these were more impressive—or more legendary—than the Knights Templar, also known as the Templar Order. Bearing a red cross upon their white tunics, the Knights Templar existed almost purely for the purpose of crusading, and they became an emblem of the Church's power.

That power included wealth. When the Crusades had still been the in thing among Europe's nobility, they had poured vast amounts of money into donations to the Templar Order. This wealth would turn out to be part of the Knights' downfall. Upon their return from the last crusade, Philip IV borrowed an almost unimaginable sum from the Knights Templar without any intention of ever paying it back. When the Knights started to get restless about the debt, Philip responded by issuing an order to have them all arrested on charges that were likely all false. Still, the nature of the charges succeeded in turning the very Church against the Knights Templar. It was on a dark Friday, the 13th of October, 1307, that the arrests were made. The date of Friday the 13th has gone down in history as an unlucky one ever since.

Tortured by a cruel inquisition, most of the Knights confessed to their false crimes, and dozens were burned at the stake. But one—the Grand Master of the Knights Templar, Jacques de Molay—recanted his confession. It would be seven years before Philip succeeded in destroying the Templar Order once and for all, which made Jacques guilty by association and allowed Philip to burn him at the stake at last.

Jacques' execution was to be a display of Philip's power, a final assertion of the fact that the French Crown was now stronger than the Church. And what place would be more befitting for such an execution than the most majestic cathedral in the capital of France? So it was, on March 18th, 1314, as the sunset painted the incomplete twin towers of Notre-Dame's western facade in perfect gold, that the last of the Grand Masters was tied to a wooden stake in the square in front of the mighty church. In the shadow of the institution for which he had fought so long and hard, Jacques de Molay watched as the wood surrounding him was set on fire. His executioners had specifically built the fire to burn for a long time so that Jacques would be slowly and excruciatingly killed. And as the flames licked at his hands and feet, as the blisters spread across his body and his clothes melted into his skin in the face of the flame, Jacques lifted up his voice and cursed King Philip, the pope, and everyone else who had partaken in his execution. He cursed Philip most of all, prophesying that the House of Capet—which had stood firm as the royal family of France for three centuries—would end with him.

Jacques' curse may have been simply the desperate anger of a dying man. Yet there is something chilling in the events that followed. Within a little more than a month, the pope was dead. That same year, King Philip IV died. And in 1328, Charles IV, Philip's youngest son, died without an heir. The Capetian dynasty died alongside him, and from the ashes of his death rose the ugly era of the Hundred Years' War.

117 years later, the boy king of England would be crowned King of France only a few yards from the place where Jacques de Molay had been killed. But Henry VI's coronation was not the Hail Mary that the English regency had hoped it would be. Instead, it was the last gasp of a failing war effort. Joan of Arc's influence had been too strong to die with her; it lived on in French efforts until, finally, the last battle of the Hundred Years' War was won in 1453.

France had narrowly escaped falling into English hands. Now a proudly independent nation, it raised itself from the rubble left by the devastating war. Notre-Dame would rear her proud and gorgeous head over a liberated Paris.

But Notre-Dame's troubles were far from over. In fact, for the beautiful church itself, they were just beginning. An era of saints and crusades, a time of powerful popes and Gothic cathedrals, was coming to an end. And as the Roman Catholic Church lost its power, its cathedrals would find themselves in great peril.

Chapter 4 – The First Ransacking

Grotesques, like this chimera on the roof of Notre-Dame, were meant to symbolize the
evil consequences of disobeying God's commands, specially designed to help educate
illiterate medieval peasants. Huguenots, however, saw them as abominations

In 1517, after centuries of the Roman Catholic Church reigning supreme over all of Western Europe's Christians, a man named Martin Luther was the first to openly challenge the status quo.

The Roman Catholic Church was the first organized religious institution to rise from the band of wanderers that called themselves the apostles. With bare feet and empty hands, this handful of men and women, the first Christians, moved throughout their world to spread the Gospel. Bands of believers gathered together and became known as "the Church," but it would be a long time before actual church buildings would first become part of the Christian faith. It was only once the Roman Empire itself adopted Christianity that churches and basilicas began to be built in large numbers, and when the Western Roman Empire fell apart, the Roman Catholic Church remained. It would survive for decades as the Middle Ages came and went, and it still survives today, but not alone. Now, hundreds of different denominations have opened churches all over the world. And the Reformation began with a man named Martin Luther who began to question Catholicism as a whole.

While the Church had declined in power since the early Middle Ages, it still remained not only a religious organization but also an important political entity. And, as politics often does, it had become deeply corrupted. Men in positions of power quickly found a way to abuse that power, regardless of whether they were priests or popes. Worse still, in Luther's eyes, were some of the Church's doctrines—and primary among them was the practice of making icons. These little artworks depicting saints or even Jesus Himself were central to the Catholic faith, but to Luther, they were idols, directly breaking the Second Commandment.

Luther was driven to take action. His vision was one of a new type of faith, one that relied on the words of Scripture instead of on the teachings of priests or popes. And so, in 1517, he published his *Ninety-five Theses* calling for change.

Times were, indeed, changing in France and elsewhere. The era of the medieval knight had come to an end; cannonballs now whistled in battle where once swords had clashed, and an era of innovation and discovery was being ushered in. Spain had discovered America (although they didn't know it yet), golf games were being played, and Leonardo da Vinci's world-shaking ideas had started to encourage the world to think outside the box. The Roman Catholic Church was very much inside the box, and when Luther proposed a change, thousands of people followed him. And Notre-Dame, herself a magnificent emblem of the Church's pomp and power, would be in terrible danger.

* * * *

The mighty Notre-Dame towered over France, its details etched in the brilliant sunlight. From the Old Testament kings decorating its tympanum, to the shining stained glass scenes from the Bible in its windows, and to the priceless artworks hanging on its walls, Notre-Dame was filled with images of saints, martyrs, and people from the Bible. To the Catholics who worshiped there, these were icons that they used to focus their minds on their worship. But to the Protestants lurking in the streets outside, they were abominable idols, sinful images that directly broke the rules of God.

It was the year 1548, and the Protestant movement had been gathering momentum ever since the day that Martin Luther nailed his *Theses* to the door of a German church. Spreading all over Europe, his ideas had inspired a vast following, including John (Jean in French) Calvin—a Frenchman who would later become one of the greatest protagonists of the Reformation. Calvin's followers in France had become known as Huguenots by their enemies, and they had already endured relentless persecution. Anger boiled in them for the Catholic Church that they viewed as gluttonous and immoral. And in their eyes, Notre-Dame, standing in the center of Paris, with all of its paintings and its statues, was an unbearable symbol of that immorality.

While the day and time are unknown, we do know what the Huguenots did next, sometime in that fateful year. They gathered together, a huge band of furious men and women, ready to do what they perceived to be justice. And then they stormed the mighty Notre-Dame. Their target was not the people serving inside the church, but the icons that those people had treasured for decades. And the Huguenots were merciless with them. Statues were beheaded, windows smashed; they even stormed the roof and cast down the snarling gargoyles from their perches. Stone smashed and shattered on the street, artworks that had taken years to complete irreparably broken in mere minutes. The Huguenots were filled with righteous rage, and they didn't care.

By the end of the ransacking, many of Notre-Dame's artworks had been all but destroyed. Her walls and towers still stood proud, but great holes gaped where her stained glass windows had proudly shone. As for the Huguenots, they would soon face a tidal wave of relentless persecution, a cruel and bloody era in history during which they were butchered for their different faith. Yet the Protestants did not give up, and the Reformation would change the face of religion forever. The Roman Catholic Church, however, like Notre-Dame, would not be removed. Both still stand today as they have stood for centuries.

Chapter 5 – Louis Times Two

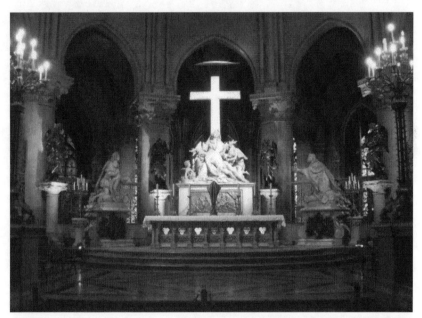

The high altar. The gilded fence added by Robert de Cotte is visible in the background

By the mid-17th century, most of the religious fighting was over. The Huguenots had been scattered to the four winds, some as far away as the southern tip of Africa. A kind of peace had been reached after the Protestants and their English allies suffered a heart-wrenching defeat at the Siege of La Rochelle in 1628; the

Protestants were ostensibly free to worship in any way they wished, even though their army had to be disbanded.

The peace would not last long, however. Notre-Dame stood guard over a Paris that would soon come under intense threat from a war that would claim eight million lives: the Thirty Years' War. It was an extension of the French Wars of Religion that had blossomed all over Europe, triggered by the election of Ferdinand II, a Holy Roman Emperor whose slant was strongly pro-Catholic. His attempts to suppress Protestantism in his empire resulted in a bloody, drawn-out war that dragged several other European countries into the conflict, including, most notably, France.

The Thirty Years' War ended in 1648, a hundred years after the Huguenots first desecrated Notre-Dame. Its sheer destruction was on a scale hitherto unheard of; plague, war, and famine had defaced Europe's people in much the same way as Notre-Dame was stripped of her treasures. For France, the war ended in a victory, establishing the nation as the mightiest in Europe.

By the time the war was over, France had ushered in a new age of greatness, led by King Louis XIV. Known as the Sun King, Louis was one of the longest-reigning monarchs of all time. He was passionate about arts and literature and was an able ruler; under his guidance, France grew into one of the major powers on the continent. He was also able to secure territories in North America. His keen interest in the arts would greatly affect Notre-Dame herself—and not in a way that many historians consider to be positive.

Robert de Cotte, a prestigious architect, was chosen for the task of renovating Notre-Dame in order to reflect the wealth and power of the Sun King. Work on the cathedral began in 1699, focusing on the sanctuary and high altar of the church. De Cotte designed a luxurious wrought-iron fence, overlaid with pure gold, to replace the rood screen that had once shielded the choir; he also entirely removed the high altar—including the tombs that were located beneath it—and replaced it with a new one. This one, extravagantly decorated with a pietà, was flanked by two kneeling statues of Louis XIV and his father Louis XIII.

Notre-Dame was now thoroughly stylish. While many of its medieval features had been removed or destroyed, it was entering into a new age in the history of France, an age in which art had risen to an entirely new height of importance. This was reflected in the sudden flood of artwork that was brought to the great cathedral. 76 paintings —some of them priceless masterpieces—were donated. One of these was Charles de la Fosse's *Adoration of the Magi*, a famous depiction of the three wise men worshiping the Baby Jesus, painted in 1715.

Gold and jewels were in abundance as well; the goldsmiths' guild of Paris had agreed to donate a gleaming altarpiece every year. As these were due to be donated on the first of May each year, they became known as the *grands Mays*. Depicting scenes from the biblical book of Acts, they were wrought by only the most skilled goldsmiths, and many of these works remain in Notre-Dame today. They would complement an altar that was already built from the most precious Egyptian marble.

As the 18th century wore on, changes to Notre-Dame continued, always overseen by Louis XIV and his successor Louis XV. The doorways were widened to allow royal processions to pass through more easily; even more of the gargoyles were removed, and their lead guttering along with them. More positively, some of Notre-Dame's structures were further strengthened and repaired where necessary, allowing the mighty cathedral to stand for centuries to come.

By the time the renovations were completed in the mid-18th century, Notre-Dame was at the height of its beauty. The art and materials within it were immensely, immeasurably valuable; its structure had been restored to even more than its original strength. France was a glorious and mighty power, and Notre-Dame, towering at the heart of the nation's capital, was a symbol of it. With colonies in the Americas, an unrelenting grip on its own nation, and coffers overflowing with wealth, France was a force to be reckoned with. It was proud, it was lavish, and it was luxurious— as were its kings.

Yet pride comes before a fall. And no monarchy would fall harder than the rulers of France. The French Revolution was coming, and it was going to be ugly—for the monarchy, for the people, and even for the innocent and beautiful Notre-Dame.

Chapter 6 – Surviving Revolution

An artist's depiction of the Storming of the Bastille
https://commons.wikimedia.org/wiki/File:Prise_de_la_Bastille.jpg

In the shadow of Notre-Dame, trouble was brewing.

It was the year 1789. The age of the Sun King was long gone; now Louis XVI was on the throne. Enlightenment had brought new ideas to France, and with them came a threat to the old order.

Absolute monarchy and feudalism, as well as the constant intersection between church and state, were old news. The population of France was seeking something new, and their king was not going to give it to them. In fact, their king was not going to give anything to them except for raised taxes. France had given great support to America during the American Revolutionary War, and now the French were feeling the pinch of the costly war.

As always, it was the common people who had to take the brunt of it. They watched as their king and queen dined upon the most sumptuous delicacies, could only stare as the nobility continued with their lives as if nothing had changed in several hundred years. The peasants starved, and the nobility barely noticed that their nation had been brought to the very brink of bankruptcy.

Something had to give. And on the sunshiny summer day of July 14th, 1789, it gave.

The Bastille was located less than half a mile from the spires of Notre-Dame. A frowning fortress and state prison, it towered over Paris, its stern balustrades and impregnable towers a loud reminder to the Parisians that only the royalty held any real power. It was a symbol of the tyranny of those who ruled by virtue only of their ancestry. It was, in the eyes of the people, a disgrace and a blight on their lives. And so, as its military governor watched with trepidation from behind its mighty drawbridges, the Parisians gathered in the streets. They clutched weapons of every ilk: everything from the deadly muskets that characterized the age, to sharp-edged swords that flashed brilliantly in the summer sun, to half bricks and bits of stone and butcher's knives and wooden clubs and anything else that they could get their hands on. Notre-Dame watched, a pillar of grace and beauty, as anger and resentment bubbled in the streets below.

The crowd continued to grow until, at last, its members decided that they were ready. They rushed forward, half-armed peasants throwing themselves in baying fury against the stern stone walls of the hated Bastille. The soldiers within defended themselves, and gun smoke rose up past the arching windows of Notre-Dame as, just below, a relentless slaughter began. At first, the attempt appeared laughable. How could a handful of peasants overcome the strength of a fortress that had stood since the Middle Ages? But as Parisians continued to flock to the scene, their sheer numbers became overwhelming. At last, the governor had no choice. He raised the white flag of surrender. The Bastille had fallen.

If the governor had hoped that his surrender would lead to his survival, he was sorely mistaken. The revolutionaries captured him and started to lead him toward the Hotel de Ville where they planned to try him for what they perceived to be his crimes against them—even though the only thing of which he was really guilty was his association with the hated monarchy. But he never made it there. The group that had taken the Bastille was not an army but an angry, disorganized mob, and part of it swooped down upon the governor, beheading him, impaling his disembodied head upon a stake, and then parading it through the streets of Paris, right past the doorways of Notre-Dame. And if the great cathedral could have known that this act of violence was only the beginning, if she could have guessed at what was coming next, then her very buttresses would have shivered in fear.

* * * *

The storming of the Bastille was only the beginning of the French Revolution—an ugly, violent, and brutal event in France's history, taking place a little over a full decade and causing thousands of gruesome deaths.

After the Bastille fell, Louis XVI realized that military resistance against the revolutionaries would be fruitless. Instead, for several years, he followed a course of attempting to compromise with the citizens. Ultimately, however, it ended in failure. The first constitution of France—written in 1791—was met with contempt. Nothing but a total victory and a complete change in the government would do for the revolutionaries; they wanted the monarchy gone, and they succeeded in their goal, guillotining first Louis and then his queen, Marie Antoinette, in 1793. The Revolution had now dissolved into an angry and hateful bloodbath known as the Reign of Terror. The radical Jacobins had taken power and sent enemies of the Revolution to the guillotine in terrifying numbers. They went so far as to change the calendar, and they viewed the pompous Church as being just as bad as the monarchy that they had so triumphantly ended. So, their next target was a vast one: Christianity itself.

Notre-Dame, the beautiful cathedral where generations of Parisians had worshiped their God, a shining testimony to architecture, the gleaming home of the Roman Catholic Church in France, became a gigantic target. Disgusted by everything that the great cathedral stood for, revolutionaries fell upon it with no shadow of mercy in 1793. Notre-Dame—so long revered, so carefully treasured—had nobody left to defend her now, not with church leaders and royals alike being beheaded in front of baying crowds. The church was ransacked, and the destruction wrought by the Huguenots was nothing compared to what these revolutionaries did. The statues of the biblical kings were ripped down, beheaded, and carried off as nothing more than rubble; the artworks depicting scenes from the Bible were destroyed and pillaged. The church became a hollowed-out shell of the great cathedral that it once was.

Once the church was stripped of its treasures, it was rededicated but not to a different form of Christianity—in fact, it wasn't even to a religion. Instead, it was made a temple of the Cult of Reason. This new cult was designed to take Roman Catholicism's place in the minds and government of France. Instead of the sober Mass that had once been conducted there, a Festival of Reason was held instead, where a scantily dressed young woman would be placed on a pedestal and dance seductively as revolutionaries worshiped her as the Goddess of Reason.

It was a good thing that Maurice de Sully had been dead for almost 600 years. Had he seen what had become of his beloved Notre-Dame, one can only imagine the heartache and pain that he would have suffered.

For the cathedral, it would seem that all hope was lost. But a savior was coming, one who would put together the pieces of post-Revolution France, one who would become famous all over the world and throughout history, one whose name would become synonymous with strategic brilliance: Napoleon Bonaparte.

Chapter 7 – The Emperor and the Hunchback

Golden morning light streamed into the heart of Notre-Dame, filtered by its tall windows. The light sparkled upon the gilded wrought-iron fence and slid across the surfaces of restored artworks that decorated its interior. Outside, the beheaded statues of the Kings of Judah had been returned to their rightful places. Crosses and cherubim, virgins and kings once again adorned the mighty church.

Ever since the revolutionaries first destroyed her majesty in 1793, Notre-Dame had found itself housing various cults and even being used for completely non-spiritual purposes. The Cult of Reason had been supplanted by the Cult of the Supreme Being in mid-1794, and a mixture of philosophy and pagan rituals continued to be celebrated inside the venerated walls for years. That was until Napoleon Bonaparte rose to power. A military genius who had been serving France during the Revolution, Napoleon's vision of post-Revolution France did not align with that of the radical Jacobins that were then in control of the government. He staged a coup in 1799, overthrew the French Directory, and established a Consulate, naming himself as the First Consul.

By that point, Napoleon was the most powerful man in France. But First Consul was not enough for him. He wanted a higher title with more power that was preferably a hereditary one. Being king would take a step back into the days before the Revolution, so Napoleon aimed even higher. He decided to have himself crowned emperor.

And so, on December 2nd, 1804, Notre-Dame was packed with people. Years of restoration work had gone into turning it from the hole of pagan worship it had been during the Revolution back to its former glorious self. Napoleon had chosen it as the perfect venue for his coronation: beautiful, majestic, and at the center of France's capital, but not bearing the same negative connotations as Reims, the historic location for the coronations of the very kings that the revolutionaries had just overthrown.

Napoleon had also decided to restore Christianity to a legal and acceptable religion in France. The revolutionaries had been unsuccessful in eradicating it. Only the most radical of the French people agreed to join their cults; most still clung to their beliefs despite persecution from the revolutionaries. While the church and state were now separate once and for all, Napoleon himself remained a Roman Catholic and saw his coronation as a statement about his divine appointment to the rank of emperor.

The coronation ceremony was in full swing. Music rose up, sweet hymns once again filling the air inside the belly of Notre-Dame. Its bells rang once more, their clear and poignant peals echoing across a restored Paris. Pope Pius VII anointed Napoleon's head and hands, a sacred ceremony that he would have performed on a new king if the monarchy had not been destroyed. But one thing was different about this ceremony, a stark reminder that the old glory days of Catholicism were gone. Instead of placing the crown upon Napoleon's head, Pius handed it to him and stepped back. To roars of appreciation from the audience, Napoleon, seated on his throne, took the crown and crowned himself.

* * * *

Napoleon's rule over France brought stability to the nation, if not the freedom that the revolutionaries had wanted. Although he was widely known as a despot and centralized power for himself, he did succeed in dragging France, kicking and screaming, into the modern era. Education, military, taxation, and other aspects of the administration were all streamlined and modernized under his rule. And while the Church no longer held the administrative power that it did before the Revolution, religious tolerance was widespread. Catholics, Protestants, atheists, and Jewish alike were allowed to worship openly without fear of persecution.

After his coronation, however, Napoleon's focus turned to warfare. His famous campaigns were widely successful, but they left little room to focus on the church where he had been crowned. Notre-Dame, although given a rest from the looting it had suffered in the past centuries, was neglected. Not all of the damage done by the revolutionaries had been repaired before Napoleon's coronation; for example, instead of repairing damages done to the walls, Napoleon's workers had simply covered obvious blemishes with tapestries or drapes. Besides that, the church was already centuries old, and its age was beginning to show. Hundreds of years of wind, weather, and filth were starting to take their toll.

By 1831, Notre-Dame's interior had practically fallen to pieces, as had French politics. Napoleon had abdicated in 1814 after successive military defeats left him with little choice. The monarchy returned to power with the guillotined Louis XVI's younger brother being crowned Louis XVIII, although many of the Revolution's reforms remained in place. Kings were still regarded with some suspicion, and turbulence had taken hold of France. An economic downturn was inevitable—and Notre-Dame was not exempt from feeling the pinch.

The cathedral's proud exterior was more or less intact, apart from the headless kings that now decorated it. Its spire, however, had crumbled due to sheer age. And within, Notre-Dame was almost as decrepit as the church of Saint Etienne that it had replaced. While Mass was still being held inside the church, its interior was filled with crumbling masonry, cracked glass, and remnants of the Revolution's vicious desecration.

Parisians had just suffered the most violent fifty years in the city's history. Now, however, despite the turmoil in the government, daily life had become largely peaceful. They were able to turn their hearts and minds back to things like art and worship, and the state of Notre-Dame tugged at their hearts.

No one was more affected than Victor Hugo. He was disgusted by the destruction that the Revolution had wrought, and he responded in the only way that his writer's soul knew how: he wrote a novel. Titled *Notre-Dame de Paris*—and later published in English as *The Hunchback of Notre-Dame*—it told the story of the unfortunate foundling Quasimodo, a bell-ringer of Notre-Dame in the Middle Ages at the height of the cathedral's glory. The story tugged at the hearts and minds of people all over France, and public outcry demanded for the restoration of Notre-Dame. The French king, Louis Philippe I, had little choice but to respond. He ordered renovations to begin in 1844, and under the guidance of two architects—Jean-Baptiste-Antoine Lassus and Eugène Viollet-le-Duc—work began.

In an era when freshly minted Neo-Baroque architecture was taking over most of the cities, Lassus, Viollet-le-Duc, and their colleagues went against the grain. Their vision was to restore Notre-Dame the way it was when it had just been completed, recreating the cathedral that had so captured the collective imagination in Hugo's novel. This did not stop them from adding a few embellishments, however. While they worked from old drawings of the cathedral in its Gothic splendor, they also added a famous line of stone chimeras along the roof and built a new spire that has become an icon of Notre-Dame's beauty.

The renovations took two decades to complete. By 1865, Notre-Dame was once again restored to its full and splendid glory. Victor Hugo actually survived to see the renovations complete. He would go on to finish many dramas, poems, and books, but none would be so famous as the story that saved a cathedral—*The Hunchback of Notre-Dame.*

Chapter 8 – Two Warrior Women

"*Au Nom de Dieu!*" *In the Name of God!* The cry rose high above the battlefield, piercing through the screams of the dying and the clash of weapons. Dead men and horses sprawled all over the muddy banks of the Loire, their blood trickling into the river, as the French and English clashed in violence. The siegeworks of the English were being rapidly breached, and the city of Orléans anticipated its liberation as French knights surged into the relentless tide of their foe. Grunts of effort, bellows of pain, and barked orders echoed across the bloodied battlefield—but one voice rose above them all, not because of its volume but because of its ringing purity. It was like the sound of a church bell among the echoes of war. "*Au Nom de Dieu!*"

From where they tried desperately to hold their ground, the English soldiers could see a shining white banner snapping above the heads of the French guard. Moments later, bursting brilliantly forth between the swarm of soldiers, came a charging white horse. Its rider gleamed in their burnished armor, but this metal suit followed a set of shapely curves. From beneath the raised visor of the helmet, a youthful young face gazed out, smooth cheeks

---

framed by a torrent of dark hair and with blue eyes unnerving in their brightness.

"The witch!" the English soldiers cried among themselves. "The witch!"

But to the French, the girl who rode at their head, armed only with her white banner, was everything but a witch. She was a savior, a beacon of hope, an angel—perhaps even a saint. Her name was Jeanne d' Arc, although the English called her Joan. And she was going to save them all.

* * * *

Science and history combined still fail to explain why Joan of Arc was able to so dramatically turn the tide of a war that had been raging for almost a century. The Hundred Years' War was a bitter and drawn-out conflict, and its most definitive turn came when this innocent maiden from a tiny village rode up to the French Dauphin and told him that God had sent her. Joan would proceed to lead a series of victorious battles, never actually striking a blow herself, but her sheer presence inspired the French soldiers to the point where they seemed to believe themselves invincible.

The war was all but won by the French when the English finally captured her. Joan was tried by a corrupt court and sentenced to death for the only charge they could get to stick—cross-dressing. She was burned at the stake in 1431, 22 years before the battle that would bring the great war to an end at last.

Joan had been condemned to death by the Catholic Church. But almost 500 years later, that very same Church would recognize her as a hero and a martyr. Joan's mother, Isabelle, was the first to raise her voice in indignation that a girl who had been viewed as a heroine of the faith had been killed by the Church itself. She appealed to have Joan's name cleared in 1455, shortly after the end of the war. Her appeal was granted, and Joan was exonerated in 1456.

Over the centuries, although the revolutionaries destroyed Joan's sword and banner as symbols of both Catholicism and the monarchy, her identity as France's great national hero would endure. Napoleon definitely viewed her as a hero, and she has been widely celebrated by the people ever since his ascension. And despite initial resistance from some of the clergy, in 1909, the Church finally agreed that Joan was more than a hero—she was a saint. The first step toward declaring Joan's sainthood was to beatify her, a way to officially recognize her as blessed.

Notre-Dame, located in the heart of the country that Joan had sworn to save, was chosen as the best venue for her beatification. Fresh from its renovations, the cathedral was more beautiful than ever before. The beatification ceremony was held on April 18th, 1909, and was attended by some of the most important people in the whole of France as well as descendants of some of the people she had known in her life—most notably the Duke of Alençon, who had been one of her staunchest supporters and most courageous friends.

In 1920, Joan was officially canonized and entered the records of the Roman Catholic Church as a fully-fledged saint. 30,000 people attended the ceremony at St. Peter's Basilica in Rome, proving that Joan was more than just a historical figure to them: she still remained as a symbol of France's courage, resilience, and faith, even in the face of hopelessness.

* * * *

On February 11th, 1931—a decade after Joan of Arc was made a saint—a gunshot rang out in the sanctuary of Notre-Dame.

Nobody had believed María Antonieta Rivas Mercado when she'd told them that she was depressed. After all, why should she be? She was everything: beautiful, young, rich, and famous.

Born in 1900 to a wealthy family in Mexico City, Antonieta grew up in a turbulent Mexico. While the president, Porfirio Díaz, seemed to be a strong and able administrator, he had also been fraudulently elected. The corruption was too much for Mexico's citizens who staged a ten-year revolution that ended in 1920. Revolts would continue, however, as Antonieta grew up, fell in love, and gave birth to her son. In the face of the continued violence and chaos throughout the country, citizens found themselves teetering between anarchy and subservience to the traditional, old ways. New ideas were hard to find, and when they did occur, they were not welcomed by the people; as a result, the arts suffered. Worse, Mexico's neighbor, the United States, had granted women the right to vote while feminism itself was only in its infancy stage in Mexico.

Antonieta spent her life trying to change that. She threw herself into supporting literature, theater, and other forms of art. Financing theaters and supporting all kinds of artists, Antonieta was herself a writer and a vocal advocate for the rights of women and children. In a time when Mexico was focused on survival, Antonieta was asking for more than that: she wanted progress.

Today, she is credited with greatly aiding the survival of Mexican culture. She might not have been a Catholic or even a rider on a white horse like Joan of Arc was, but she was a warrior in her own right, fighting tooth and nail for everything she believed in. And she won many of her fights, but one victory was permanently denied her.

Antonieta's personal life was often in chaos. Her marriage to Albert Edward Blair, an engineer, had ended in unhappiness, her love affair with painter Manuel Rodríguez Lozano had been one-sided, and now she loved a man who was married to someone else. It was this man, a politician named José Vasconcelos, that she had followed all the way across the world from Mexico to Paris to find that he wasn't willing to leave his wife for her.

The dark cloud that had hung over Antonieta's head ever since her hateful marriage grew thicker and thicker. At last, one day, she asked her lover, "Tell me if you really need me."

Tragically, he didn't recognize the real implication of her words. Instead, he considered it a philosophical question, something intellectual instead of the raw and desperate cry of a soul looking for a reason—any reason—to stay alive.

"No soul needs another," he responded, trying to impress her with his wisdom. "No one, neither man nor woman, needs more than God."

His words were the last straw for Antonieta. Later that day, after he had left, she stole the gun that he kept in his desk. Then she walked down toward the banks of the Seine and gazed up at the majestic facade of Notre-Dame. Her father, a renowned architect, had told her enough about his work that she knew the great cathedral was one of the best in the world. Its towering spire, its gleaming statues, its gilded details—it was exquisite, and it still couldn't help her. Her mind filled with a dark turmoil and a deadly certainty, Antonieta mounted the steps, entered the cathedral, and walked up to where a statue of Christ dominated the high altar.

It was there that she shot herself. One bullet, directly into her heart. And for the first time, Notre-Dame's interior was awash with blood.

* * * *

In later decades, others would commit suicide by jumping from the roof of Notre-Dame. But Antonieta's death was even more brutal, its location even more heart-wrenching. Notre-Dame, the venue for a thousand happy occasions over the hundreds of years of its history, was now a giant and silent witness to a young, preventable, and appalling death.

Chapter 9 – Withstanding the War

Ringing out across the city, breaking the silence that had enveloped Paris for four long and frightening years, tolled the tenor bell of Notre-Dame. Its sweet and somber tone echoed throughout the streets, bouncing off the wreckage of the hard battle that had just been fought there.

Paris was a pathetic sight compared to the bustling city that it had been just a few years ago before World War II began. The capital of France had weathered the First World War behind the lines, serving as an oasis of relative peace despite occasional bombings and the rationing that had characterized wartime Europe. Now a republic, it had experienced a relatively easy interwar period, not feeling the pinch of the Great Depression as bad as some other countries. Culture, art, and Parisian life had blossomed at the feet of Notre-Dame as before, and the cathedral itself was still in good condition after its restorations less than a century before.

Then the Nazis came.

They rolled over the French landscape, bitter and fascist and unrelentingly powerful. For a year, France held out against them with all of its might, supported by its Allied friends. But it was not enough. In 1940, France fell, forced to surrender to Germany, and Paris became a part of what Hitler hoped would become an empire. The great city was subjected to terrible humiliation as Nazis set up shop wherever they wished. Its population—once purged of those unfortunates whom the Nazis deemed to be less than human—was largely unmolested physically, but the very spirit of Paris—its artistry, its passion, its sophistication—was crushed. Witnesses would later tell how the streets of the City of Lights fell silent. There was no music. There were no singers. There was only a kind of muffled terror as Parisians struggled through their daily lives, their food rationed, every corner watched by their looming enemy. And they waited for the sound of bombs or sirens—anything that would indicate that the Nazis had tired of them and decided to eradicate them anyway.

The mighty Notre-Dame now stood guard over a city that seemed to have lost its soul. While Mass was allowed to continue, frightened citizens often opted to stay home instead. Ceremonies had lost their pomp and passion with the clergy seeming to be going through the motions. Notre-Dame used to be a symbol of French craftsmanship and power. Now it was mocked by the swastikas on every flag, its people defeated. None of its statues had been cast down, as this time, the damage was unseen. Notre-Dame was still beautiful, yet it was no longer the pride of the French people. They had lost their pride long ago.

For four terrible years, the cathedral watched as France lay beaten. But though France had surrendered, many of its people had not given up. Rallied by army officer Charles de Gaulle, they formed the French Resistance, a secret underground force that stood against everything the Nazis wanted. And in 1944, the Resistance rose at last. Common Parisians blocked the streets with bits of furniture and chunks of wood then stormed upon their enemies as Allied support rushed in from beyond the city walls. Finally, Paris was free.

To celebrate, the bells of Notre-Dame were rung, and the city erupted into a celebration of noise that had been straining to be free through the four years of silence. Joyous, the bells tolled, singing out their sweet message across the rescued city. Notre-Dame was more of a monument now than ever before: she stood now for a people who had saved themselves. A people who, even in the face of defeat, were never truly defeated.

* * * *

From the ashes of the Second World War rose France's Fourth Republic, which soon gave way after a few years to the Fifth Republic and was led by the same Charles de Gaulle who had sparked the Resistance in the first place. A steady and capable president, de Gaulle succeeded in freeing many of the countries that were still French colonies, established good relations with Germany, and even made France the fourth nuclear power during the Cold War.

One of his other acts as president was to appoint a new culture minister: Georges André Malraux. This highly controversial man had been fascinated by historical artifacts, works of art, and literature ever since he was young, and he quickly set his sights on one of Paris' most famous landmarks—Notre-Dame. The cathedral had suffered only a few superficial bullet holes during the Liberation of Paris, and most of its priceless beauty had survived both world wars unscathed. However, the industrial era—and the pollution that came with it—had been far less kind. Over the past hundred years, as factories began to crop up all over France and the world, spewing noxious gases and smoky fumes, a layer of grime had begun to accumulate over Notre-Dame's proud visage. The dirt was so bad that it transformed the pale stone from a creamy white to a dull gray. In 1963, as the world was just starting to settle down after decades of global warfare, Notre-Dame celebrated its 800ᵗʰ birthday. Malraux's anniversary gift to the cathedral was a thorough cleaning. It took hours of labor and multitudes of workers, but by the end of the year, Notre-Dame sparkled once more.

With the cathedral now beautifully restored, its artworks all in their proper place, and its walls shining, a young daredevil named Philippe Petit decided that it was the perfect location for his first great stunt in 1971. Stringing a tightrope between the two towers of Notre-Dame's western facade, Petit stepped out onto the wire over an awed crowd gathered below. With no safety net and no harness, he walked the distance from one tower to the other with nothing but a balancing pole. His successful stunt made him famous—and also got him arrested. He was soon released, however, and would make an even more famous appearance by walking a tightrope between the Twin Towers of the World Trade Center in New York three years later.

The year that the Soviet Union fell and the Cold War finally ended—1991—Notre-Dame was once again extensively renovated. Much of its masonry was beginning to show signs of wear after almost 830 years, which was not helped by air pollution and pigeon droppings, and the famous gargoyles were even in danger of falling clean off the cathedral's walls. The exterior was extensively restored, always staying as true as possible to the original; while new stone had to be brought in, it was carved to be the exact similitude of the crumbling blocks it came to replace. These restorations took eight years to complete.

By the beginning of the 21ˢᵗ century, Notre-Dame was looking as glorious as could be expected considering its advanced age. In fact, it had become a monument of everything that France had survived. The great cathedral had stood guard as the tumultuous Middle Ages devolved into the brutal Hundred Years' War; it had survived the savage Revolution and seen Napoleon crowned; and even the two world wars could do little to change the steadfast landmark that had become the most famous in all of Paris.

France had now entered a new era, one where it would stand side by side with the free world in combating the terrorism that had now become a global threat. Less than thirty years after Petit's famous walk across the World Trade Center, the Twin Towers were bombed by Middle Eastern terrorists, starting the War on Terror. Paris became the target for smaller attacks. Notre-Dame herself came perilously close to suffering the same fate as the Twin Towers: in 2016, a group of terrorists was arrested near the cathedral with explosives found inside their car.

Yet some of the greatest destruction that would ever be wrought upon Notre-Dame was not an intentional attack. After surviving Huguenots, revolutionaries, and enemy invasions, the over eight-century-old cathedral was about to face her greatest threat yet. And this time, it would be by accident.

Chapter 10 – Part of Us Burning

Robbed of its iconic spire, Notre-Dame is at the mercy of the blaze
*LeLaisserPasserA38, CC BY-SA 4.0 <https://creativecommons.org/licenses/by-sa/4.0>,
via Wikimedia Commons
https://commons.wikimedia.org/wiki/File:Incendie_Notre_Dame_de_Paris.jpg*

On April 15th, 2019, Notre-Dame burned. 400 firefighters rushed to the rescue of the cathedral that had captured the world's heart as smoke belched into the air, rising from somewhere behind the great towers that had stood guard over 800 years of history. Orange flames combined with white smoke, the greedy fingers of the flames reaching up to grasp the spire with strangulating force. Crowds gathered, crying out in horror as the fire licked and then roared upon the roof. The oak was hundreds of years old; it was a part of the original structure, hewed by medieval hands and sawed from the ancient strength of 5,000 oak trees. It was priceless, it was carefully preserved, and it was a part of French history. But the fire didn't know. The fire didn't care. It simply devoured it, centuries of beloved art crumbling into ash in mere hours. Lead melted and dripped onto the street, and the gargoyles' snarling faces appeared transfixed by pain as the fire lapped around their feet.

Hurrying to try and quench the blaze, the firefighters soon had to face a terrifying possibility. Despite the jets of water that they kept constantly directed on the heart of the flames, fighting a fire of this scale on a building of this age was almost impossible. There were no fire safety features installed here, none of the modern sprinkler systems that newer buildings have to protect against just such a tragedy. Access would be difficult; to try and save the cathedral without destroying it by water damage would be even more so. Dismayed, some firefighters had to tell the press the frightening truth: They might not be able to save Notre-Dame at all. Paris might have to watch its favorite cathedral burn to nothing but rubble.

Centuries of skill, passion, and care had gone into building the cathedral and its many restorations. Time, effort, money, even love—it had all been poured into Notre-Dame over hundreds of years as the French people rallied time and time again to save and protect it and everything that it stood for. Never had they had to fight as hard as that day, a day when firefighters risked their own lives to try to rescue a chunk of history, a piece of Paris' own heart.

As the night wore on, the firefighters kept working. They had suffered a terrible setback that evening when, with a crack whose echoes rang out across the world, the great spire fell. Viollet-le-Duc had built it after the French king had ordered it, after Parisians had demanded it, after Victor Hugo had inspired them. Decades of work, hours of dedication—gone in a moment, in the flash of a flame.

But the firefighters refused to give up. Even after one of their own was sent to the hospital after suffering serious injuries, they continued to fight for the cathedral that France loved. And finally, in the small hours of the next morning, the flames were stilled.

* * * *

The whole world had watched as Notre-Dame burned. The President of France himself dropped everything and rushed to the scene to watch in silent horror. When that spire fell, the hearts of millions tumbled alongside it. Indeed, the damage was horrifying. Two-thirds of the roof had been completely destroyed, alongside the lead guttering that had been there for centuries. The spire was gone, consumed by flame. Smoke damaged many of the paintings within, and even the stained glass windows' lead joints melted and caused further damage. Pews that had seated generations of Parisians at every Mass had been reduced to nothing but ash.

Yet in the cold light of day, as the sun rose for the first time on a Notre-Dame gutted by destruction, workers began to sift through the wreckage, and what they found surprised them. It was hope. For even though the spire was gone, the roof destroyed, and much of the interior had been irreparably damaged, much of Notre-Dame was left. Her facades and towers remained standing as they had for centuries; the ancient stonework was largely untouched. The organ, main cross, and altar, the gorgeous rose windows, and every last relic—including some reported to be from the Crucifixion itself—had all survived almost unscathed. This was largely thanks to the ribbed stone vault that formed much of the cathedral's ceiling; the stone was virtually impervious to the fire, saving much of the interior. Many of the artworks had been salvaged, either already removed due to the construction taking place prior to the fire or rescued by a determined team of individuals who had formed a human chain and carried relics and artworks alike to the safety of the Louvre one by one. And the largest of all of Quasimodo's bells had survived intact.

The cathedral had been desperately wounded, but it lived, and its soul seemed to live on in the people of Paris. They gathered in the streets because their cathedral had burned and sang "Ave Maria" as investigators began to filter through the rubble.

The cause of the fire, at the time of writing, is still under investigation, as is the true extent of the damage—the water, smoke, and structural damage have not yet been fully assessed. Preliminary results, however, suggest that it was a horrible accident, potentially the result of electrical wiring or of the renovations that were underway when the fire began.

The fire had not yet been put out when millionaires and people of power started to pledge money and time in order to rebuild and restore Notre-Dame. Over one billion euros have already been donated for the rebuilding. Notre-Dame's burning was a horrific tragedy, but one that both Notre-Dame and its people will survive, cut to the quick though they both might be. It has been estimated that the reconstruction could take decades, a disappointing number for those who may have hoped to see the iconic cathedral during the 2024 Paris Olympics. Plans for rebuilding are already well under way, however, including an architectural design competition for the new spire.

The French president, Emmanuel Macron, seemed to sum up the feelings of an entire nation in a social media post on the day of the fire. "Emotion of a whole nation," he wrote. "[...] Like all our compatriots, I am sad this evening to see this part of us burning."

Conclusion

The massive donations that came rolling in after Notre-Dame's tragic fire became controversial in many circles. In a time when forests, seas, and countless other natural environments are under threat, a time when people still go hungry and humanitarian crises still abound, the absurdity of spending such vast sums of money on an ancient building seems like an insult. Why would it be important to rebuild some old church instead of using that kind of money for other good causes?

The answer lies not only in Notre-Dame's story but in what she means to the nation that built her. Maurice de Sully envisioned building a majestic cathedral in the newest style, a beautiful building where people could worship their God and admire the power of human achievement. Yet Notre-Dame has become so much more than that. It became a beacon of hope throughout the past 850 years of the long and messy history of the human race. As the French and English killed one another, as France rose up in revolt against itself, as Nazi Germany overwhelmed France and crushed Paris under merciless oppression for four long years, Notre-Dame stood unshaken. She may have suffered a few bullet holes and lost many of her statues, but what the cathedral stood for was something that no amount of war or tragedy could change. It was a symbol of hope, an emblem of the fact that there is something more to this life than mere survival.

Now covered in soot and ash, Notre-Dame still manages to rear its proud facade over the city that grew up around it. Over a billion euros have been pledged to rebuild it, although it remains uncertain whether a full restoration would even be possible. Yet looking back on the centuries of suffering that lay behind, one cannot help but look into the future with an unexpected optimism. Notre-Dame might not have survived much worse than this, but France certainly has. And so, France, tenacious, passionate, and enduring, can be trusted to rebuild the cathedral that the whole world loves so dearly.

Here's another book by Captivating History
that you might like

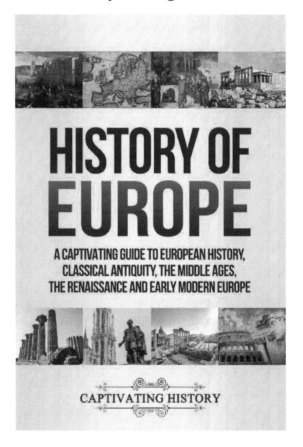

Free Bonus from Captivating History (Available for a Limited time)

Hi History Lovers!

Now you have a chance to join our exclusive history list so you can get your first history ebook for free as well as discounts and a potential to get more history books for free! Simply visit the link below to join.

Captivatinghistory.com/ebook

Also, make sure to follow us on Facebook, Twitter and Youtube by searching for Captivating History.

Appendix 1: The Fourteen Points, a simplified list of Wilson's guidelines for peace

Open covenants of peace, openly arrived at

Freedom of the seas

The removal so far as possible of all economic barriers

The reduction of national armaments to the lowest point consistent with domestic safety

Impartial adjustment of all colonial claims

The evacuation of all Russian territory

The evacuation and restoration of Belgium

The liberation of France and return of Alsace and Lorraine

Readjustment of the frontiers of Italy to conform to clearly recognizable lines of nationality

The peoples of Austria-Hungary should be accorded the freest opportunity of autonomous development

Evacuation of occupation forces from Romania, Serbia, and Montenegro; Serbia should be accorded free and secure access to the sea

Autonomous development for the non-Turkish peoples of the Ottoman Empire; free passage of the Dardanelles to the ships and commerce of all nations

An independent Poland to be established, with free and secure access to the sea

A general association of nations to be formed to guarantee to its members political independence and territorial integrity (the genesis of the League of Nations)

Bibliography

Andress, David. *The Terror: The Merciless War for Freedom in Revolutionary France*. London: Macmillan, 2006.

Anonymous. *The Song of Roland*. North Chelmsford: Courier Corporation, 2012.

Blanning, T. C. *The Nineteenth Century: Europe, 1789-1914*. New York: Oxford University Press, USA, 2000.

Blanning, Tim. *The Pursuit of Glory: The Five Revolutions that Made Modern Europe: 1648-1815*. London: Penguin, 2007.

Bridgeford, Andrew. *1066: The Hidden History in the Bayeux Tapestry*. New York: Bloomsbury Publishing USA, 2009.

Caesar, Julius. *The Conquest of Gaul*. London: Penguin, 1983.

"Cahiers." Accessed January 1, 2021. https://pages.uoregon.edu/dluebke/301ModernEurope/Cahiers.html.

Carey, John. *Eyewitness to History*. New York: HarperCollins, 1997.

"Charlemagne's Travels." Wayback Machine. Accessed November 25 2020. https://web.archive.org/web/20160419073559/https://aethelraed.ddns.net/charlemagne/intro.html

Chereau, P. (Director). (1994). *Queen Margot* [Dramatic retelling of the events of the St. Bartholomew's Day Massacre].

Cronk, Nicholas. *Voltaire: A Very Short Introduction.* New York: Oxford University Press, 2017.

Danton. Directed by Andrzej Wajda. 1983. Film. (Starring Gerard Depardieu)

Davies, Peter. *France and the Second World War: Occupation, Collaboration and Resistance.* Psychology Press, 2001.

Durant, Will, and Ariel Durant. *The Age of Louis XIV: The Story of Civilization.* New York: Simon & Schuster, 2011.

"France Unveils Stunning Replica of Lascaux Cave Paintings." Artnet News. Last modified December 12, 2016. https://news.artnet.com/exhibitions/lascaux-cave-paintings-replica-780452.

Geary, Patrick J. *Readings in Medieval History, 5th ed.* Toronto: University of Toronto Press, 2015.

Harrison, Kathryn. *Joan of Arc: A Life Transfigured.* Anchor Books, 2014.

Home · Liberty, Equality, Fraternity: Exploring the French Revolution. Accessed November 2, 2020. https://revolution.chnm.org/

Howarth, David. *1066: The Year of the Conquest.* 2002.

Jackson, Julian. *De Gaulle.* Cambridge: Harvard University Press, 2018.

"Jazz Liberates Paris." American Heritage. Accessed February 22, 2021. https://www.americanheritage.com/jazz-liberates-paris

Mansel, Philip. *King of the World: The Life of Louis XIV.* Chicago: University of Chicago Press, 2020.

"Portraits: Louis XIV." Amazon.com. Accessed December 28, 2020. https://www.amazon.com/gp/video/detail/B07CSJJQXS/ref=atv_hm_ho m_1_c_iEgOEZ_2_4

Roche, Daniel. *France in the Enlightenment.* Translated by Arthur Goldhammer. Cambridge: Harvard University Press, 1998.

Schama, Simon. *Citizens: A Chronicle of the French Revolution.* Toronto: Vintage Canada, 1990.

Sebald, W.G. *Austerlitz.* New York: Modern Library, 2011.

Simpson, Howard R. *Dien Bien Phu: The Epic Battle America Forgot.*

Lincoln: Potomac Books, 2005.

The Sorrow and the Pity. Directed by Marcel Ophuls. 1969. Paris, FranceFilm.

Tiersky, Ronald. *François Mitterrand: A Very French President*. Lanham: Rowman & Littlefield, 2003.

"Treasures from Versailles – An Encounter of the Richest Kind." The Culture Concept Circle. Last modified January 13, 2017. https://www.thecultureconcept.com/treasures-from-versailles-an-encounter-of-the-richest-kind

Various. The Portable Enlightenment Reader. London: Penguin, 1995.

Wawro, Geoffrey. *The Franco-Prussian War: The German Conquest of France in 1870-1871*. Cambridge: Cambridge University Press, 2005.

Wilson, Derek. Charlemagne. New York: Vintage, 2007.

Kreis, S. 2006, *The Conversion of Clovis*, The History Guide, viewed 24 April 2020, <http://www.historyguide.org/ancient/clovis.html>

Rickard, J. 2012, *Battle of Soissons, 486*, History of War, viewed 24 April 2020, <http://www.historyofwar.org/articles/battles_soissons.html>

History.com Editors 2018, *Huns*, A&E Television Networks, viewed 15 April 2020, <https://www.history.com/topics/ancient-china/huns>

Pruitt, S. 2018, *8 Things You Might Not Know About Attila the Hun*, A&E Television Networks, viewed 15 April 2020, <https://www.history.com/news/8-things-you-might-not-know-about-attila-the-hun>

Pelegro, B. 2017, *Rome Halts the Huns*, National Geographic, viewed 15 April 2020, <https://www.nationalgeographic.com/history/magazine/2017/01-02/roman-empire-decline-attila-the-hun/>

Stoddard, B. C. 2014, *Attila the Hun & The Battle of the Catalaunian Plains*, Warfare History Network, viewed 15 April 2020, <https://warfarehistorynetwork.com/2014/08/27/attila-the-hun-the-battle-of-the-catalaunian-plains/>

Cavendish, R. 2011, *Death of Clovis I of the Franks*, History Today, viewed 15 April 2020, <https://www.historytoday.com/archive/death-clovis-i-franks>

Mingren, W. 2016, *The Commanding Clovis I: King of the Merovingian Dynasty and Founder of France*, Ancient Origins, viewed 15 April 2020, <https://www.ancient-origins.net/history-famous-people/commanding-clovis-i-king-merovingian-dynasty-and-founder-france-005777>

Violatti, C. 2014, *Franks*, Ancient History Encyclopedia, viewed 15 April 2020, <https://www.ancient.eu/Franks/>

Gascoigne, B. 2001, *History of the Franks*, viewed 15 April 2020, <http://www.historyworld.net/wrldhis/plaintexthistories.asp?historyid=ab74>

Wiener, J. 2013, *The Merovingians: The Kings and Queens of the Franks*, Ancient History Encyclopedia, viewed 15 April 2020, <https://etc.ancient.eu/interviews/the-merovingians-the-lords-and-ladies-of-the-dark-ages/>

Khan, S. M. 2020, *The Umayyad Dynasty*, Ancient History Encyclopedia, viewed 30 April 2020, <https://www.ancient.eu/Umayyad_Dynasty/>

History.com Editors 2019, *Battle of Tours*, A&E Television Networks, viewed 30 April 2020, <https://www.history.com/this-day-in-history/battle-of-tours>

Anonymous 2018, *Who Was Charles Martel and Why Is He Called the Hammer?*, History Hit, viewed 30 April 2020, <https://www.historyhit.com/day-charles-martel-dies/>

Hickman, K. 2019, *Biography of Charles Martel, Frankish Military Leader and Ruler*, ThoughtCo, viewed 30 April 2020, <https://www.thoughtco.com/muslim-invasions-charles-martel-2360687>

Shipley Duckett, E. 2019, *Pippin III*, Encyclopedia Britannica, viewed 30 April 2020, <https://www.britannica.com/biography/Pippin-III#ref5592>

Cybulskie, D. 2018, *Childhood in the Middle Ages*, Medievalists, viewed 30 April 2020, <https://www.medievalists.net/2018/11/childhood-middle-ages/>

Rendfeld, K. 2018, *Himiltrude: Charlemagne's First Ex-Wife*, Kim

Rendfeld, viewed 1 May 2020,
<https://kimrendfeld.wordpress.com/2018/09/12/himiltrude-charlemagnes-first-ex-wife/>

Schedel, H. 1493, *The Nuremberg Chronicle*, Morse Library, Beloit College, viewed 1 May 2020,
<http://digicoll.library.wisc.edu/cgi/t/text/text-idx?c=nur;cc=nur;view=text;idno=nur.001.0004;rgn=div2;node=nur.001.0004%3A8.150>

Rendfeld, K. 2013, *The Last Lombard King*, Historical Fiction Research, viewed 3 June 2020,
<http://historicalfictionresearch.blogspot.com/2013/01/the-last-lombard-king-kim-rendfeld.html>

Rendfeld, K. 2013, *Queen Mother Gerberga: Protecting Her Sons – And Her Power*, Kim Rendfeld, viewed 3 June 2020,
<https://kimrendfeld.wordpress.com/2013/05/28/queen-mother-gerberga-protecting-her-sons-and-her-power/>

Rendfeld, K. 2012, *Family Feuds: Charlemagne and the Fate of the Church*, Unusual Historicals, viewed 3 June 2020,
<http://unusualhistoricals.blogspot.com/2012/04/family-feuds-charlemagne-and-fate-of.html>

Rendfeld, K. 2013, *The Insulted Princess: Charlemagne's Second Wife*, Kim Rendfeld, viewed 3 June 2020,
<https://kimrendfeld.wordpress.com/2013/12/18/the-insulted-princess-charlemagnes-second-wife/>

Snell, M. 2018, *The Lombards: A Germanic Tribe in Northern Italy*, ThoughtCo, viewed 3 June 2020, <https://www.thoughtco.com/the-lombards-defintion-1789086>

Mark, J. J. 2014, *Lombards*, Ancient History Encyclopedia, viewed 3 June 2020, <https://www.ancient.eu/Lombards/>

Anonymous 2015, *Ancient DNA cracks puzzle of Basque origins*, BBC News, viewed 4 June 2020, <https://www.bbc.com/news/science-environment-34175224>

Rodriguez, V. 2019, *Andorra*, Encyclopedia Britannica, viewed 4 June

2020, <https://www.britannica.com/place/Andorra>

Hickman, K. 2017, *Charlemagne: Battle of Roncevaux Pass*, ThoughtCo, viewed 4 June 2020, <https://www.thoughtco.com/charlemagne-battle-of-roncevaux-pass-2360883>

Sundqvist, O. 2015, *An Arena For Higher Powers: Ceremonial buildings and strategies for rulership in Late Iron Age Scandinavia*, BRILL via Google Books, viewed 5 June 2020, <https://books.google.co.za/books?id=CSdzCwAAQBAJ&dq=irminsul+pillar&source=gbs_navlinks_s>

Anonymous 2020, *Paganism, Anglo-Saxon*, Encyclopedia.com, viewed 5 June 2020, <https://www.encyclopedia.com/environment/encyclopedias-almanacs-transcripts-and-maps/paganism-anglo-saxon>

Packer, J. I. 2000, *131 Christians Everyone Should Know*, Holman Reference

Sass, R. 2018, *Saxon Paganism for Today*, Lulu Press, Inc. via Google Books, viewed 5 June 2020, <https://books.google.co.za/books?id=OZg6CgAAQBAJ&dq=fritzlar+church+saxon+burn&source=gbs_navlinks_s>

Violatti, C. 2014, *The Saxons*, Ancient History Encyclopedia, viewed 5 June 2020, <https://www.ancient.eu/Saxons/>

Anonymous 2018, *Widukind, Saxon thorn*, The Eighth Century and All That, viewed 5 June 2020, <http://www.8thcentury.com/widukind-saxon-thorn/>

Anonymous 2018, *Saxon Wars I*, The Eighth Century and All That, viewed 5 June 2020, <http://www.8thcentury.com/the-saxon-wars-i-lets-do-this/>

Anonymous 2018, *Saxon Wars 2: Charles, lawgiver and butcher*, The Eighth Century and All That, viewed 5 June 2020, <http://www.8thcentury.com/saxon-wars-2-charles-lawgiver-and-butcher/>

Anonymous 2018, *Saxon Wars 3: The war is over! Right?*, The Eighth Century and All That, viewed 5 June 2020, <http://www.8thcentury.com/saxon-wars-3-the-war-is-over-right/>

Evans, G. R. 2014, *Charlemagne vs. the Saxons*, Christian History

Magazine, viewed 5 June 2020,
<https://christianhistoryinstitute.org/magazine/article/charlemagne-vs-the-saxons>

Hourly History 2016, *Charlemagne: A Life from Beginning to End*, Hourly History via Google Books, viewed 5 June 2020, <https://books.google.co.za/books?id=9JKeDwAAQBAJ&dq=battle+of+trsat&source=gbs_navlinks_s>

Story, J. 2005, *Charlemagne: Empire and Society*, Manchester University Press via Google Books, viewed 5 June 2020, <https://books.google.co.za/books?id=vTbvq_8HFPUC&dq=charlemagne+slavs&source=gbs_navlinks_s>

Violatti, C. 2014, *Slavs*, Ancient History Encyclopedia, viewed 5 June 2020, <https://www.ancient.eu/Slavs/>

Mark, J. J. 2014, *Avars*, Ancient History Encyclopedia, viewed 5 June 2020, <https://www.ancient.eu/Avars/>

Pohl, W. 2018, *What is So Fascinating About the Avars?*, Osterreichische Akademie der Wissenschaften, viewed 5 June 2020, < https://www.oeaw.ac.at/imafo/read/what-is-so-fascinating-about-the-avars#:~:text=The%20Avars%20are%20interesting%20not,great%20powers%20in%20early%20medieval>

Bachrach, B. 2013, *Charlemagne's Early Campaigns (768-777): A Diplomatic and Military Analysis*, BRILL via Google Books, viewed 5 June 2020, <https://books.google.co.za/books?id=k0B92eRh2-EC&dq=charlemagne+bavaria&source=gbs_navlinks_s>

Anonymous 2020, *Louis I*, Encyclopedia.com, viewed 6 June 2020, <https://www.encyclopedia.com/people/history/french-history-biographies/louis-i-louis-pious>

Editors of the Encyclopedia Britannica 2019, *Carolingian dynasty*, Encyclopedia Britannica, viewed 6 June 2020, <https://www.britannica.com/topic/Carolingian-dynasty>

Freeman, J. A. 2014, *Alcuin of York*, Christian History Institute, viewed 6 June 2020, <https://christianhistoryinstitute.org/magazine/article/alcuin-of-york-and-charlemagne>

Fleener, M. 2005, *The Significance of the Coronation of Charlemagne*, Medievalists, viewed 6 June 2020, <https://www.medievalists.net/2010/12/the-significance-of-the-coronation-of-charlemagne/>

von Hellfold, M. 2009, *Charlemagne is crowned emperor – December 25, 800*, DW.com, viewed 6 June 2020, <https://www.dw.com/en/charlemagne-is-crowned-emperor-december-25-800/a-4614858-1>

Loughlin, J. 1907, *Pope Adrian I*, Catholic Encyclopedia, viewed 6 June 2020, <https://www.newadvent.org/cathen/01155b.htm>

Editors of the Encyclopedia Britannica 2020, *Adrian I*, Encyclopedia Britannica, viewed 6 June 2020, <https://www.britannica.com/biography/Adrian-I>

Mann, H. 1910, *Pope St. Leo III*, Catholic Encyclopedia, viewed 6 June 2020, <https://www.newadvent.org/cathen/09157b.htm>

Snell, M. 2017, *Pope Leo III*, Thoughtco, viewed 6 June 2020, <https://www.thoughtco.com/pope-leo-iii-profile-1789101>

Editors of the Encyclopedia Britannica 2020, *Pippin, King of Italy*, Encyclopedia Britannica, viewed 6 June 2020, <https://www.britannica.com/biography/Pippin-king-of-Italy>

Sullivan, R. E. 2020, *Charlemagne*, Encyclopedia Britannica, viewed 6 June 2020, <https://www.britannica.com/biography/Charlemagne/Military-campaigns>

Biography.com Editors 2014, *Charlemagne*, Biography.com, viewed 6 June 2020, <https://www.biography.com/royalty/charlemagne>

Brondou, C. 2011, *Charlemagne, King of the Franks and Holy Roman Emperor*, Finding Dulcinea, viewed June 2020, <http://www.findingdulcinea.com/features/profiles/c/charlemagne.html>

History.com Editors 2019, *Charlemagne*, A&E Television Networks, viewed June 2020, <https://www.history.com/topics/middle-ages/charlemagne>

Mark, J. J. 2019, *Charlemagne*, Ancient History Encyclopedia, viewed

June 2020, <https://www.ancient.eu/Charlemagne/>

Illustration I:
https://commons.wikimedia.org/wiki/File:Charlemagne_Notre_Dame.jpg

Illustration II:
https://commons.wikimedia.org/wiki/File:Charlemagne_and_Pope_Adrian_I.jpg

Illustration III:
https://commons.wikimedia.org/wiki/File:Ary_Scheffer,_Charlemagne_re%C3%A7oit_la_soumission_de_Widukind_%C3%A0_Paderborn,_(1840).jpg

Illustration IV: By Lokilech - Own work, CC BY-SA 3.0,
https://commons.wikimedia.org/w/index.php?curid=2236671

Illustration V:
https://commons.wikimedia.org/wiki/File:Charlemagne_et_Alcuin.jpg

https://enacademic.com/dic.nsf/enwiki/991965

http://www.historyofinformation.com/detail.php?id=2908

http://www.medievalists.net/2015/07/how-christianity-came-to-europe/

https://www.discoverfrance.net/France/History/DF_history.shtml

https://www.thoughtco.com/france-a-historical-profile-1221301

https://www.ancient.eu/gaul/

https://www.britannica.com/place/Gaul-ancient-region-Europe

http://www.messagetoeagle.com/pillar-of-the-boatmen-carved-by-brotherhood-of-mariners-in-lutetia-that-became-paris/

https://quatr.us/medieval/notre-dame-st-etienne.htm

https://www.catholic.org/encyclopedia/view.php?id=11148

https://www.encyclopedia.com/religion/encyclopedias-almanacs-transcripts-and-maps/maurice-sully

http://www.henrysixth.com/?page_id=150

https://www.historytoday.com/archive/coronations-henry-vi

https://history.howstuffworks.com/european-history/notre-dame-cathedral.htm

https://www.designingbuildings.co.uk/wiki/Notre-Dame_de_Paris

http://www.indiana.edu/~paris10/ParisOSS/Day_1_Early_Paris/Medieval/McGregor_Building_of_Notre_Dame.html

https://www.dominicselwood.com/trial-of-the-templars/

https://www.ancient-origins.net/history-famous-people/powerful-curse-jacques-de-molay-last-grand-master-templars-005431

https://pulpitandpen.org/2019/04/16/historic-nugget-the-last-time-it-was-calvinists-who-vandalized-notre-dame/

https://www.historyextra.com/period/medieval/notre-dame-cathedral-facts-history-built-fire/

https://www.history.com/topics/france/huguenots

https://www.huguenotsociety.org.uk/history.html

https://www.history.com/topics/france/louis-xiv

http://rodama1789.blogspot.com/2019/04/the-cathedral-of-notre-dame-in-18th.html

https://www.encyclopedia.com/people/literature-and-arts/architecture-biographies/robert-de-cotte

https://www.history.com/this-day-in-history/french-revolutionaries-storm-bastille

http://time.com/4402553/bastille-day-history-july-14/

https://www.bl.uk/learning/timeline/item106472.html

https://www.history.com/topics/france/french-revolution

https://www.britannica.com/event/French-Revolution

https://www.encyclopedia.com/religion/encyclopedias-almanacs-transcripts-and-maps/reason-cult-goddess

https://www.history.com/news/notre-dame-fire-french-revolution

https://www.history.com/this-day-in-history/napoleon-crowned-emperor

https://www.napoleon.org/en/history-of-the-two-empires/articles/napoleons-consecration-and-coronation/

https://shannonselin.com/2016/12/coronation-of-napoleon/

https://www.history.com/topics/france/napoleon

https://www.britannica.com/event/Coup-of-18-19-Brumaire

https://www.napoleon.org/en/magazine/places/cathedral-of-notre-dame-in-paris/

https://inews.co.uk/culture/books/hunchback-of-notre-dame-paris-cathedral-victor-hugo-fire-repairs/

https://www.vox.com/culture/2019/4/15/18311758/notre-dame-fire-victor-hugo-hunchback

https://qz.com/quartzy/1596085/notre-dame-fire-victor-hugo-wrote-hunchback-to-save-the-cathedral/

https://www.jeanne-darc.info/biography/canonization/

http://www.maidofheaven.com/joanofarc_beatification.asp

https://www.tolucanoticias.com/2019/04/antonieta-rivas-mercado-the-mexican-woman-who-committed-suicide-at-notre-dame.html

http://artdaily.com/news/25209/Tribute-For-Late-Antonieta-Rivas-Mercado-at-Palace-of-Fine-Arts#.XNUsnrPv7ak

https://wend.ca/?p=63683

https://allthatsinteresting.com/liberation-of-paris

https://www.washingtonpost.com/opinions/a-history-of-paris-during-nazi-occupation/2014/08/29/fce9e112-222c-11e4-958c-268a320a60ce_story.html?utm_term=.1754489bb236

https://www.france24.com/en/20140820-paris-wwii-liberation-nazi-occupation-battle-france-world-war-two-webdoc

https://www.discoverwalks.com/blog/paris-during-wwi/

https://www.bbc.com/news/world-europe-47946675

https://www.apollo-magazine.com/the-many-lives-of-andre-malraux/

https://www.britannica.com/biography/Andre-Malraux

https://www.vintag.es/2019/04/philippe-petit-notre-dame-1971.html

https://www.biography.com/athlete/philippe-petit

https://www.france24.com/en/20190415-liveblog-fire-paris-france-notre-dame-cathedral?ref=tw_i#link

https://www.cbsnews.com/live-news/notre-dame-cathedral-fire-paris-collapse-live-updates-today-2019-04-15/

https://www.cnet.com/news/notre-dame-cathedral-fire-what-caused-it-and-what-happens-next/

Illustrations:

Illustration I: By Anonymous - Marsyas 08:50, 7 March 2006 (UTC), CC BY 2.5, https://commons.wikimedia.org/w/index.php?curid=617778

Illustration II: Image by Ian Kelsall from Pixabay: https://pixabay.com/photos/notre-dame-cathedral-paris-france-4150231/

Illustration III: Image by Peter H. from Pixabay: https://pixabay.com/photos/organ-instrument-cathedral-church-3599447/

Illustration IV: Image by Bartlomiej Koc from Pixabay: https://pixabay.com/photos/city-panorama-paris-france-498368/

Illustration V: By Benchaum - Own work, CC BY-SA 3.0, https://commons.wikimedia.org/w/index.php?curid=6531394

Illustration VI: By Jean-Pierre Houël - Bibliothèque nationale de France, Public Domain, https://commons.wikimedia.org/w/index.php?curid=106405

Illustration VII: By Ian Kelsall from Pixabay: https://pixabay.com/photos/notre-dame-paris-architecture-4132071/

Illustration VIII: By Nuno Lopes from Pixabay: https://pixabay.com/photos/notre-dame-columns-974864/

Illustration IX: By digital341 from Pixabay: https://pixabay.com/photos/notre-dame-paris-france-religious-4131864/

Illustration X: By LeLaisserPasserA38 - Own work, CC BY-SA 4.0, https://commons.wikimedia.org/w/index.php?curid=78064310

Made in United States
Troutdale, OR
10/01/2024

23289405R00235